PREACHING
THE
NEW COMMON
LECTIONARY

PREACHING
THE
NEW COMMON LECTIONARY

YEAR A

Advent, Christmas,
Epiphany

Commentary by:

Fred B. Craddock
John H. Hayes
Carl R. Holladay
Gene M. Tucker

ABINGDON PRESS
Nashville

Preaching the New Common Lectionary
Year A Advent, Christmas, Epiphany

This book is printed on acid-free paper.

Library of Congress Cataloging in Publication Data

Main entry under title:
   Preaching the new common lectionary. Year A, Advent, Christmas, Epiphany.

   Includes index.
   1. Bible—Homiletical use. 2. Bible—Liturgical lessons, English. I. Craddock, Fred B.
   BS534.5.P727   1986   251   85-30712

ISBN 0-687-33851-4
(pbk.: alk. paper)

Scripture quotations unless otherwise noted are from the Revised Standard Version of the Bible, copyrighted 1946, 1952, © 1971, 1973 by the Division of Christian Education of the National Council of the Churches of Christ in the U.S.A., and used by permission.

Those noted NEB are from The New English Bible, © the Delegates of the Oxford University Press and the Syndics of the Cambridge University Press 1961, 1970. Reprinted by permission.

Those noted JB are from The Jerusalem Bible, copyright © 1966 by Darton, Longman & Todd, Ltd. and Doubleday & Company, Inc. Used by permission of the publisher.

Those marked NIV are from the Holy Bible, New International Version. Copyright © 1973, 1978, 1984, International Bible Society.

Those noted NJPSV are from *Tanakh: A New Translation of the Holy Scriptures According to the Traditional Hebrew Text.* Copyright © 1985 by the Jewish Publication Society of America.

The charts on pages 217-37 are from *Common Lectionary: The Lectionary Proposed by the Consultation on Texts.* The Church Hymnal Corporation. Used by permission of the copyright holder, James M. Schellman.

MANUFACTURED BY THE PARTHENON PRESS AT
NASHVILLE, TENNESSEE, UNITED STATES OF AMERICA

Contents

Epiphany

Special Days

Introduction

It might be helpful to the reader if we make a few remarks about our understanding of our task and what we have sought to accomplish in this volume. The following comments will touch on four topics.

The Scripture in Preaching

There is no substitute for direct exposure to the biblical text, both for the preacher in preparation and for the listener in worship. The Scriptures are therefore not only studied privately but read aloud as an act of worship in and of itself and not solely as prelude to a sermon. The sermon is an interpretation of Scripture in the sense that the preacher seeks to bring the text forward into the present in order to effect a new hearing of the Word. In this sense the text has its future and its fulfillment in preaching. In fact, the Bible itself is the record of the continual rehearing and reinterpreting of its own traditions in new settings and for new generations of believers. New settings and new circumstances are properly as well as inescapably integral to a hearing of God's Word in and through the text. Whatever else may be said to characterize God's Word, it is always appropriate to the hearers. But the desire to be immediately relevant should not abbreviate study of the text or divorce the sermon from the biblical tradition. Such sermons are orphaned, released without memory into the world. It is the task of the preacher and teacher to see that the principle of fidelity to Scripture is not abandoned in the life and worship of the church. The endeavor to understand a text in its historical, literary, and theological contexts does create, to be sure, a sense of distance between the Bible and the congregation. The preacher may grow impatient during this period of feeling a long way from a sermon. But this time of study can be most fruitful. By holding text and parishioners apart for a while, the preacher can hear each more clearly and exegete each more honestly. Then, when the two intersect in the sermon, neither the text nor the congregation is consumed by the other. Because the Bible is an ancient book, it invites the preacher back into its world in order to understand; because the Bible is the church's Scripture, it moves forward into our world and addresses us here and now.

The Lectionary and Preaching

Ever increasing numbers of preachers are using a lectionary as a guide for preaching and worship. The intent of lectionaries is to provide for the church over a given period of time (usually three years) large units of Scripture arranged according to the seasons of the Christian year and selected because they carry the central message of the Bible. Lectionaries are not designed to limit one's message or restrict the freedom of the pulpit. On the contrary, churches that use a lectionary usually hear more Scripture in worship than those that do not. And ministers who preach from the lectionary find themselves stretched into areas of the canon into which they would not have gone had they kept to the path of personal preference. Other values of the lectionary are well known: the readings provide a common ground for discussions in ministerial peer groups; family worship can more easily join public worship through shared readings; ministers and worship committees can work with common biblical texts to prepare services that have movement and integrity; and the lectionary encourages more disciplined study and advance preparation. All these and other values are increased if the different churches share a common lectionary. A common lectionary could conceivably generate a community-wide Christian conversation.

INTRODUCTION

This Book and Preaching

This volume is not designed as a substitute for work with the biblical text; on the contrary, its intent is to encourage such work. Neither is it our desire to relieve the preacher of regular visits to concordances, lexicons, and commentaries; rather it is our hope that the comments on the texts here will be sufficiently germinal to give direction and purpose to those visits to major reference works. Our commentaries are efforts to be faithful to the text and to begin moving the text toward the pulpit. There are no sermons as such here, nor could there be. No one can preach long distance. Only the one who preaches can do an exegesis of the listeners and mix into sermon preparation enough local soil so as to effect an indigenous hearing of the Word. But we hope we have contributed to that end. The reader will notice that, while each of us has been aware of the other readings for each service, there has been no attempt to offer a collaborated commentary on all texts or a homogenized interpretation as though there were not four texts but one. It is assumed that the season of the year, the needs of the listeners, the preacher's own abilities, as well as the overall unity of the message of the Scriptures will prompt the preacher to find among the four readings the word for the day. Sometimes the four texts will join arm in arm, sometimes they will debate with one another, sometimes one will lead while the others follow, albeit at times reluctantly. Such is the wealth of the biblical witness.

A final word about our comments. The lections from the Psalter have been treated in the same manner as the other readings even though some Protestant churches often omit the reading of the psalm or replace it with a hymn. We have chosen to regard the psalm as an equal among the texts, primarily for three reasons. First, there is growing interest in the use of Psalms in public worship, and comments about them may help make that use more informed. Second, the Psalms were a major source for worship and preaching in the early church and they continue to inspire and inform Christian witness today. And third, comments on the Psalms may make this volume helpful to Roman Catholic preachers

9

who have maintained the long tradition of using the Psalms in Christian services.

This Season and Preaching

This book deals with the Seasons of Advent, Christmas, and Epiphany. It is our hope that this three-in-one format will not lure the preacher into moving through these services with a kind of sameness of spirit that fails to acknowledge and embrace the various changes in the seasons of the spirit. For observing advent, which begins the Christian year, we have biblical texts that speak of promise, preparation, hope, and anticipation. Those who preach on these texts will want to capture their moods of restrained excitement. Christmas differs from Advent as fulfillment differs from expectation, as today differs from both yesterday and tomorrow. Having is an experience quite different from hoping, for having moves the spirit down the road of reflection, asking, Now what? Then comes Epiphany, the celebration of the manifestation of Christ to the nations. Themes and images of light, revelation, and public proclamation abound in these texts. Nothing is subdued or veiled here; "This is my beloved Son" is the word from heaven. Advent's whisper in Bethlehem is now a shout in the streets of every city. Good preaching will not only say the words but will also attempt to carry the tune.

Fred B. Craddock (Gospels)
John H. Hayes (Psalms)
Carl R. Holladay (Epistles)
Gene M. Tucker (Old Testament)

First Sunday of Advent

Isaiah 2:1-5; Psalm 122; Romans 13:11-14; Matthew 24:36-44

On this day that is the turning point of the year all of the assigned texts direct the attention of the church to the future. They begin the preparation for Christmas, to be sure, but they also stress the eschatological dimensions of the coming of Jesus. A new age is dawning, already present but not yet consummated. The Old Testament lesson is a vision of peace for all peoples, that peace on earth announced by the angelic host to the shepherds in Luke's account of the birth of Jesus (Luke 2:13-14). The responsorial psalm sets the tone for celebration of that peace which has its center in Jerusalem. The reading from Romans reminds the faithful that they are living between the ages, and should be prepared at all times for the end of the present age. The Gospel likewise calls for watchfulness, for only the Father knows the day and hour. The expectation, mystery, and celebration of the reign of God are the leading themes for the day.

Isaiah 2:1-5

These words here attributed to Isaiah of Jerusalem appear in virtually identical form in Micah 4:1-4. There is no way of determining which prophet depends on the other. Indeed, it is quite likely that both occurrences are either citations from an older tradition, known at the temple in Jerusalem, or later additions to the words of the two eighth-century prophets. The liturgical dimensions of the passage lend support to the view that the tradition is older than Isaiah and Micah, but the particular eschatology expressed in the poem is more consistent with perspectives of the exilic or early postexilic eras.

11

Our reading contains three distinct parts, a superscription in verse 1, the announcement of salvation in verses 2-4, and a call to the congregation to respond in verse 5. The superscription, similar in many respects to the one in Isaiah 1:1 and the others that begin prophetic books, is the heading for a collection of prophetic addresses, and not simply for the passage before us. Its presence indicates that some part of the Book of Isaiah that begins here—either through the end of chapter 4, through 9:7, or perhaps as far as the end of chapter 4, through 9:7, or perhaps as far as the end of chapter 11—once circulated independently. The call to the congregation (verse 5) applies the good news of the announcement to the addressees.

It is the lines in verses 2-4 that attract our attention, and with good reason. While there are liturgical allusions and even hymnic features—the implicit praise of Yahweh, his temple and Zion—the passage is not a hymn but an announcement or promise of salvation. The words are not addressed to God, but are indefinite, to any who listen. Nor is God the speaker, but a prophetic voice announces what will happen and what Yahweh and others will do. The sequence of events is important. First, "the mountain of the house of the Lord," that is Zion, will be elevated and exalted (2*ab*). Second, there will be a pilgrimage of all peoples to the holy mountain (verses 2*c*-3*a*). Third, as they come the people will sing a call to pilgrimage that expresses their reasons for approaching Zion, namely, that the God of Jacob may teach them his ways (verse 3*b*). Fourth, the motivation for the pilgrimage, or the attraction of Zion is stated: the law (or instruction) and the word of Yahweh go forth from Jerusalem (verse 3*c*). Finally, the results of all that has transpired thus far are specified: Yahweh shall "judge between the nations," who will make their instruments of war into farming tools, inaugurating a permanent reign of peace (verse 4).

Note that some of the events are characterized passively and others actively. The mountain "shall be established,. . . . raised," (verse 2) and the law and the word of the Lord "shall go forth" (verse 3). The only actors in the drama of peace are Yahweh and "the nations," or "many peoples" (verses 3, 4). Yahweh takes on the role of teacher or instructor (verse 3) that traditionally was held by the priests in ancient Israel, and the duties of judge and administrator of justice (verse 4). The role of the nations is crucial. They come to Zion seeking instruction and revelation, and they—not God—destroy the weapons of war. Their acknowledgment of and trust in God is the basis for peace.

What is the role of the people of God, those people of Judah and Jerusalem mentioned in the initial verse? At some stage in the transmission and liturgical use of our text—if not when it was originally composed—that same question arose, and was answered with the lines in verse 5. The announcement is a vision of peace for all peoples, in which the foreign nations come to Jerusalem to learn the ways of justice. Having heard that proclamation, the congregation of the faithful in Jerusalem is called to "walk in the light of the Lord." The point seems clear: those who already live in the presence of God are admonished to take the first steps on the path that all the nations will one day tread. "The light of the Lord" thus refers to the vision of God's reign just announced. The appropriate response to this vision is to be guided by it.

The reading is rich in themes for theological and homiletical reflection. (1) Above all, there is the announcement of the future reign of God. This is good news in the Old Testament prophetic sense. The time is not specified, but the announcement is concrete. The poem is not a prediction, but a statement of the certainty that history will reach its goal, its culmination. That divine reign will involve the utter transformation of existing conditions, from nationalism and conflict to unity and peace. Resources will be turned from weapons to tools for harvesting food. (2) This vision has international political if not universalistic dimensions. The expectation is that all nations will come to Jerusalem to know the one true God, and peace will be the result. (3) Especially important in this hope is the understanding of God as judge (verse 4a). This is not the typical image of the Lord as judge, handing out punishment after establishing guilt or innocence. Like that image, the view here has deep roots in the view of Yahweh as just, and in the prophetic calls for justice and righteousness. But the divine judge here is the one who settles the disputes among the nations, resolving their differences so that peace can be established and maintained.

It is tempting for us, in an era of military conflict, nationalism, and international mistrust, to simply write off such an announcement as this one, either as unrealistic or as applicable only to an era beyond history and not within it. It probably is unrealistic to expect peace among all nations in the immediate future. Should one then capitulate to such realities? Our reading, like so much of the Bible, holds forth the assurance that God will one day reign, and in peace. Moreover, the passage brings home to us the power of expectation. Who can read or hear these lines and not have his or her hope for peace kindled? Surely such a reign of God could not come among us unless we have—and keep alive in each generation—a vision of that reign.

Psalm 122

Psalms 120 to 134 form a collection in which each of the psalms bears the heading "a song of ascents." Although the meaning of the term "ascents" has been much debated, it is now widely agreed that the expression (literally, "going up") refers to pilgrimage. Thus these are pilgrim songs. (Other interpretations include "a song of going up" [from exile], "a song of graduated vocalization," "a song of graduated expression," "a song for the temple steps" [the ascents], and so on.)

This collection of fifteen psalms may once have existed as a small songbook for use on pilgrimages to Jerusalem. Some of the psalms appear to have been adopted secondarily for use on pilgrimage, some having initially been composed for other occasions. (Psalm 130, for example, is a lament which may have been written for use in some specific time of trouble.) After the move by kings Hezekiah and Josiah to close all sanctuaries except for Jerusalem (see II Kings 18, 22-23), pilgrimages would have become more important in the life of the people. If they were to worship in a temple, some had to travel long distances on foot to get to the capital city.

The tractate *Bikkurim* ("First Fruits") in the *Mishnah* tells us about features involved in going on pilgrimage. The persons in a district would assemble in the main village/town in the area, sleep outside (to avoid contamination) the night before setting out, move out together (men in one group, women in another) under the supervision of a pilgrimage director (see Ps. 42:4), and make their way to the temple.

There are many ways of thinking of a pilgrimage and its symbolism. The book of Hebrews conceives life as a pilgrimage. The pilgrimage reflected in Psalm 122 was a periodic and repeatable pilgrimage, a recurring event frought with meaning, like Advent.

The thought of a pilgrimage conjures up many images—the movement from the periphery to the center, from the ordinary to the holy, from the mundane to the meaningful, from the normal to the highly symbolic, from the loosely organized to the highly concentrated, from obsession with the present to the wellsprings of memory, from the low voltage of the everyday to the high voltage of celebration, from the famine of the ordinary to the festivities and feasting of the special. To return on pilgrimage is like homecoming or reunion time, a return to the roots, to the source, to the "mother" that still sustains and nourishes.

Now to the psalm. Like many of its companions in Psalms 120–134, this composition gives indication of being sung on the way to the temple. Antiphonal singing, with individual and group participation (the director–pilgrims' participation?), is suggested by the movement from first person singular ("I") to first person plural ("our"). The rapturous joy of departing on pilgrimage is expressed in the opening lines. Verse two anticipates the joy of arriving at the object of pilgrimage—two totally different sets of emotions but related sentiments nonetheless. The arrival is anticipated by recalling a previous experience of standing in Jerusalem. In addition to the joy of the experience of visiting Jerusalem, three things should be noted about this psalm's content.

1. First of all, the psalm stresses the unity that is symbolized by the city (verses 3-4). This is done in two ways: (a) with reference to the city's architecture and (b) with reference to the city as the object of tribal pilgrimage. In antiquity, every major city was compactly built, nestled atop some defendable elevation, and no doubt gave the impres-

sion of houses stacked one upon another. Such towns, surrounded by a defense wall, were frequently no more than ten to twenty acres in size. Streets within the towns were merely passageways for humans and an occasional beast of burden. Intimacy and communal knowledge, familiarity and gossip were characteristics of every such town but also there were sharing and a sense of common fate. Not only was the city compactly built and thus knit together but also the city was the central goal of pilgrimages for the various components (the tribes) of Israelite society. A common place of worship manifested and helped create a sense of national unity. In going on pilgrimage, the people were fulfilling the divine command (see Exod. 23:14).

2. Jerusalem is also the place of judgment (verse 5). The Davidic family who ruled in Jerusalem was responsible, like all kings in antiquity, to see that justice prevailed in the land. (Note Jer. 21:11-12 where the prophet reminds the ruler of this ongoing royal responsibility.) The reference in the plural to the "thrones for judgment," "the thrones of the house of David" has baffled scholars. The plural is perhaps best understood as referring to the throne of the king and to the throne of the queen-mother who, instead of a wife of the reigning monarch, served as first lady of the realm. This had the practical effort of eliminating competition for the post by the various wives of the king. The importance of the queen-mother and her possible role in the administration of justice in Jerusalem are suggested by two facts. For all the Judean kings, with only two exceptions, the biblical historian has provided us with the name of the king's mother. (This is not given for the northern or Israelite kings.) First Kings 2:19 reports that Bathsheba had a throne alongside that of her son Solomon and it may have been she who was the first Judean queen-mother. (Note I Kings 15:9-13 with regard to the importance of the queen-mother.)

3. The peace of Jerusalem is a burning concern of the psalm (verses 6-9). It is widely assumed that the name Jerusalem is built on the Hebrew word for peace, *shalom*, and as such incorporates in its very name a plea for or an affirmation about peace. The opening line of verse 6 reads in Hebrew *shaalu shelom yerusalayim* and such assonance suggests that it

may have been a proverbial expression—"ask about [or pray for] the peace of Jerusalem." Jerusalem, a city sacred to all three of the world's monotheistic religions (Judaism, Christianity, and Islam) and a symbol of peace, has proven throughout history to be one of the most fought over cities in the world. One scholar has calculated, for example, that between 323 B.C. (the death of Alexander the Great) and 63 B.C. (the capture of Jerusalem by the Roman general Pompey), over two hundred major military campaigns were fought in and across Palestine and against or in the vicinity of Jerusalem. Almost one per year! In modern times, the city is still frequently a battleground. As in days of old, so today too we should remember and pray for the peace of Jerusalem, the mother of us all.

As we move into Advent, we can see it as also a pilgrimage, as a journey back to the center, to a place of meaning, to the manger where kings bring their gifts and human hearts are wrapped in swaddling clothes.

Romans 13:11-14

Advent themes are boldly stated in this arousing call to vigilance. We are reminded "what hour it is" (verse 11, RSV), "how critical the moment is" (NEB), that "'the time' has come" (JB). The text confronts us with the eschatological *kairos*—the impending Day of God when salvation comes. Elsewhere Paul reminds his readers that the *kairos* has grown very short (I Cor. 7:29).

Such reminders reflect the common early Christian expectation of the speedy return of Christ (I Cor. 7:26, 31). The death and resurrection of Christ had ushered in the period of the "last days" (Acts 2:17), the new era of God's reign. In one sense, this new period could be understood as calendar time, but it was more than that. It was a different era qualitatively, for salvation was now possible in an unprecedented manner. For Paul, the Christ-event now confronted everyone with "the acceptable time . . . the day of salvation" (II Cor. 6:2). In Johannine Christianity this new time saw the ushering in of "eternal life" (John 5:24). This time was often regarded as "the hour" that was at hand (John 5:25; I John 2:18; cf. John 4:23).

The call to "wake up" is a call for us to be awake to this new set of realities. As one age dawns, another age is eclipsed. Hence an age of darkness gives way to an era of light (cf. I John 2:8). The light of God's new revelation has broken through time, with the Christ-event as the dawning moment (II Cor. 4:6). Our options for living are sketched in dualistic terms common to early Jewish apocalyptic, well attested in the Qumran community, and shared by many early Christians. It is a choice between light and darkness, day and night, good and evil (I Thess. 5:4-8). Such dualism reflects the common notion that evil flourishes at night but flees before the coming day. The metaphor is graphic but should not lead us to the naïve view that light and darkness are to be equated with day and night. It is rather the case that good and evil cut across all time—through the day and into the night.

The call here is to "cast off the works of darkness" (verse 12; cf. Eph. 5:11). Instead we are to "put on the armor of light" (verse 12; cf. Eph. 6:11-17; also II Cor. 6:7; 10:4). The metaphor of donning new clothing is continued in verse 14 as we are urged to "put on the Lord Jesus Christ" (cf. Gal. 3:27; Eph. 4:24; Col. 3:12-14). It is a charge to clothe ourselves in the new being of Christ. So clothed, we are warmed, protected, and adorned.

The text does not leave us guessing as to the profile of the new life in Christ. Conduct "becoming the day" is sketched as eliminating certain vices from our lives (cf. Matt. 15:19; Rom. 1:29-31; I Cor. 5:10-11; 6:9-10; II Cor. 12:20; Gal. 5:19-21; Eph. 4:31; 5:3-5; Col. 3:5, 8; I Tim. 1:9-10; 6:4-5; II Tim. 3:2-4; Tit. 3:3; I Pet. 4:3; Rev. 9:21; 21:8; 22:15). Three pairs of vices are listed: no "reveling and drunkenness" (RSV), or "drunken orgies" (JB); no "debauchery and licentiousness" (RSV) or "sexual immorality and debauchery" (NIV); no "quarreling and jealously" (RSV). We should note that social sins, or sins against community and the common good, rank alongside various forms of personal indulgence, or sins against the self.

Today's text calls us to develop a Christian sense of time. This entails more than knowing the time of day, the season of the year, and even making good use of the time we have (cf. Eph. 5:16). It certainly requires more than the art of circling the calendar and trying to predict the time of Christ's coming. This is a misguided venture not only because it is bound to fail but mainly because it misconstrues the true nature of Christian time. The New Testament is fairly uniform in urging us to be alert, always prepared for Christ's coming, not because we know when it is but because we know what it means. Living with an eye toward Advent is living preparedly and expectantly.

To develop a Christian sense of time is to live in a new understanding of time. Christ's first coming allows us to see that time is not just a matter of clocks and calendars. It is to sense the tension between the divine will and human ways, the ongoing struggle between good and evil that goes on around us. It is to recognize that Christ's coming has begun to make a difference in this conflict between light and darkness. Things may be dark but not as dark as they would have been otherwise. The light of Christ has provided significant illumination. This is not only true on the grand, historical scale of human history; it is also true within us as communities of believers and as individuals. The Christian sense of time finally translates into a way of life whose contours are clear—and for that reason offers a clear set of options for everyone of us who has experienced within ourselves the tension between good and evil, day and night, light and darkness.

Matthew 24:36-44

Advent is not a period of Christmas preliminaries but a season in itself, with its own integrity and its own announcement. Advent proclaims the coming of the Lord, but that is not the same as saying that Christmas is coming. Lest Advent melt too easily into the birth stories, the first Sunday of this season calls upon biblical texts that are not at all associated with the nativity. In fact, they are most usually understood as pointing to the "Second Coming." The preacher would do well to disengage from thinking first coming or second coming and announce that which all Scripture affirms: our God is the one who comes to the world. The question is, How shall the day of the Lord be? Will it be darkness or light, joy or dread, judgment or redemption? It is this thought that stirs the people of God and reminds us that not only joy and anticipation but also repentance mark the observance of Advent.

In all three cycles of the lectionary, the Gospel for the First Sunday of Advent is drawn from Jesus' apocalyptic discourse (Mark 13:5-37; Matt. 24:4-36; Luke 21:8-36). However, unlike the readings from Mark (Year B) and Luke (Year C) which describe the nature of the Lord's coming along with the attendant cosmic and historical signs, today's lection contains only the closing verse of Matthew's version of the discourse (24:36). The verse is joined to an extended call for watchfulness in view of the uncertain time of the Lord's coming (verses 37-44). It could well be that Matthew intended verses 37-44 to be included as a part of the apocalyptic discourse. The reasons for this judgment are two: one, Matthew has taken material (verses 37-44) that Luke has scattered through the travel narrative (17:26-27, 34-35; 12:39-40) and placed it here immediately after declaring that only God knows when the Son will come (24:36). As we shall see, the calls to watchfulness are appropriate to this setting. Two, Mark's ending to the discourse (13:33-37), which Matthew does not repeat, is a call for watchfulness. While Matthew depends heavily on Mark's account (Matt. 24:36 is almost an exact following of Mark 13:32), he replaces Mark's concluding exhortation to be alert with his own version of essentially the same message.

Matthew 24:36-44 consists, then, of two statements: the uncertain time of the Lord's advent (verse 36) and the behavior of the faithful in view of that uncertainty (verses 37-44). That the time of the Lord's appearing is not known by angels or even by the Son, but by God alone is a statement congenial to other words of Jesus to the effect that some matters are hidden within God's own purposes. "It is not for you to know times or seasons which the Father has fixed by his own authority" (Acts 1:7). In fact, Matthew states elsewhere that Jesus regarded not only the time of the Parousia as God's own business but also the granting of place in the kingdom (20:23). Some scribes, however, found it offensive to their Christology to speak of what the Son did not know, and so they deleted "nor the Son" from 24:36. And throughout church history there have been those unwilling to permit times and places to remain in the knowledge of God alone and who, therefore, have arranged certain texts so as to create a calendar of the last days.

The call for watchfulness (verses 37-44) consists of three parts with different images and emphases. Verses 37-39 employ the catastrophe of the flood as an analogy. However, it is not the wickedness at the time of the flood (Gen. 6:5-7, 12-13) but rather the lack of preparedness that is Matthew's concern. In verses 40-41 the theme of an all-encompassing destruction is dropped and replaced by the image of the one taken, the one left. Here the accent is on the suddenness and the finality of the two fates that will occur "then"; that is, at the coming of the Son of man (verse 39). The form of the third part of the exhortation to watchfulness (verses 42-44) is that of a parable. If the householder had known when to be alert, his house would not have been burglarized. The image here is the much-used one of the thief coming in the night (I Thess. 5:2-9; Rev. 16:15).

A flood, a kidnapper, a thief: all are sharp, intrusive, disturbing images with which to begin Advent. But they are effective in instructing us in alertness, in making preparation for uncertain certainties. Watch, stay awake; the Lord is coming.

Second Sunday of Advent

Isaiah 11:1-10; Psalm 72:1-8; Romans 15:4-13; Matthew 3:1-12

Preparation for Christmas continues with readings that kindle hope for the future reign of God in all the world, a reign of justice and righteousness. The Old Testament reading is one of the classic announcements of a future king in the line of David, one who will inaugurate a rule of peace with justice, especially for the poor. Psalm 72, a petition to God that the king rule with righteousness and justice, continues the same themes. A major motif in the epistolary lection, which cites Isaiah 11:10, is hope, based on the confirmation of the Old Testament promises by the coming of Jesus. The apocalyptic dimensions of the season are dramatized in the Gospel lesson, the account of the appearance of John the Baptist with his announcement of the kingdom of God.

Isaiah 11:1-10

Advent, the time of expectation, is a good season for Old Testament texts, and especially those that anticipate the future reign of God. All the Old Testament readings for Advent and for Christmas itself in Year A are from the Book of Isaiah. Today's selection continues the vision of the future expressed in last week's reading (Isa. 2:1-5), and is a direct extension of the text used in all years on Christmas, First Proper, the announcement of the birth of the messianic king in Isaiah 9:2-7.

When we recognize the parts of Isaiah 11:1-10 and their relationship to one another, the meaning and implications of our reading become more clear. While everything in it concerns the future, three distinct parts comprise the passage. The first section, verses 1-5, is an announcement of the birth or ascension of a new king from the Davidic line. Verses 6-9 contain an announcement of peace and tranquility in the natural order. It is possible that these two units arose independently, or that verses 6-9 were composed after the first section. There are actually very few internal links between the two parts. In the context, however, the cosmic peace of the second unit is viewed as the consequence of the rise of the king in the line of David. Verse 10 is yet another announcement concerning the descendant of David, in this case that he will be an ensign around which all nations will unite. The fact that this final verse is prose while the preceding lines are in poetry supports the conclusion that it is secondary to the original unit or units, serving the purpose of linking 11:1-9 to 11:11 ff.

The question of the authorship and date of this passage has been the subject of considerable debate and disagreement. Does the passage, or any of its parts, come from Isaiah in the eighth century B.C., or from a later hand? The answer, at least for verses 1-5, turns primarily on the interpretation of "the stump" (or "stock," NEB) of Jesse in verse 1. Those commentators who take the passage to be late see this as an allusion to a time when the dynasty had been cut down, that is, in the exilic or postexilic era. While that is the meaning that would have been heard in those later times, the language more likely refers simply to the lineage—the family tree—of David. Nothing in verses 1-5 in particular is inconsistent with the thought of Isaiah of Jerusalem. The vision of cosmic peace in verses 6-9 may be later, but even that could have come from Isaiah.

In ancient Israel, confidence in the reign of a Davidic king in Jerusalem was based on the promise expressed in II Samuel 7 and celebrated regularly in worship (cf. Pss. 2; 45; 110). Prophets such as Isaiah saw the Davidic monarchy as Yahweh's means of implementing his will first for Judah and Jerusalem, and then for the world as a whole. In later centuries the hope for such a messiah ("anointed one") was linked more and more to the culmination or fulfillment of God's will for human history.

Verses 1-5 of our reading announce a new Davidic king

(verse 1) and then describe him and his rule (verses 2-5). The lines do not comprise an oracle, for the words are not attributed directly to Yahweh. Instead, a prophetic voice proclaims what will happen in accordance with the divine will. The character of the ruler (verses 2-*3a*) will be shaped by the "Spirit" of Yahweh. This spirit (*ruah*) represents the active and creative divine presence known at creation (Gen. 1:2) and in the inspiration of prophets (II Kings 2:9; Mic. 3:8) as well as kings (I Sam. 11:6) and other leaders (Judg. 6:34). Here that divine spirit provides the king with the gifts necessary for just rule and evokes from the anointed one true piety ("fear of the Lord"). The description of this king's administration (verses 3*b*-5) concentrates on his establishment of justice. As one who sees and hears deeper than the surface, he will ensure that the "poor" and the "meek," that is, those least able to protect themselves, have full rights before the law. The character and administration of the king here are those that the people hoped for—but never fully realized—in each new descendant of David to take the throne in Jerusalem.

As the first five verses characterize the rule of justice in human society, verses 6-9 picture a transformation in the natural, cosmic sphere. Natural enemies in the animal world will live together in peace. There are echoes of a return to a world without violence among creatures, such as that assumed in Genesis 1:29-31. The goal of this transformation is for human beings to live without fear (verses 6, 8). The "little child" (verse 6), the "sucking child," and the "weaned child" (verse 8) represent children generally, human beings at their most vulnerable stages, rather than any particular individual. The center of the peaceful cosmos is the same as that in Isaiah 2:1-5, Yahweh's "holy mountain," that is, Mount Zion in Jerusalem. And as a consequence of the rule of justice and the transformation of nature, "the earth shall be full of the knowledge of the Lord" (verse 9).

The juxtaposition of verses 1-5 and 6-9 evokes reflection on the relationship between justice, mercy, peace, and harmony in the natural order. Thus the preacher may be moved to remind the congregation, as Reinhold Niebuhr and many others have said, "If you want peace, work for justice." That would not be inconsistent with John the Baptist's call for repentance in today's Gospel lesson. However, one should not lose sight of both the contents and the mood of these powerful lines. They bring unqualified good news. Whether in this world and history or beyond, they cry joyfully that God wills—and will one day bring about—justice and peace.

Psalm 72:1-8

This lection forms part of an intercessory prayer offered by the community on behalf of the king at his royal coronation. Thus it is a royal psalm expressing aspects of the theology of kingship—what the people believed, expected, and hoped for the ruling Davidic monarch—and forming the basis for messianic speculations about the future—what might be expected from the ideal ruler in the future.

The component features and actions in the coronation of the Judean king can be partially reconstructed from I Kings 1 (the account of Solomon's coronation) and II Kings 11 (the account of the coronation of the young boy king Jehoash). We cannot be certain, however, about the exact sequence of events (compare I Kings 1:38-40 with II Kings 11:9-12).

1. A significant feature was the *anointment*, or the "messiahing" since the messiah was the anointed one, a title that would have been used for the reigning king. The anointing with holy oil set the new king apart from normal humanity.

2. The *acclamation*, with trumpet blowing and public shouts, affirmed the population's support. These two events, the anointment and acclamation, occurred either at the pool of Gihon (thus with Solomon), the sacred water source for the city of Jerusalem, or in the temple (so with Jehoash whose life, however, was in danger).

3. The *procession* to the throne marked the king's assumption to power.

4. The *homage* of the officials may have been offered in the throne room. These events formed the skeleton of the ritual. No doubt, spoken components formed significant parts of the ceremony.

Psalm 78 would have been one of the spoken parts of the

coronation liturgy. Perhaps after the new king was enthroned, the community offered prayer in his behalf. The petitions in Psalm 78 reflect many of the basic beliefs associated with the Davidic ruler, the reigning messiah. (1) The king was considered the representative of God's justice and righteousness (verse 1). (2) He was responsible for ruling over the people with equity (verse 2). (3) The new reign was hailed as the dawn of a new era in which prosperity was expected (verses 3, 6-7). (4) The king was the special custodian of the poor, the defender of the powerless, and the opponent of the unscrupulous and the oppressor (verse 4, 12-14). (5) The king was Yahweh's representative (God's son; see verse 1*b*) on earth and thus was the potential ruler of all of creation, a dominion extending from sea to sea (verses 8-11, 15).

The extravagant imagery and idealistic expectations associated with the Davidic monarchy almost exceed the bounds of normal life and illustrate the flowery speech and language used at the royal court. (Note the sort of speeches and the claims made at presidential inaugurations in the U.S.) Long life is requested for the king in totally unrealistic terms—"while the sun endures, and as long as the moon," "till the moon be no more" (verses 5, 7).

For further discussion of Psalm 72 see remarks on Epiphany, pages 104-6.

Romans 15:4-13

Advent is above all a time of hope. As we reflect on the Lord's coming in its many dimensions, our mood is expectant. Our eyes are cast forward as we lean into the future, and we see the future as a time of promise.

Today's epistolary lection sounds the note of hope. It opens by reassuring us of our hope (verse 4) and closes by anchoring human hope in "the God of hope" (verse 13).

We all realize how fragile hope can be. We wonder whether it is an illusion. What might be competes with what never will be. Hope dances on the edge of wishing, comes close to expecting, but retreats to wishing. We do not want to be disappointed, so we wish instead of hope. The one flirts with the future, the other flings itself toward the future. On what, then, can we rest our hope? Two things, according to Paul in today's text.

First, "whatever was written in former days . . . the scriptures" (verse 4). We are reminded that these "ancient scriptures" (NEB) were written for our benefit—to instruct us. In view here, of course, are the Jewish Scriptures, which later came to be called the Old Testament. These were the Scriptures early Christians had at their disposal. The writings that later came to be called the New Testament were only being composed at this period. Paul's writings were among the earlier of these writings. Since Judaism provided the setting in which early Christianity originated and took root, it was understandable for the earliest Christians to look to the Jewish Scriptures for guidance and instruction. It was their conviction that these writings were written "for our sake" (I Cor. 9:10; Rom. 4:23-24; cf. I Cor. 10:11). Accordingly, these inspired writings provided guidance for righteous and obedient living before God (II Tim. 3:16).

One of the chief values of the sacred Scriptures is "the encouragement they give us" (verse 4, NEB; cf. I Macc. 12:9). The stories they tell help us "maintain our hope with fortitude" (verse 4, NEB), or give us examples of "how people who did not give up were helped by God" (verse 4, JB).

Early Christians read the Jewish Scriptures in terms of promise and fulfillment. Here they saw unfolded the story of God's promises to Israel and the fulfillment of those promises. What moved the story along was the promise God gave and the hope that it would be fulfilled. It was God's fidelity in keeping promises that provided the source of encouragement. But it was not a story without breaks. Sometimes Israel proved unfaithful to the covenant. Sometimes fulfillment took awhile. The singular virtue turned out to be "steadfastness" (verse 4, RSV), or "endurance" (NIV). To receive the promise can mean to wait, and wait patiently.

Second, our hope is rooted in "the God of steadfastness and encouragement" (verse 5), "the God of hope" (verse 13). Paul insists on "God's truthfulness" (verse 8), or the absolute fidelity of God, and in doing so stands firmly within the Old Testament tradition (cf. Ps. 88:3; Mic. 7:20). Elsewhere, Paul insists that the "gifts and the call of God are irrevocable" (Rom. 11:29; cf. II Pet. 1:19).

Some thought that God's integrity had been called into question by the mission to the Gentiles. But Paul insists that God's fidelity to the divine promise remained in tact. True, God had given promises to the patriarchs, but the fact that Christ was a Jew merely confirmed that God kept the promise. The Jews thus remained part of God's saving work. But God's promise had not been one-sided. It had also extended to the Gentiles, as the numerous Scripture quotations make clear (verses 9-12; Ps. 18:49; II Sam. 22:50; Deut. 32:43; Ps. 117:1; Isa. 11:10). It was just as important for God to keep faith in extending salvation to the Gentiles as it was to keep the promise made to the patriarchs. Paul's mission to the Gentiles attests God's truthfulness.

If our hope is predicated on God's record in fulfilling divine promises, we can be reassured by the way in which God has extended salvation to include both Jews and Gentiles. What God has done in the past, in the arena of human history, gives substance to our hope. It is not as if our hope is rooted only in who God is, or whom we believe God to be, but also in what God has done. The being of God is rooted in the acts of God.

Our text, then, confronts us with our hope as embodied in Scripture, and our hope as embodied in God. In both instances, we have reason to "abound in hope" (verse 13).

In conclusion, we might note that our common conviction and expression of hope has a unifying force (verses 5-6). What results from our common hope is a genuine form of community, which in its best form is harmonious as it, with one voice, glorifies God (cf. Rom. 12:16; II Cor. 13:11; Phil. 2:2; 4:2; I Cor. 1:10; I Pet. 3:8). Concretely, this translates into forms of genuine hospitality (verse 7; Rom. 14:1; Philem. 17). Hope turns out not to be ethereal but practical as it binds us into a community where we extend our love to one another, as we learn to "accept one another as Christ accepted us" (verse 7, NEB).

Matthew 3:1-12

On the second Sunday of Advent, the Gospel reading each year treats the person and work of John the Baptist. All four Evangelists deal at some length with John, not primarily because he was a significant religious leader who had disciples (Mark 2:18), who suffered martyrdom (Mark (6:14-29), and who became the central figure in a continuing sect (Acts 18:24–19:7), but because the church understood John's function to be the one preparing for the Advent of Christ. He was the one of whom Isaiah spoke (Matt. 3:3; Isa. 40:3), and the returned Elijah (Matt. 11:14; 17:13; Mal. 4:5-6) who was to prepare the people for "the great and terrible day of the Lord." But the preacher will not want to rush past John to Jesus. There is yet time. The accents of last Sunday continue in our text today: the time of the Lord's coming is near and preparation for that event is of primary importance. If one is true to today's lection, Jesus is not yet introduced as the Coming One. Matthew leaves Jesus a child in Nazareth (2:23), and we do not learn he is now an adult until 3:13. There is no indication at 3:11-12 that John knew at that time the identity of the One to come who was mightier than he.

For his presentation of John the Baptist, Matthew had access to Mark 1:1-8 and had in common with Luke a source of information about the content of John's preaching (Matt. 3:11b-12; Luke 3:16b-17). Much briefer than Mark or Luke is Matthew's introduction of the narrative: "In those days" (verse 1). The phrase is chronologically vague but is used later by Matthew as a reference to the last days (24:19, 22, 29) and therefore, may have eschatological overtones here. John comes announcing the last days, the messianic age, the time that is ushered in by the Advent of Christ.

Matthew introduces John in verses 1-6, and he does so in this way: (a) by name and location; (b) by activity and message; (c) as the one fulfilling the prophecy of Isaiah 40:3 (Matthew omits Mark's awkward use of Mal. 3:1 in connection with Isa. 40:3); (d) by description of personal appearance, on the model of Elijah (II Kings 1:8); (e) by the public response to John. By this brief sketch Matthew makes it clear that while he assumes the readers already know of

John the Baptist, it is important that they see him as introducing the messianic age and, therefore, as the eschatological prophet of Isaiah and the returned Elijah. He functions as preparer of the way through the preaching of repentance and baptism.

Both Matthew (verses 7-10) and Luke (3:7-9) at this point present a summary of John's preaching of repentance. They use a common source but Luke has John address the multitudes (all Israel together) while in Matthew's account John directs his words to the religious leaders, the Pharisees and Sadducees. The sermon is a strong indictment of a "brood of vipers" (Isa. 11:8; 14:29; 30:6) and a compelling call for the bearing of good fruit. The bearing of good fruit is a familiar image from the Gospels (Matt. 7:16-20; 12:33-37) implying the demand not only for conduct and activity appropriate to repentance and faith but also for integrity; that is, the tree and its fruit should be of the same kind. Before the searching and judging word of God neither ritual (John does not seem anxious to see how many he can baptize) nor genealogy (God is able from stones to raise up children to Abraham) provide valid claims or grounds for exemption from the wrath to come (verse 7; I Thess. 1:10; Amos 2:4-16).

Matthew concludes his presentation of John with a brief summary statement of his messianic preaching (verses 11-12).

John does not identify this person to come by name (we are thinking "Jesus" but the narrative asks us to exercise restraint and let the story unfold in its own time) or by title but rather as "he who is coming after me" and as "mightier than I." The identification of the One whose Advent is near is sharpened by contrast with John's person ("whose sandals I am not worthy to carry") and John's baptism (water, as distinct from the Holy Spirit and fire).

While Mark speaks only of a promised baptism with the Holy Spirit (1:8), Matthew has the stronger image of judgment in the phrase "with the Holy Spirit and with fire." Verse 12 makes it clear that "wind and fire" are judgment images in the sense of making distinctions between wheat and chaff. The Advent of the Messiah means that the differences among persons and their futures will become evident.

John's preaching makes it abundantly clear that one aspect of the Lord's Advent is the full revelation of the kind of persons we are and of the consequences of character and conduct that await us.

Third Sunday of Advent

Isaiah 35:1-10; Psalm 146:5-10; James 5:7-10; Matthew 11:2-11

As the church anticipates celebrating the Incarnation, the readings for the day highlight eschatological themes. The effect is to recall that the birth of a particular baby is an event of the end-times, of the culmination of God's will for the world and human history. With the exception of the Epistle, the texts have in common the healing of the sick as signs of the new order. Isaiah 35:1-10 celebrates the transformation of the wilderness into a fertile land; the healing of the blind, the deaf, the lame, and the dumb, and the restoration of Zion. The psalm is a song of praise to the God who sets prisoners free and opens the eyes of the blind. James 5:7-10 affirms that the coming of the Lord is at hand, and counsels patience. In the Gospel lection John the Baptist is confirmed as the one who prepared the way for Jesus, and Jesus is confirmed as the Messiah through his healing of the sick and the preaching of good news to the poor.

Isaiah 35:1-10

Last week's Old Testament reading from Isaiah 11:1-10 left us with a vision of nature transformed, a vision in which natural enemies of the animal kingdom and human beings live together in peace. Today's lesson complements that one, but now it is the land, and especially the wilderness, that has become a supportive environment for human beings. In Isaiah 11:1-10 Zion was the center of the peaceful kingdom; in Isaiah 35 it is the goal of a pilgrimage of the elect through lands that once were hostile.

Because of its similarities to the poetry in Isaiah 40–55, some commentators have attributed Isaiah 35 to the same prophet, Second Isaiah in 539 B.C. On closer examination, however, it appears that the author of Isaiah 35 knew and depended upon Second Isaiah. He frequently cites but often reinterprets expressions from that prophet of the end of the Babylonian Exile: "highway" (verse 8) from 40:3, "streams in the desert" (verse 6) from 43:19, the appearance of the "glory of the Lord" (verse 2) from 40:3, 5, and more. However, while Second Isaiah had announced the return of the Judean exiles from Babylon along a highway in the desert, the poet of chapter 35 expects more. The dispersed of Israel from throughout the world shall return to Zion, and the desert will become a fertile garden. The vision in our passage is more cosmic and eschatological than that of Second Isaiah. Since it depends upon Second Isaiah, the chapter can be dated to the postexilic age, and perhaps relatively late in the Persian period.

The question of the place of this chapter in its context in the book is closely related to the issue of its date of composition. Isaiah 35 stands in sharp contrast to the immediately preceding chapter, a harsh prophecy of judgment with almost apocalyptic overtones against Edom, Judah's neighbor. Isaiah 36–39 is an appendix to the prophetic collection with narrative accounts concerning Isaiah of Jerusalem. It thus seems likely that at one stage in the growth of the book, our chapter stood either as its conclusion or as the transition to the words of Second Isaiah in chapters 40–55.

The poem before us today closely resembles a prophetic announcement of salvation, but its contents are more apocalyptic in character. Its two main parts, linked by their attention to wonderful changes in nature, present distinct but closely related themes.

1. Verses 1-6a, with all the language about the transformation of the desert, concerns the coming of "the glory of the Lord" (verse 2). The words actually seem to be addressed to the Lord's messenger or messengers, urging them to call for the wilderness to celebrate and the desert to bloom (verses 1-2). They also are to encourage the weak (verses 3-4). There are echoes here of the old tradition about the theophany, the arrival of God and the dramatic and terrifying effects of his coming on nature, but here nature is transformed by the

coming of God's glory, and then the sick are healed (verses 5-6).

2. Verses 6b-10, on the other hand, concern the return of the redeemed, that is, the dispersed people of Israel, to Zion. Here, too, nature is transformed, made into a well-watered land and fitted with a highway called "the Holy Way" (verse 8). The familiar threats to travelers in the desert—dry land, wild beasts, and enemies—no longer exist. The final lines (verse 10) catch the tone of the entire poem: joy and gladness, for "sorrow and sighing shall flee away."

Psalm 146:5-10

The Old Testament lection holds out hope in a grand and glorious transformation of world orders and in a reversal of fate for both human beings and the world of creation. As one of the Hallelujah psalms (Pss. 146–150), Psalm 146:5-10 breathes the air of praise and trust in the divine. In its descriptions of the qualities and acts of God, the psalm shares many of the hopes and expectations of Isaiah 35:1-10.

The psalm is structured around two opposites. The negative, cast as a warning, in verses 3-4, admonishes the audience not to trust human leadership, princes or a son of man, who cannot aid and whose efforts and plans are destined to sleep with him in the same tomb. (The NJPSV translates verse 3 as "Put not your trust in the great, in mortal man who cannot save.") The best laid plans, the highest hopes, the grandest designs die with their architects; they dissipate with their discoverer's demise. The one who trusts and hopes in such is doomed to disappointment since the son of man (*adam*) always returns to earth (*adamah*).

The opposite end of the spectrum is viewed in verses 5-9. Over against the human, the transitory, the disappointing, the inadequate stands the divine, the eternal, the satisfying, the sufficient.

Verse 5 declares "happy" anyone whose help and hope lie with the Deity. The term "happy" denotes a state of well-being and contentment but not necessarily a state of extravagance and luxury. Beginning in verse 6, a series of four characteristics of God are presented as supporting the contention that happy is the one whose help and hope is in God. (1) First of all, appeal is made to God as creator. As the one who made heaven, earth, and sea—that is, the totality of the universe—God is not bound by the structures and limitations of creaturehood. As creator, he is owner and ruler. (2) Second, appeal is made to the fidelity and constancy of the Creator "who keeps faith for ever." Unlike humans whose plans and programs die with them, God and his help endure forever. Unlike humans, God is not threatened by the possibility of non-being. (3) God is the one who is not only concerned for but also executes (guarantees) justice for the oppressed. In this affirmation and throughout verses 7-9, one finds a consistent emphasis of the Old Testament: God takes a special interest in and acts on behalf of the downtrodden, the powerless, and the despairing. (4) The satisfaction of physical needs is also the concern of God who "gives food to the hungry." As the maker of heaven and earth, God does not will that humans be oppressed or that they should suffer from hunger.

Following these four divine characteristics, the psalmist speaks of seven activities of God in which the Divine acts to alleviate human distress and to defend those without rights. Most of those noted as the object of God's care are persons without full authority and potential to assume responsibility for and to exercise rights for their own welfare: the prisoners (at the mercy of the legal system or perhaps in slavery), the blind (at the mercy of the seeing), those who are bowed down or with bent backs (in debt or oppressed by others thus carrying burdens not their own), the righteous (the innocent in the legal system who however were at the mercy of the upholders of justice), the sojourners (foreign settlers or visitors, nor members of the native culture and thus aliens), and the widow and fatherless (who were without the support of a male patriarch in a male-dominated culture). God is declared to be committed to the care of all these while at the same time God sees to it that the wicked come to their just reward—ruin.

The psalmist here obviously presents the basic nature and character of God but does not claim that conditions and circumstances conform to this idealized divine will. In the list of attributes, God is primarily contrasted with human leaders (verses 3-4 over against 5-9). Verse 10 adds an eschatological note to the text and points to the future as the time when the intervention of God on behalf of society's rejects and subjects will occur. In this forward-looking thrust, the psalm participates in and contributes to the expectations of Advent.

James 5:7-10

This passage overlaps with the epistolary lesson (James 5:7-11) for Proper 21 in Year B, and the reader may wish to consult our remarks in *Year B, After Pentecost.*

In the setting of Advent, it is our text's strong emphasis on the Lord's future coming that we hear most loudly. By the third week of Advent, ordinarily our thoughts have begun to shift toward the Lord's first coming, the Incarnation. Today's other lections lay special stress on the healing miracles that accompany the coming of the Lord. Our text, however, moves in another direction. Its orientation is still eschatological, reminding us that "the coming of the Lord is at hand" (verse 8). In a similar mood and tone, we are warned that "the Judge is standing at the doors" (verse 9). These are salutary reminders that throughout Advent the eschatological note is present. It may be dominant, it may be recessive, but it is always there.

The fundamental message of our text is a call to patience. Twice are we told, quite straightforwardly, "Be patient" (verses 7 and 8). Even though this is deemed necessary in view of the return of Christ, the need for patience was generally recognized in the early church. Patience was recommended as a standard feature of Christian exhortation (I Thess. 5:14; cf. II Cor. 6:6; Gal. 5:22; Eph. 4:2; Col. 1:11; 3:12; II Tim. 3:10). As a natural outgrowth of love (I Cor. 13:14), patience was seen to reflect the very nature of God (Rom. 2:4; 9:22; I Pet. 3:20; II Pet. 3:9, 15) and the work of Christ (I Tim. 1:16). It was the special capacity by which the patriarchs distinguished themselves. Only after Abraham "patiently endured" did he receive the promise (Heb 6:15).

Our text recognizes that awaiting the Lord's final Advent requires an extra measure of patience. To be sure, the coming of the Lord was an event expected in the near future (I Thess.

2:19; 3:13; 4:15; 5:23; II Thess. 2:1, 8). Because the interim was seen to be short, it led to anxiety. Some apparently stopped working, deciding to remain inactive during the remaining time (I Thess. 5:14; II Thess. 3:10). Others became troubled when relatives and friends died during the interim, wondering what was to become of them (I Thess. 4:13-18). With so much uncertainty, it is easy to see how grumbling could become the order of the day (verse 9). In similar circumstances, where the future was unknown, the Israelites turned to grumbling (I Cor. 10:10; cf. Exod. 16:2; 17:3; Num. 14:2; Ps. 106:25). Paul also recognizes that those who are unable to wait patiently tend to become factious (Rom. 2:7-8). The antidote to grumbling is a stern reminder that we stand under God's judgment (cf. 4:12; Heb. 12:12; II Tim. 4:8). Indeed, the judge stands at the door (Matt. 24:33; Rev. 3:20).

We are given two examples of those who know how to wait. First, the farmer who plants the seed and waits patiently for the rains, then the harvest (cf. Deut. 11:14; Jer. 5:24; Hos. 6:3). The essence of farming is to "plow in hope . . . thresh in hope" (I Cor. 9:10). For those who must have immediate results, farming is the wrong profession. Second, "the prophets who spoke in the name of the Lord" (verse 10). Not only did they wait, they suffered while they waited (cf. Matt. 5:12; 23:31; Acts 7:52; Heb. 11:33-38). Yet the essence of their prophetic task was to speak in hope, even if they did not live to see their promises fulfilled.

Being patient means that we must "establish our hearts" (verse 8, RSV), or be "stout-hearted" (NEB). Ultimately this comes as God's gift to us (I Thess. 3:13), but expresses itself in our capacity to maintain equanimity in the face of anxiety. We will all be impatient at one time or another, for one reason or another, but if impatience becomes an ingrained pattern of behavior, it is a sure mark of weak-heartedness. The true test of strength is to wait before the Lord, letting the Lord come when the Lord wills.

Matthew 11:2-11

The Gospel lection for today continues last Sunday's attention on John the Baptist, but now his ministry is over

37

and it is being seen in retrospect. What did that man and his ministry mean for the Advent of Jesus Christ? He deserves a second look, not because he was a fascinating figure, but because he prepared minds and hearts for the One whose coming meant the end of John's era, standing as he did at the doorway of the new. Through the words of Jesus our text offers us the early church's understanding of the one who prepared the way.

Matthew 11:1 concludes a discourse of Jesus with the repeated formula "when Jesus had finished" (7:28; 11:1; 13:53; 19:1; 26:1). Our lection follows immediately that transition and constitutes a portion of Jesus' conversation about John, first with John's disciples (verses 2-6) and then with the crowd (verses 7-19). This material is absent from Mark but is shared with only slight alterations with Luke (7:18-28). That John is in prison at the time (verse 2) is information shared with the reader casually and without explanation. Since this is the first mention of it in Matthew (Luke tells his readers as early as 3:19-20; Matthew supplies details later at 14:3-12), we can only assume that Matthew knew his readers knew enough not to be stalled at this point in the narrative.

Verses 2-6 consist of a question from John to Jesus and the reply to be carried to John by his disciples. The question, "Are you he who is to come, or shall we look for another?" (verse 3) is not at all clear, either in what is being asked, or why. John does not ask if Jesus is the Messiah. Earlier John had announced that one was to come after him who would be mightier (3:11), but even then he did not identify that one as the Messiah, but only that he would baptize with the Holy Spirit and with fire. Perhaps he had in mind Elijah who would return in the last days to turn people again to God (Mal. 4:5). Jesus said John himself was the Elijah to come (11:14), but according to the fourth Evangelist John did not claim that role (John 1:20). But our uncertainty about John's question does not explain John's uncertainty about Jesus. Matthew says that when Jesus came for baptism, John recognized him as greater and without need of baptism (3:13-15), and following the baptism, John (and others?) was told from heaven, "This is my beloved Son" (3:17). How, then, are we to understand the question? That even the revelation at the baptism was not clear to John? That John, for all his courageous preaching, is now pressed by prison, persecution, and the prospect of death into doubt and uncertainty? That the difference between John's image of the One to come and the actual style and nature of Jesus' ministry was so radical as to generate this question to Jesus?

Perhaps in all these answers there is some truth. Certainly this text prompts in an Advent community the reflection: As we await the coming of Christ, what kind of person, what kind of ministry, what kind of relation to us are we anticipating? Christ disappoints the expectations of some.

Jesus' reply to John is a summary of Jesus' ministry, leaving John to arrive at his own conclusion based on what is heard and seen (verses 4-6). This summary echoes Isaiah 29:18-19 and 35:5-6. Healing lepers and raising the dead are not in Isaiah but are added from the accounts of Jesus' activity. Scholars are divided on the interpretation of the beatitude in verse 6. Does it or does it not imply a criticism of John?

Whatever one's interpretation of verse 6, verses 7-11 leave no doubt about Jesus' estimate of John. He was, said Jesus, no weather vane, turning with the wind, nor was he a fashion setter. John was not just a prophet but more than a prophet. "More than a prophet" apparently refers to John's introduction of the One toward whom the other prophets pointed and to John's unique place at the door of the messianic age. Yet even John's greatness pales before that great life which belongs to even the least among us who are Jesus' disciples.

Through public sermon and private doubt John has introduced us to the One who is to come. And like John, we will have to respond on the basis of what we hear and see.

Fourth Sunday of Advent

Isaiah 7:10-16; Psalm 24; Romans 1:1-7; Matthew 1:18-25

As Christmas approaches, the Gospel accounts of the birth of Jesus command our attention more and more. Today's reading from Matthew, with its report of Joseph's marriage to Mary who is "with child of the Holy Spirit," is the most obvious selection for the last Sunday of Advent. The Old Testament lesson contains the lines quoted by Matthew, Isaiah 7:14. Psalm 24 is an entrance liturgy—appropriate for the advent of the Messiah—that celebrates the coming of the Lord as king to the temple and has the congregation asking who may enter with that divine king. The key lines of the epistolary lection for this day are those of the christological confession in Romans 1:2-6 that set the coming of Jesus in the context of God's activity in history.

Isaiah 7:10-16

Texts such as this one, when read in the context of Christian worship, sharpen the tension between the historical meaning and the homiletical or theological interpretation of the Bible, and of the Old Testament in particular. What Isaiah 7:10-16 meant in its original context and what it means in the shadow of Matthew 1:18-25 may be quite different. Matthew quotes Isaiah 7:14 as a prophecy of the conception and birth of Jesus, while Isaiah himself almost certainly had in mind a particular woman and child in his own time. Because the church's commitment to the Bible includes the Old Testament, we should seek to allow the words from Isaiah to be heard in their own terms first.

Some of the literary and historical questions concerning our passage can be answered with relative certainty. It is one

40

of a number of reports of encounters in Jerusalem between Isaiah and King Ahaz at a particularly critical moment in the history of Judah. The historical situation is summarized in Isaiah 7:1-2 and spelled out further in II Kings 16:1-20. When the Assyrian king, Tiglath-pileser III, began to move against the small states of Syria and Palestine, the leaders of those states began to form a coalition to oppose him. Apparently because Ahaz of Judah refused to join them, the kings in Damascus and Samaria moved against Jerusalem (about 734 B.C.), to topple Ahaz and replace him with someone more favorable to their policies. In the passage (7:1-9) that immediately precedes our reading, Isaiah counseled non-resistance based on faith in the ancient promise to David that one of his sons would always occupy the throne in Jerusalem.

Seen in that historical situation, Isaiah 7:10 ff is an announcement of salvation to the king and the people of Judah, concerning the immediate future. Within a short time ("before the child knows how to refuse the evil and choose the good," verse 16), the threat from the "two kings"—that is, Rezin of Damascus and "the son of Remaliah" of Israel—will be ended. The passage is one of a number of sign acts or symbolic action reports in the context, and it is not even the only one to see the birth of a baby as a symbol of hope (see Isa. 9:1-7). When Ahaz refuses Isaiah's invitation to ask for a sign, the prophet gives one. The birth of a child is a sign of salvation, of deliverance from a specific political and military threat. The good news is carried by the child's name, "Immanuel," (verse 14), "God is with us." Deliverance will come, not through alliances or military might, but through divine intervention, by a God who keeps promises.

Also clear are the reading and translation of the Hebrew text of verse 14. The Hebrew word is 'almah, correctly rendered by the RSV and almost all other modern translations "young woman." The term is neutral with regard to her marital status. It was the Greek translation of the Book of Isaiah, the Septuagint, that read "virgin" (Greek *parthenos*), thus setting the stage for the particular messianic interpretation expressed in the New Testament. The bridge between the eighth century and the early church is thus yet another historical and theological context, the translation of the

Hebrew scriptures for Jews in a Hellenistic, pre-Christian culture.

Other aspects of the unit are less clear, including the point where it ends. Is verse 17 a part of the original sign act, or a later addition, and what does it mean? Highly disputed is the identity of the child and his mother. In view of a context that stresses the significance of the Davidic dynasty, many commentators have taken the child to be the crown prince, and the woman as the wife of Ahaz. Others, seeing the passage in some ways parallel to Isaiah 8:1-4, have argued that the woman was the wife of the prophet, and the child his son. It is quite likely, however, that the "young woman" was simply a pregnant woman whom Isaiah saw as he was addressing the king.

Regardless of the extent and limits of our understanding of the passage in its own literary and historical context, it is hardly possible for a Christian congregation to hear the Immanuel prophecy without thinking of the birth of Jesus. What, then, are we to do with the tension between the ancient and the Christian meanings? It is difficult, but essential, to sustain the tension, to refuse to resolve it quickly by choosing the one while rejecting the other. Even a typological interpretation should be attentive to what it is that has been reinterpreted.

Living with Isaiah 7:10-16 itself keeps our feet on the ground of history and human experience. The particular kind of good news proclaimed here by the ancient prophet should not be forgotten. It is a message that sees pregnancy and birth—even when not understood as miraculous—as signs of God's concern for his people. That good news comes into a world with such concrete problems as international politics and threats of war. The fact that the prophet and his message are so directly involved in political events may move us to ask if such expectations as his—along with the message of the coming of Jesus—are legitimate hopes for the people of God.

Psalm 24

Portions of this entrance psalm are used in each of the years in the lectionary cycle (Proper 8, Year B; Presentation (alt.), Year A, All Saints, Year B). This reflects the fact that in the course of church history, the psalm has assumed a number of different contexts being applied to the Incarnation (Christ's entrance into flesh), the saints' entry into the heavenly world, and Christ's ascension. The psalm's acclamation of the advent of God and the divine ascent into the temple make it appropriate to express the Advent theme and to celebrate the entrance of the Messiah into the world.

The psalm is a liturgical composition, written for use in a litany at the temple gate. Thus, it gave expression to communal concerns rather than to personal piety, and it functioned as the spoken component of a ritual occasion rather than as an individual prayer or praise.

In temple services during the second temple period, this psalm was sung as part of the Sunday morning sacrificial ritual. That is, it was used as the psalm for the first sacrificial service of each new week. Thus, it served to open the weekly routine of worship. (Psalms used during the rest of the week were, in order of usage: 48, 82, 94, 81, 93, and 92.)

Psalm 24 begins with a two-verse hymnic acclamation that proclaims the divine ownership of the world with all its inhabitants and substantiates such a claim with reference to God's establishment or creation of the world. In elucidating the expression, "The earth is the Lord's and the fulness thereof," the rabbis noted that a man may own a ship and the cargo not be his or one may own the cargo but not the ship. God, however, owns both the ship (the earth) and the cargo (the fullness thereof).

Creation is here presented, not as the formation of the world from nothing (creation *ex nihilo*) or as the production of the occupants and orders of the universe, but as the anchoring and securance of the world in the midst of the waters. (Springs and wells as well as the sea and lakes suggested that the world "sat" amidst the waters.) Jonah 2:5-6 notes the roots of the mountains thrusting down through the waters.

In verse 3, pilgrims coming to the temple raise the question, "Who can be Yahweh's guest in his house?" The response, probably by the priests inside the sacred precincts, points to four qualifications: purity in action ("clean hands")

43

purity in inward truthfulness ("pure heart"), purity of unadulterated devotion and worship ("does not lift up his soul to what is false [idols]"), and purity of speech ("does not swear deceitfully"). (Such emphases on ethical standards and personality traits illustrate that the cult and morality in ancient Israel went hand in glove.) Those confessing such moral standards and religious virtues, as these pilgrims claim to be (verse 6), are declared to be the recipients of God's blessing and vindication (verse 5).

With verse 7, the focus shifts away from the human world of pilgrims who came to worship and falls upon God who is entering triumphantly as the God of war and power. One must think in rather concrete terms here: God, probably represented by the ark, enters with the pilgrims. (For further discussion of the entry ritual, see Presentation pages 210-11.)

Mount Zion where the temple was built and which is the concern of the psalm came to be identified with Mt. Sinai. Just as the people in the original narrative about Sinai are described as making preparation for their assembly (see Exod. 19:14-15) so the pilgrim in this psalm must be prepared for the presence of God. And so must the worshiper for the Christmas season. The God who came to Sinai in thunder and lightning (Exod. 19:16-24) and to Zion as the "strong and mighty" (Ps. 24:8) comes at the Christmas season as the king enthroned in a manger hailed by shepherds, heralded by angels, and worshiped by wise men.

Romans 1:1-7

With the Fourth Sunday of Advent we edge closer to the celebration of Christ's coming in the Incarnation. This is seen especially clearly in the Old Testament and Gospel readings, both well-known incarnational texts. In the epistolary lection, it is verse 3 that figures most prominently in this regard. With our ears attuned to Advent themes, we are especially eager to hear "the gospel concerning his Son."

As the Gospel reading calls attention to the Davidic lineage of Christ (Matt. 1:20; also 1:1), so our text stresses that Christ was "descended from David" (verse 3). Deeply embedded in the Old Testament was the expectation that a descendant of

David would establish another kingdom (II Sam. 7:12; Ps. 89:3-4; Jer. 23:5). Early Christian faith saw Jesus Christ as the descendant of David who fulfilled these expectations (Matt. 22:42; John 7:42; Acts 13:23; II Tim. 2:8; Rev. 22:16).

Our text also echoes incarnational themes with its insistence that Christ was descended "according to the flesh" (verse 3). Like the Gospel text, this places Christ squarely within human history and guards against all forms of Gnosticism that deny or deemphasize the humanity of Christ (cf. I John 4:2-3). It also conforms to the recurrent New Testament emphasis on Christ's full participation in humanity (Rom. 8:3; 9:5; Eph. 2:14-15; Col. 1:22).

Even though these incarnational themes are especially prominent in this Fourth Sunday of Advent, they by no means exhaust this text. We should note first the unusual form of the text. It is an epistolary greeting, but unlike most opening greetings in the Pauline Letters, it is lengthy and does far more than identify the author and addressee (cf. I Cor. 1:1-3; II Cor. 1:1-2). At the center of the passage is a summary of the early Christian faith in which Paul traces God's activity from the time of the prophets down to his own apostolic ministry. The language is clearly confessional, with each phrase virtually echoing early Christian worship. It is generally agreed that the language is pre-Pauline, which suggests that Paul is citing earlier christian tradition that he had received. This was an especially appropriate move since Paul had not visited the Roman church. By aligning himself with a widely accepted Christian creed, he naturally commended himself and his gospel.

Several features of the confessional summary are worth noting. First is the emphasis on the gospel as expressing the age-old purpose of God (Rom. 16:25-26; Tit. 1:2). The promise was expressed through the prophets whose message became embodied in the scriptures (cf. Luke 1:70). Second is the resurrection as the point when Jesus is certified as Son of God (verse 4; cf. Acts 13:33; I Tim. 3:16). A Pauline note is sounded in the emphasis on the Holy Spirit as that which mediates the power of the resurrection (Rom. 8:11).

Apart from these more formal features, the text is also revealing for what it tells us about Paul. He identifies himself as servant of Christ (cf. Phil. 1:1; Gal. 1:10; also James 1:1; II Pet. 1:1; Jude 1), who was called to be God's apostle. The language Paul uses to describe his "setting apart" by God is reminiscent of Old Testament prophetic calls, suggesting that he understood himself in terms of prophetic vocation (cf. Isa. 49:1; Jer. 1:4-5; also Gal. 1:15; I Cor. 15:10). The object of his commission was "the gospel of God" (cf. Rom. 15:16; II Cor. 11:7; I Thess. 2:2, 8; cf. Mark 1:14; I Pet. 4:17). His specific mission, of course, was to extend the gospel to the Gentiles (verse 5: cf. Rom. 15:18; 16:26; Gal. 2:7-8). Those who respond obediently are called by God to affiliate with Christ (verse 6; cf. Rom. 8:28; 9:24; I Cor. 1:9).

The final verse of our text is the greeting addressed to the saints in Rome (verse 7). Unlike the first part, it conforms to the standard Pauline form of greeting (cf. I Cor. 1:2; II Cor. 1:2; Gal. 1:3; Eph. 1:2; Phil. 1:2; Col. 1:2; I Thess. 1:1; II Thess. 1:2; Philem. 3).

Homiletically, the most natural point of entry to today's text will be verse 3, with its emphasis on the Davidic descent of Christ and his coming in the flesh. But since the overall framework of the epistolary text is much broader than this, extending from prophetic times to the Pauline present, it may serve to balance the more narrow focus of the other lections. In this sense, the epistolary text serves the legitimate function of sketching the larger story within which is set the single event of Christ's Incarnation.

Matthew 1:18-25

For two Sundays the question of who Jesus is has been answered by John the Baptist: "the one to come" and "he who is mightier than I" (3:11). Now Matthew in four stories expands on that answer: Jesus is descended from Abraham and David (1:1-17); Jesus is the child of the virgin Mary, wife of Joseph (1:18-25); Jesus is king of the Jews and hope of the nations (2:1-12); Jesus is God's Son called out of Egypt (2:13-23). The reader who is left with many questions of historical details unanswered needs to remember that the Evangelist is concerned only to give the Christian community's response to the question, Who is Jesus, founder and

Lord of the church? Today's lection is the second of these four stories.

Notice how much Matthew assumes is already known by the community. The conception and birth are very briefly and only indirectly told. That Jesus was born in Bethlehem of Judea is not mentioned until later (2:1) in connection with the cycle of Herod stories (2:1-23) and the circumstances under which Jesus of Bethlehem came to be Jesus of Nazareth. (Notice this is the reverse of Luke's concern to show how Jesus of Nazareth was actually from David's town of Bethlehem, 2:1-7.) From what Matthew records in this brief account, it seems that he wanted to respond to three questions which were prompted by the church's claims about Jesus: How can Jesus be the son of David when his genealogy is traced through Joseph (1:16) who was not his father? In what way can it be claimed that this unusual birth was of God's doing? And where does this child fit into the divine scheme of promise and fulfillment? Our discussion will pursue these three questions.

The Evangelist places upon himself the burden of explanation when he states, "and Jacob the father of Joseph the husband of Mary, of whom Jesus was born, who is called Christ" (1:16). That is, Joseph is the son of David (1:20) but how can Jesus be? The answer is twofold. First, at the time of Jesus' conception Joseph is betrothed to Mary (verse 18) and therefore, her husband (verse 19). Betrothal was not an engagement to be married in the modern sense. Betrothal was a legal bond that could be broken only by divorce (verse 19). A woman betrothed, if bereaved of her "husband," was considered a widow, and if she, during her betrothal, had an affair with another man, it was regarded not as fornication but as adultery. Second, Jesus is the son of David because at the time of his birth Joseph is Mary's husband (verse 24) and, therefore, the legal father of Jesus.

The second question is, How can the Christian community claim that this unusual birth was God's doing? The response of the Evangelist is fourfold. First, he simply asserts that the conception was "of the Holy Spirit" (1:18). That expression is rather restrained and does not provide historical detail. However, Mary is a virgin (verses 23, 25) and God is the giver of children (Gen. 18:10-12; 25:21; 29:31; 30:2, 22-23). Second, Matthew uses the passive voice to speak of the conception (verses 18, 20), the traditional way of referring to divine activity. Third, Matthew appeals to Joseph's character, "a just man and unwilling to put her to shame" (verse 19). "A righteous man" in that tradition should not be translated "a nice guy" in ours. And finally, God is related to these events by means of revelation. An angel of God, coming to Joseph through a dream (verses 20, 25) explains Mary's condition, calms Joseph's fear, directs him to marry her, and gives the name for the child (Jesus-Joshua-salvation from the Lord).

And the final question, Where does this child fit into God's divine plan? is answered by the use of Isaiah 7:14. The quotation formula concerning "what the Lord had spoken by the prophet" (1:22) is found about twelve times in Matthew (among them 2:6, 15, 17, 23) and is important for the Evangelist not simply as a proof pattern but as a declaration of God's faithfulness. Isaiah 7:14 was in its original context a promise and a fulfillment, and so is it here in a new setting. Here, however, the fulfillment is more broadly understood than in its context in Isaiah, for here the word "Emmanuel" capsules the central meaning of Jesus as son of David and Son of God: "God with us." That is the promise containing all promises, the fulfillment containing all fulfillments.

Christmas, First Proper
(Christmas Eve/Day)

Isaiah 9:2-7; Psalm 96; Titus 2:11-14; Luke 2:1-20

The texts for all the Christmas services are the same every year, but the story never grows old. The Lucan account of the birth of Jesus, the shepherds, and the angels concludes with Mary pondering all these things in her heart and the shepherds glorifying and praising God for what they had heard and seen. Isaiah 9:2-7 sings of good news that accompanies the birth of one to sit on the throne in Jerusalem, and the responsorial psalm is an exuberant song of praise for God's reign. The epistolary text speaks of living between the times, between the appearance of the glory of God in the Incarnation and the return of the Lord.

Isaiah 9:2-7

This poem, so distinctive in many ways, closely resembles the thanksgiving songs in Psalms (e.g., Pss. 18:5-20; 32:3-5). There is an account of trouble and the deliverance from it and a thanksgiving service in celebration of that deliverance. But the song also is similar in important respects to prophetic announcements of the future. While it concerns events that have happened and are happening, it announces at the end the implications of those events for the future. In effect, the deliverance from trouble is a sign of what God intends for the future.

Although many commentators in the late nineteenth and early twentieth centuries took the present passage to be a postexilic addition to the Book of Isaiah, it is now widely accepted that it comes from Isaiah in the eighth century B.C.

The precise date is difficult to establish; there doubtless are historical allusions within the poem itself, but they are obscure. Isaiah 9:1 refers to the territories taken by Tiglath-pileser in 733–32 but this verse probably was added when the book was compiled, and in any case the poem speaks of events after the Assyrian invasion. Some scholars have seen the poem as part of the coronation ritual for a particular Judean king, most commonly identified as Hezekiah in 725 B.C. However, it is more likely that the prophetic hymn was composed to celebrate the birth of a new crown prince some time after 732. The sign of God's deliverance is the birth of a new descendant of David.

In terms of literary and grammatical structure, there are two major parts to the poem. Verses 2-3 present an account of release from trouble and the accompanying celebration. Verses 4-7 give three reasons for that celebration, each introduced by "for." Those reasons are the deliverance from an oppressor (verse 4), the destruction of the gear of battle (verse 5), and the birth of the special child (verses 6-7). Most of the verbs are properly translated as present or past tenses, but the final lines are future.

One may also analyze and interpret this passage as a series of graphic images, each with its accompanying moods and tones.

First, there are the contrasting images of darkness and light (verse 2). Darkness is a metaphor for depression and death. The NEB makes that explicit in the final line: "dwellers in a land as dark as death" (compare Ps. 23:4). Light symbolizes life and joy.

Second, in the language of prayer the prophet sketches a scene of celebration. One can almost see and hear the festivities. People shout and sing to their God, as if it were the thanksgiving festival at the end of a good harvest, or the spontaneous expressions of joy when a war has been won.

Third, contrasting images again come to the fore, the harsh pictures of the instruments of war and oppression and a gathering lighted by a fire in which those instruments are burned. The mood of joy and celebration from the previous images continues. What begins as the immediate deliverance from a particular oppressor—doubtless the heel of Assyria—

becomes a vision of perpetual peace: war boots and bloody uniforms are burned.

Fourth, there is the image of a messenger emerging from the royal palace with the good news that a son—a crown prince—has been born. This birth-announcement image is the central scene of the poem. Like the symbolic-action reports in the immediate context in the Book of Isaiah (7:10-16; 8:1-4), the birth of a baby is a sign of God's saving activity on behalf of his people.

Finally, and with no dramatic transition, the scene moves to the throne room of the king and beyond. The newborn baby is now seen as the righteous and just king, sitting on the throne of David. This son of David will administer justice, establish righteousness, and inaugurate a reign of peace, all of which corresponds to the will of God and thus will extend forever.

One way for the preacher to proclaim the good news of this passage is to simply present these graphic images to the congregation. Good news is preached not only by what is said but also by establishing a mood of celebration, and these scenes do just that. Or one could explore the specific contents of the passage. Those would be God's deliverance from oppression, the establishment of peace, and the reign of justice and righteousness. Any or all of these would carry forward the message of Christmas.

Psalm 96

The psalms for the three propers of Christmas are the same throughout the three years of the lectionary, namely Psalms 96, 97, and 98. All of these psalms belong to the same genre or type. They are hymns proclaiming and celebrating the kingship of Yahweh, the Hebrew Deity. To be more specific, they celebrate the enthronement of God. As such they may be seen as proper responsorial psalms to the arrival of Jesus, the Messianic-Davidic king. Christmas is a time when "heaven and nature sing," and these psalms call upon the whole of nature to join in the celebrative chorus.

Psalm 96 actually consists of two extended calls to praise and proclamation (verses 1-3 and 7-9) and two series of imperatives characterize each of the calls: sing, sing, sing, tell, declare (verses 1-3), and ascribe, ascribe, bring an offering and come, worship, tremble (verse 7-9).

One of the early rabbis said the following about the first three of these imperative verbs: "The three times that the word *sing* is used in this psalm correspond to the three prayers during which the children of Israel sing praises every day to the Holy One, blessed be He. Thus *sing* in *O sing to the Lord a new song* corresponds to the morning prayer during which the children of Israel sing praises to the Holy One . . . because He renews daily the work of creation; *sing* in *sing to the Lord, all the earth* corresponds to the afternoon prayer, because during the day all the inhabitants of the earth enjoy the sun and its beams; and *sing* in *Sing to the Lord, bless his name* corresponds to the evening prayer when the Holy One . . . is praised because He brings in the evening twilight" (*Midrash Tehillim* on Ps. 96).

The center of this psalm is verse 10a: "Say among the nations, 'The Lord reigns!'" Here we have the shout or acclamation (perhaps better translated, "Yahweh has become king") which proclaimed the enthronement of God probably celebrated in an annual enthronement ritual.

The preceding verses declare the impotency of other gods and extol the greatness of Yahweh. Other deities are merely idols (the products of human handiwork and thus of no ultimate value to humans) while Yahweh is the creator of the heavens (hardly the consequence of someone else's creation). Yahweh is the one "to be feared above all gods." (The NJPSV here translates: "He is held in awe by all divine beings.")

The proclamation of praise and ascription of the honor due Yahweh terminate in submission. Recognition of Yahweh's status as reigning king should, according to the psalm, eventuate in submission to God. This is the emphasis of verse 8b-9 which the NJPSV translates: "bring tribute and enter His courts. / Bow down to the Lord majestic in holiness; / tremble in His presence, all the earth!"

The verses following 10b speak of the conditions and consequences of Yahweh's reign as king. Verses 10b and c may be seen to embody both present and eschatological affirmations. The present is described as secure since Yahweh has established (or reestablished) the earth (10b). Again the NJPSV provides a translation that brings out the emphases of the text: "the world stands firm; it cannot be shaken." Human lives are thus not at the whim of irrational forces, not at the mercy of senseless powers, not the pawn of some cosmic game between divine beings, not the object of some supercilious deity. The belief that Yahweh was in control meant for the ancient Hebrew that life could make sense, that life could be lived in some consistency and hope, and that even consolation could be found in calamity. The eschatological or future dimension can be seen in 10c: "he will judge the peoples with equity."

The consequences of these conditions are that heaven and nature should sing and rejoice: the heavens, the earth, the sea, sea creatures, the field, wild animals, and the trees of the forest.

Titus 2:11-14

Since this is the epistolary lection for Christmas Day in all three years, the reader may wish to consult our remarks on this passage in Years B and C.

This passage has been chosen because of the prominence of the "appearing" motif. In fact, two appearings are mentioned. The first "appearing" occurred when God's grace was manifested to everyone in the sending of Christ (verse 11). The second "appearing" lies in the future when Christ will come again as the God and Savior of the redeemed people of God (verse 13). Here we see the dual themes of Advent interlocked—the Incarnation as the First Coming and Parousia as the Second Coming. This serves as a reminder that even when our attention is centered on the birth of Christ as the moment of Incarnation, we are never far removed from that future moment of God's revelation.

This epistolary reading is not a Christmas text in the sense that it makes explicit reference to the birth of Christ, as is the case with the Gospel reading. It does not. Rather than seeing God's coming into the world as a single event in the life of Jesus, it views the entire life and work of Christ as a time of divine visitation. Taken as a whole it was nothing less than a demonstration of divine grace (verse 11). Nor was it merely for the sake of God's making an appearance in the world. The purpose was salvific—to make "salvation possible for the whole human race" (verse 11, JB).

We should note the force of this claim. This divine epiphany, or appearance of God, was not a moment of private revelation. Such was the case when God revealed himself to Jacob, an epiphany memorialized in the name El-bethel (Gen. 35:7). Similar appearances occurred with other Old Testament figures, including Abraham, Moses, and others. We also know of other instances where a dramatic appearance of God occurred, localized in a particular place (cf. II Macc. 3:30). But our text for today places the appearance of the grace of God through the coming of Christ in a different category. It was not merely a moment of private revelation, limited to one person and one place. It was universal in scope. It is for everyone (I Tim. 2:4; 4:10).

The redemptive work of Christ receives special emphasis in today's text: he "gave himself for us to redeem us from all iniquity" (verse 14). This is of course a reference to the sacrificial work of Christ (Gal. 1:4; 2:20; Eph. 5:2, 25; I Tim. 2:6; I Pet. 1:18). It recalls last week's Gospel reading and its reference to Jesus who would "save his people from their sins" (Matt. 1:21). In this respect, Christ the Savior now fills the role of Yahweh as the one who redeems us from all our iniquities (cf. Ps. 130:8). His sacrifice also has a purifying effect. The promise that God's people would be cleansed and purified is now fulfilled in Christ (Ezek. 37:23).

The final effect of the redemptive work of Christ is to create a people for himself. A people for God's own possession is a frequent Old Testament hope (Exod. 19:5; Deut. 7:6; 14:2). It is now realized in the people of God redeemed by Christ. The moral effect of Christ's redemptive work is to create a people "zealous for good deeds" (verse 14; 3:8, 14; I Pet. 3:13; Heb. 10:24).

In a sense, the real test of how we appropriate God's grace is the life we lead. As our text suggests, God's grace has an educative function. It actually trains us in a form of life that renounces evil and pursues the good (verse 12). Standing, as we do, between the two moments of God's appearing—the First Coming in the Incarnation and the Second Coming in the Parousia—we are urged to adopt a form of life that befits divine grace. If Christ sacrificed himself to redeem and purify us, we are expected to extend his salvific work into our own being. It is in this posture that we face the future and await "our blessed hope" (verse 13).

Even though today's epistolary text is not a Christmas text in the narrow sense, it is in the truest sense. Seen through Christian eyes, the birth of Christ is nothing if not a manifestation of divine grace.

Luke 2:1-20

The Gospel lesson for Christmas each year is the ever familiar, ever new story in Luke 2:1-20. The account consists of two parts, verses 1-7 and verses 8-20, the former stating quite simply the event, the latter announcing its significance. The two units together reveal a common trait of Lukan writing: a straightforward narration that could have been written by a disinterested historian joined to material highly confessional that hides nothing of the writer's world view and faith. (As other examples, see 3:1-9 and Acts 23:1-11.)

To say that verses 1-7 read as lines composed by a disinterested historian is not to say that this brief record is free of historical problems. Every serious commentary on Luke struggles with the chronological difficulties spawned by the reference to a census under Quirinius, governor of Syria. Luke sets his nativity story in the days of Herod, king of Judea (1:5) and yet it was not until after the reign of Herod's son Archelaus (A.D. 6) that Judea was placed under the governor of Syria. Added to that is the whole question of whether a Roman tax decree required subjects to return to ancestral homes. Those two questions hang over the text. But Luke, having done his research (1:1-4), writes as a historian, providing an event with time, place, principal characters, and circumstance. No angels, no wise men, no stars invade the story, alerting the reader to its peculiarly Christian promptings. Not even the manger scene is given any special halo. The census enrollment had crowded the city, the inn was full, a manger had to suffice; it was as simple as that.

However, to say that verses 1-7 have the style of a disinterested historian is not to say that the writer has pulled from the account the interests of faith. On the contrary, within the historian's style are to be found many Christian affirmations. In addition to answering the question, How could Jesus of Nazareth qualify as the prince to be born in David's city? (Mic. 5:2), the passage is full of allusions to the Old Testament (Mic. 5:2; Isa. 1:3; Jer. 14:8). Likewise, the reference to Caesar Augustus and Quirinius is more than a method of dating; it is also a way of affirming that God uses emperors, governors, and kings to carry out the divine will even though those authorities are unaware of their roles in God's purposes. (Acts 23–28 dramatically illustrates this perspective in Paul's arrest, official protection, and voyage to Rome.) And finally, the description of the baby in the manger is Luke's way of affirming what Matthew says with "Emmanuel" (1:23), what John says with "the Word became flesh" (1:14), what Paul says with "born of woman, born under the law" (Gal. 4:4), and what the writer of Hebrews says with, "In the days of his flesh . . . . he learned obedience through what he suffered" (5:7-8).

Less subdued and more openly confessional are verses 8-20, which announce the significance of the event in verses 1-7. But even here amid angelic choirs and excited shepherds there is a sad silence. At the annunciation that she would bear the Christ Child, Mary had an angel visitor (1:26-38) and in the home of Elizabeth had her place in God's purpose confirmed (1:39-56). But now, away from home, in a stable, in the pain of labor and birth, there is no angel, there is no heavenly confirmation. She hears of heaven's shout from the shepherds (verses 15-20), to be sure, but one still would have wished for her that night one angel of her own, just for reassurance. But faith is usually one angel short, left to ponder these things in the heart (verse 19).

The messages of venses 8-20 are both stated and implied. The messages stated are many: Jesus is Lord, son of David, Christ, and Savior; his birth ushers in a time of joy in the good news of God's favor and a time of peace among those who please God; the good news of Jesus Christ is for "all the people" (verse 10); the sign of God's favor is not in heavenly voices or in visions of angels but in the "babe wrapped in swaddling cloths and lying in a manger" (verse 12); and appropriate responses to the child's birth are wondering, praising God, glorifying God, rejoicing, and pondering these things in the heart. Implied but no less important are other messages: God has been faithful to a promise (Mic. 5:2); as with David the shepherd (II Sam. 7:8), God visits with favor the least likely and lifts up those of low degree (1:52); the story previews the first sermon of Jesus in his home synagogue: "He has anointed me to preach good news to the poor" (4:18; Isa. 61:1-2). Both the angels of heaven and the poor of the earth will reappear often throughout this Gospel and Acts.

Christmas, Second Proper (Additional Lessons for Christmas Day)

Isaiah 62:6-7, 10-12; Psalm 97; Titus 3:4-7; Luke 2:8-20

A note reverberating through the lessons for today is that of proclamation, the making known of the good news embodied in the birth of the Christ Child. The reading from Isaiah recalls weary but alert watchmen who herald the coming news of salvation. The psalm affirms that God has become king, a kingship proclaimed by heaven and earth. The reading from Titus testifies to the experience of responding to the good news. The Gospel reading—Luke's birth story—focuses on the proclamation of good news, first heard by the shepherds at Bethlehem, good news which leads the shepherds to praise, people to wonder, and Mary to ponder.

Isaiah 62:6-7, 10-12

Many of the Old Testament readings for the season concern the dramatic transformation of Jerusalem, the holy city, into the center for the people of God in a new era of salvation. The motif is taken up in various ways, but usually as part of a prophetic announcement of salvation that ultimately affects not only all peoples but even nature itself (Isa. 2:1-5 on the First Sunday of Advent; Isa. 11:1-10 on the Second Sunday of Advent). Even the other texts that are more explicitly messianic have Jerusalem and Zion in the background, as the center from which God will reign through the descendant of David.

The Old Testament text for this occasion likewise looks to the restoration and elevation of Jerusalem, but the angle of vision is somewhat different and the range a bit more limited. Instead of announcement of salvation, the reading begins with prayers for restoration. Only in the final verses does it turn confidently to the future, but even those lines serve to remind Yahweh of the promises he has made. The perspective from which these words emerge, therefore, is quite sober. The prophetic poet knows that the present reality of Jerusalem is far from that anticipated in the ancient promises concerning the city. The city and its people are in trouble, and it is time to pray for deliverance.

Isaiah 62, as part of the collection of material (Isa. 56–66) identified as Third Isaiah, does indeed come from a troubled time, especially for the city of Jerusalem. Precise dates for the units in these chapters are difficult to establish, mainly because they do not come from a single prophet. Isaiah 56–66 rather is a collection of prophetic and liturgical materials from the postexilic era, many of them depending on and extending the message of Second Isaiah (chapters 40–55). Many of the sections, including the one before us now, appear to assume the situation in the first decades after the exiles began to return from Babylon to Judah, that is, 538–516 B.C.

Most of our evidence for the circumstances of Judah and Jerusalem in those years comes from Ezra 1–6, Haggai, and Zechariah 1–8. Haggai and Zechariah, like Isaiah 62, are concerned with the restoration of Jerusalem, and the rebuilding of the temple in particular. Serious construction work on the new building began in 520 B.C. and it was completed in 516 B.C. During this period—in fact, for the two centuries from 538 to 333 B.C.—Judah was a province of the Persian Empire. In the first years after the return, the former exiles found the city and the temple in ruins, experienced conflicts among themselves and with those who had remained in the land, and faced threats from people outside, including their former enemies. They also faced more than one crisis of faith when the new life in the Holy City fell far short of what the prophets had told them to expect.

Although a central motif in Isaiah 62 is prayer to God for the salvation of the city, it is not easy to identify the various speakers and addressees in the passage. Is the "I" of verse 1 a prophetic voice that will not be silenced, or Yahweh himself who affirms that he will now speak up? The initial speaker probably is a prophetic one, for in verse 6 that same voice first speaks to Jerusalem, appointing sentries for her walls, and then commissions them to remind Yahweh of his promises concerning the city, giving him no rest until he fulfills them. The image of "watchmen" is indebted to a tradition such as the one found in Ezekiel 33, but in that case the prophet was to warn the people and here the prophetic sentries are to be in continuous prayer to Yahweh.

In the concluding section (verses 10-12), the prophetic figure now addresses the people of Jerusalem, exhorting them to prepare "the way for the people," that is, all who will come to the Holy City. The image of a highway is familiar from Second Isaiah, but there it involved God's transformation of the dry wilderness trails into a level road with water along the way. Here those who stand in Jerusalem and those who have already returned are urged to go out and "build" the road and "clear it of stones" (verse 10). They are to work hard on behalf of other returnees.

The good news is that the Lord himself is coming to Zion, bringing "salvation," "reward," and "recompense." Throughout the entire chapter it is clear that God is asked for—and will grant—a renewal of the covenant with Jerusalem and its inhabitants. In that covenant the people themselves shall be renewed. The new relationship is like a marriage (verses 4-5). Moreover, the transformation will be effected by giving the city, the land (verse 6), and the people themselves new names that embody the new reality: "holy people," "redeemed of the Lord," "Sought out," and "not forsaken" (verse 12).

Psalm 97

Like Psalm 96, this text focuses on the kingship and reign of God and on the consequences of God's coming in judgment.

The psalm opens with a statement that "Yahweh reigns" or "has become king" and that the whole earth and the coastlands (the islands to the west) should rejoice and be glad. Such an announcement assumes the existence of a new state of being, a new reality which can only be greeted or announced but not brought into being or humanly created.

The qualities or effects of God's reign are described, in verses 2-5, using the metaphorical language of a thunderstorm (see Ps. 29). With some simplification, the reign and presence of God as king may be said to reflect the following conditions (using the NJPSV): *mystification* ("Dense clouds are around Him,/righteousness and justice are the base of His throne"), *purgation* ("Fire is his vanguard,/burning His foes on every side"), *illumination* ("His lightnings light up the world;/the earth is convulsed at the sight"), *transformation* ("mountains melt like wax at the Lord's presence,/at the presence of the Lord of all the earth"), and *proclamation* ("The heavens proclaim His righteousness/and all the peoples see His glory").

Two human responses are noted (in verses 7-8). Shame and dismay overtake the worshipers of idols who are exposed as practicing futility in their worship (since even the other gods must bow to Yahweh; verse 7c). Shame is the consequence of being discovered as something other than what we have claimed to be. On the other hand, Zion and the daughters (= towns) of Judah can rejoice in God's judgments (verse 8). Here the idea of rejoicing in judgment is based on the fact that judgment which vindicates by revealing the truth is salvation. The people proclaim their readiness to be judged with confidence in the outcome.

The final section of the psalm (verses 10-12) concentrates on God's preservation of those who belong to the people of God. They have nothing to fear. Note the three actions of God emphasized: the Lord loves, preserves, and delivers. The opening line of verse 10 has no hesitancy in declaring that God loves those who hate evil. Ancient Israel had no qualms about affirming hatred if it was hatred of that which God did not condone. The righteous and the upright in heart in verse 11 are probably synonymously used terms. The righteous were those declared in the right in judgment. Since in biblical thought the heart was the center of the will and the intellect, being upright in heart was being consistent in thought and action. (The heart's association with the intellect has been preserved when we say we memorize things "by heart.") Though the psalm closes with a call to rejoice, that is, a call to let human emotions be given free rein, it also closes with a call to worship and give thanks to God.

Titus 3:4-7

Since this same epistolary text is used for the set of additional Christmas lessons, the reader may wish to consult our remarks on this passage in the *Advent, Christmas, Epiphany* volumes for Years B and C.

Several preliminary observations are in order. First, as to the literary form of the text, some scholars see behind these verses an ancient baptismal liturgy. The strophic arrangement of these verses in Nestle-Aland, 26th ed., reflects this judgment, even though most other translations print the verses as straight prose (RSV, NEB, JB, NIV). The suggestion is plausible not only because of its context but because of its content as well. The previous verse depicts life before conversion, following the pattern of "once you were. . . ." In such a context, one might reasonably recite the words of a baptismal service to depict the change that occurs in conversion. Besides the context are the explicit references to the "washing of regeneration" (verse 5) and the renewing and receiving of the Holy Spirit (verses 5-6), both of which point in the same direction.

Second, we should take note of what immediately precedes these verses. In verse 3 we have a vivid depiction of life apart from Christ as both self-indulgent and self-destructive. Today's text presents the other side by showing us how the work of God has made a decisive difference. Taken alone, verses 4-7 appear to provide merely a capsule summary of salvation history, but when seen in their context they are far more than this. They depict the saving work of God as a dramatic response to the human condition. It is one thing to rehearse the story of God's saving work, quite another to see it as the answer to our own human dilemma. Today's text does the latter. This is well worth remembering at Christmas when we may find ourselves telling *the story* merely as story, not as saving story. We may tell the story of an accident vividly and excitedly, but we will tell it differently if it is an accident in which *we* were involved—and through which we lived.

Third, our text speaks primarily of God's work. It is God's "goodness and loving kindness" that has appeared; it is God who is "our Savior"; it is God whose uncalculated mercy has saved us and has been lavishly poured out on us. To be sure, all this has been achieved through the saving work of "Jesus Christ our Savior" (verse 6), but the prime actor in today's story is God. This too is worth remembering at Christmas when the primary focus is on Christ. And well it should be, but not if the prior work of God is eclipsed. We might note even further that the Holy Spirit figures centrally in our passage—another reminder that the Trinitarian God remains focal even in the context of celebrating the work of Christ.

Having made these preliminary observations, we might note the way in which today's text focuses on certain crucial "moments" or "events." God's saving work through Christ is taken as a whole, as that which happened at a point in time. God's goodwill "appeared" (aorist) as an event in time, notably in the person and work of Christ. In this respect, it was a decisive, visible, identifiable event that made a difference. The "moment" envisioned here is an historic moment, cosmic in scope yet historically specific.

But another moment is envisioned—our own salvation. God "saved us" (verse 5) is not a moment out there, but in here, not beyond us but within us. It is the salvific moment of the individual. We should notice this, because the text does not imply that God first saved humanity corporately, as if each of us receives our respective share. The moment in view here is our own salvation when we experienced God's rescue through baptismal regeneration and spiritual re-creation.

The tone here is thoroughly Pauline in the insistence that God's saving work has not occurred in response to or because of "deeds done by us in righteousness" (verse 5). Our text reminds us what a serious mistake it is to think that our actions—even our good actions—prompted God to act in our favor. Salvation is not a quid pro quo where God presents us with the gift of salvation in response to or in exchange for our own righteous deeds. What we have done or achieved does not commend us to God. God's saving work is prompted instead by uncalculated mercy. It is not as if God rewards us because of our religious acts but rather that God extends grace to us in spite of our irreligious nature. In the one case, plus meets plus; in the other, plus meets minus. The one can be construed as the divine responding to the human, the other as the divine rescuing the human. One is an act of reward, the other an act of mercy. What distinguishes the two is motive. To reward is to acknowledge goodness and achievement. To be merciful is to recognize need.

In the context of Christmas, today's text can prompt us to probe both the nature and mystery of our own salvation. The Gospel text can provide the christological focus, while the epistolary text can provide the theological focus. Both clearly have a soteriological focus.

Luke 2:8-20

This additional lesson for Christmas has as the Gospel lesson a portion of the reading (Luke 2:1-20) offered as the First Proper for Christmas. Luke 2:8-20 is the second of two parts of Luke's nativity story, both of which were discussed in the preceding lesson. There is no need to repeat that here. If in the Christmas season there will be a need for this additional service, it would be appropriate to use verses 1-7 as the Gospel for one occasion and verses 8-20 for the other. As we have seen, the natural division of the text welcomes such an arrangement, and both parts are certainly rich enough in thought, imagery, and proclamation so as to provide amply for different messages at the services. In fact, the preacher might welcome a briefer text, given the fact that restraint often serves to release one's faculties of thought and imagination.

Christmas, Third Proper (Additional Lessons for Christmas Day)

Isaiah 52:7-10; Psalm 98; Hebrews 1:1-12; John 1:1-14

Today's readings combine to produce a symphony of various compositions centering around the theme of redemptive good news. In the Old Testament reading, Deutero-Isaiah, the anonymous prophet of the Exile, extols the glory of the messenger who brings good news to Zion. The psalm calls for the singing of a new melody making known the victorious triumph of Israel's God. The Epistle lesson proclaims both the unique and the fulfilling quality of the coming of Christ. In the Gospel reading, the redemptive word that became flesh in Jesus is identified with the word that existed with God from the beginning.

Isaiah 52:7-10

Second Isaiah, the prophet of the end of the Babylonian Exile (539 B.C.), again both establishes the mood for our celebration and articulates the good news of the day. In fact, the contents of the reading concern the proclamation of good news to people in trouble. Although this very familiar poem is hymnic in tone and substance, and it alludes to cultic matters, it is not itself a hymn. By the time we reach its conclusion in verse 10 it is clear that it is a particular kind of announcement of salvation, one concerning the triumph of Yahweh.

The prophet, although actually in Babylon, describes a scene in distant Jerusalem. It is a powerful and captivating portrayal of a messenger arriving at the city with good news. The report of the message is overloaded with terms indicating just how positive the news is: "good tidings," "peace," "good tidings of good," "salvation" (verse 7). The actual contents of the messenger's proclamation is, however, a single line: "Your God reigns." It is the triumph of God as king that amounts to such good news.

Then (verse 8) attention shifts to the sentries on the walls of the city, shouting out that Yahweh is returning to Zion (see Isa. 40:9-10). Either the prophet himself or the sentries on the walls call for the city in ruins to sing for joy (verse 9). Here the hymnic language closely resembles a hymn of praise, typically beginning with a call to praise and then citing reasons for that praise. The reasons, introduced by "for" *(ki)*, are that Yahweh has comforted his people (see Isa. 40:1) and redeemed Jerusalem. Finally (verse 10), those reasons for praise are extended to include the entire world. The Lord has displayed his power and authority before "all the nations," so that all can see "the salvation of our God."

These four verses set before us a festival of sights and sounds, alternating from one to the other. First there is the sight of the messenger arriving with good news, seen as in a prophetic vision (verse 7*a*), and then as we look we hear the messenger's news (verse 7*b*). Next we hear the sentries on the city wall singing (verse 8*a*), and then are shown the reasons for their joy (verse 8*b*). Note the mixture of images: the city stands in ruins, but there are walls with sentries stationed on them. This picture is followed by the sounds of the song of praise (verse 9), and concluded with the most dramatic sight of all, the Lord's saving power revealed to the entire world.

A number of the words and expressions in the passage call for comment. "Him who brings good tidings" (verse 7, RSV) is a somewhat awkward translation of a single Hebrew word, and is more accurately read "herald" (NEB, NJPSV). The Hebrew *shalom* (verse 7) is read variously "peace" (RSV), "happiness" (NJPSV), and "prosperity" (NEB). In this context it does not refer so much to the absence of war as well-being. The word translated "salvation" in the RSV (verses 7, 10) could be taken as "deliverance" (NEB) or "victory" (NJPSV). In any case, it characterizes the concrete activity of Yahweh on behalf of his people.

The central themes of the passage concern the kingship of

Yahweh, his return to Zion, and the revelation of his saving power before all the world. As is usually the case in Second Isaiah, the themes are closely related to one another. Yahweh's reign is the good news; he manifests that reign by returning to Zion; in returning to Zion and redeeming his people the divine king displays his authority and power. The kingship of Yahweh is an ancient tradition, celebrated in the temple in Jerusalem. The three psalms for Christmas (96, 97, 98) all come from such celebrations, as do a great many others (e.g., 47, 93). The expression translated here "Your God reigns" (verse 7, RSV) is better read "your God is—or has become—king."

That God returns to Zion raises questions about the presence and absence of God, and the meaning of holy places. The particular motif here is known also in Ezekiel and elsewhere. With the destruction and the Exile, Yahweh was believed to have abandoned the Holy City, and even the chosen people. With the release from captivity and the return, the divine presence comes back. The announcement in this passage, then, is addressed to persons who have experienced the absence of God. Behind this understanding, moreover, stands a deep sense of Zion as a holy place, a location where God is more present than elsewhere. Various biblical traditions attempt to understand the meaning of such beliefs. In the book of Deuteronomy, Jerusalem is the place where Yahweh chooses for his "name" to dwell, that is, the place where he is known and addressed. In Priestly and other traditions, the temple in Zion is the site of God's holiness (e.g., Isa. 6).

Is this a scandal of particularity, that the God who transcends all places should be present in a special way—and even "return"—to a particular place? Here that particular presence is for worldwide visibility and for revelation, and what is revealed is God's saving activity. That, it appears, is not unlike the event celebrated on this day in the Christian Year, the Incarnation.

Psalm 98

Psalm 98 is the third of our triology of enthronement/kingship psalms (along with Pss. 96 and 97). Throughout these psalms, we find the motifs of Yahweh's kingship, the judgment of the earth, the control and stabilization of the world's orders, and the universal rule of God.

The opening stanza (verses 1-3) shows the following three characteristics. (1) The verses are filled with the imagery and metaphors of battle, warfare, and the exercise of power. Note the threefold reference to "victory." The right hand (the "clean" hand used in greeting and eating but also the symbol of favoritism and power) and the holy arm are representative of militant force. (These images may appear a bit out of order at Christmastime when attention is focused on a babe, shepherds, a family, and monarchs on a peaceful mission. Only Matthew in the birth stories speaks in violent imagery and then only with regard to the frustrated Herod whose paranoia hardly achieves anything approximating a victory.) (2) The use of the verb "to save" or "to deliver" occurs three times in these verses. Yahweh's exercise of power is a saving power. (3) Many of the central theological terms of the Old Testament appear in these verses (just as many Christian theological terms get employed in speaking of Christmas). Among these are "vindication," "steadfast love," and "faithfulness."

A special feature of these first three verses is related to the Christmas theme and has probably influenced the selection of this text (and the other enthronement psalms) for the nativity season. Here we refer to the universalism of the psalm. Note the references to "in the sight of the nations" and "all the ends of the earth." But even in light of this universalism, the particular still plays its role; God's love and faithfulness are shown to "the house of Israel."

The central section (verses 4-6) is a lengthy summons to praise addressed to all the earth. Here it is clearly the world's human audience that is addressed since the musical instruments noted are human in origin and usage. (These verses would suggest that much of the cultic, celebrative quality of Christmas has been caught best by street-corner Salvation Army bands!)

The final stanza (verse 7-9) continues the summons to praise but now the address is to the world of nature—the sea and its occupants, the earth and its inhabitants, the floods, and the hills. The reasons for such praise are found in the promise that God will come to judge and that he will judge with righteousness and equity.

Hebrews 1:1-12

Since the same epistolary text is used for Christmas, Third Proper in Years A, B, and C, the reader may wish to consult our remarks on this passage in the volume *Advent, Christmas, Epiphany* in Years B and C. Part of today's text (Heb. 1:1-4) also serves as the epistolary text for Proper 22 in Year B. The reader may find additional comments on this text in the volume *After Pentecost, Year B*.

Today's text serves as the opening section of the Epistle to the Hebrews, an anonymous writing at one time attributed to Paul. Like the epistle as a whole, which may be regarded as a lengthy, sustained christological argument, these introductory verses have Christ as their central focus. They represent a lofty meditation on Christ as the preeminent Son of God, without rival or peer either in heaven or on earth.

In the opening section (verses 1-4), we are presented with a series of contrasts: "of old . . . in these last days," "to our fathers . . . to us," and "by the prophets . . . by a Son." The first contrast signals a temporal shift, a turn of the ages, in which one era gives way to a new era. It reflects the early Christian conviction that the coming of Christ had marked the end of one age, the beginning of a new age (cf. 9:26; I Pet. 1:20; Jer. 23:20). The second contrast marks a shift in the recipients of God's revelation. In former ages, God had appeared to patriarchs such as Abraham (Luke 1:55), but now the author and his readers—and we by extension—constitute a new audience. The third contrast marks a shift in the mode of revelation. Previously, God had used prophets and other representative figures as speakers and interpreters of the divine will (Hos. 12:10-14). Now, however, there are no longer multiple witnesses, but a single witness—God's Son. God's voice is no longer heard through a multitude of human voices but is funneled through the single voice of the chosen Son.

With the mention of the sonship of Christ, there follows an

avalanche of christological claims: Christ as the legitimate heir of God, God's assistant in creation, a reflection of God's glory, the very imprint of divine essence, the one who sustains the whole universe through his powerful utterances, the high priest who offers sacrifice on behalf of the people, and the one exalted to the right hand of God (verses 2-4). This set of claims is treated more fully in our remarks on this passage in Years B and C.

These various claims about Christ gradually move toward a final argument for his superiority to angels (verse 4). This in turn is supported by a form of midrash in which various Old Testament passages are cited to show precisely how and why Christ is far superior to angels. Specifically, his status exceeds that of angels because he bears the incomparable name Son of God (cf. Eph. 1:21; Phil. 2:9). His name merely reflects his exalted status as the one who was raised from the dead and is now seated at God's right hand (cf. Eph. 1:20; I Pet. 3:22; Ps. 113:5).

The Old Testament quotations that follow appear to exhibit a certain logic, though we should not press the scheme too far. They are not unrelated to the various christological claims made in verses 2-4. We would suggest the following scheme of interpretation:

First, Christ in the preexistent state (verse 5). Psalm 2:7 and II Samuel 7:14 are cited with reference to Christ to show that he has been given the title "Son," and thereby enjoys a unique relationship with God. In his preexistent state, Christ enjoyed a father-son relationship with God which no angel had.

Second, the incarnate Christ (verse 6). We are told that God "brings the first-born into the world," an apparent reference to the Incarnation. To speak of Christ as the "first-born" is to underscore his preeminent status, not to imply that he was the first thing created (cf. Col. 1:15; Rev. 3:14). In words reminiscent of the Lukan birth narrative (Luke 2:8-20), we are told that at his birth the angels worshiped him (Deut. 32:43). Thus the angels are worshipers not the objects of worship.

Third, the resurrected Christ (verses 7-9). We next find Psalm 104:4 and Psalm 45:6-7 being applied to Christ. So understood, they appear to envision his enthroned status as

God's anointed, which would presuppose his resurrection. By contrast, the angels are but "winds, . . . and . . . flames of fire" (verse 7). His is the royal rule; theirs are accompanying signs.

Fourth, the creator Christ (verses 10-12). Here Psalm 102:25-27 is applied to Christ. He is addressed as "Lord," and is given the role of creating the heavens and the earth. In contrast to the created order, however, Christ neither changes nor perishes, but remains the same (cf. 13:8).

Fifth, the reigning Christ (verse 13). Finally, Psalm 110:1 is applied to Christ to underscore his interim reign. He sits exalted at God's right hand but waits until all his enemies are destroyed. Presumably, this envisions the period of the present between his resurrection and the final consummation.

Within the context of Christmas, the part of this passage that relates most directly to the birth of Christ is the claim made in verse 6: God "brings the first-born into the world." As noted above, the reference to God's angels worshiping him also echo familiar Christmas themes. The homilist may wish to focus on this narrow slice of the passage by relating its view of the Incarnation to that of the Gospel text for today. But other possibilities exist if one wishes to approach the text more broadly. For one thing, there are several points of convergence between the Christology of this passage and that expressed in the Johannine prologue: the finality of God's revelation through Christ, the importance of Christ's "word of power," Christ as God's agent of creation.

John 1:1-14

So significant for Christian history and Christian faith is John 1:1-14 that the minister might choose to alternate this lection with Luke 2:1-20 as the primary Gospel reading for Christmas. If that is the case, then it would be well to underscore in a message based on John 1:1-14 those affirmations that are not found in Luke's story.

Before proceeding to focus on the major themes in this text, the preacher may wish to make a decision about verses 6-8. A choice not to treat these three verses in the sermon could be justified on several grounds other than the fact that there is more than enough to occupy the preacher in verses 1-5 and 9-14. Practically speaking, verses 6-8 concern John the Baptist whose person and message were treated the second and third Sundays of Advent. Literarily speaking, these verses are an insert into the hymn to the Word as a part of the writer's polemic against the sect of John the Baptist and can be extracted without loss to the central affirmation of the passage. In fact, the move from verse 5 to verse 9 is noticeably smooth. And theologically speaking the message of the lection without verses 6-8 is God's act in Jesus Christ, the word for this and every season.

Since John 1:1-14 has been otherwise treated in cycles B and C, let us here simply call attention to five major affirmations of this text which are especially appropriate for this season.

1. John 1:1-14 reminds us that the central subject of the Bible and therefore of our faith is God. Eight times in this brief passage that fact is stated. Some christologies tend to forget God sent the Son; some pneumatologies tend to forget God sends the Spirit. God through the Word is creator (verses 2-3) and God through the Word is redeemer, the end being for us to become children of God (verses 12-13). At Christmas the spotlight is properly on the Word made flesh but the glory which faith sees in Bethlehem's child is that of "the only Son from the Father" (verse 14).

2. The larger context for the Christmas story is creation. Two important faith statements proceed from that observation. One, because the One through whom we are redeemed (verses 12-13) is the same One through whom all things were created (verse 3), then salvation is not to be understood as over against the world or out of the world as though the created order were evil and alien to the life of God's children. There is evil in the world, to be sure, but by choice not by nature. Two, all creation is involved in God's redemptive effort. Although only implied here, this theme is elsewhere developed at some length (Rom. 8:18-25; Col. 1:15-20; Eph. 1:10, 20-23).

3. The Word becoming flesh does not represent a sole and single effort of God in behalf of the world. God has

continually been life and light to the world even though the reception of God's life and light has not been universal (verses 4-5, 9-13). Ecclesiasticus (Sirach) 24 offers a beautiful portrayal of the Word (Wisdom) seeking to find a home in which to dwell on earth.

4. The eternal Word *became* flesh and dwelt among us (verse 14). That statement of identification with us is too strong and clear to be handled by analogies about being clothed as we are, or dressing as one of us, or taking on a human disguise. John 1:14 implies all the vulnerability which one finds in Luke's baby in a manger. The glory which "we" behold is that which the community of faith sees but which is not and was not openly obvious to all casual passersby. The glory of God in Jesus of Nazareth was not and is not evident to the world (14:17, 22-24). Those who will not see cannot see.

5. The birth imagery, so central to the Christmas Season, in Johannine literature is applied to all who believe. To embrace God's Word is to be born of God, to become a child of God (1:13; 3:3; I John 3:9; 5:18). The line in the carol that petitions "be born in us today" is a proper extension of the meaning and the good news of Christmas. He became as we are that we might become as he is.

First Sunday After Christmas

Isaiah 63:7-9; Psalm 111; Hebrews 2:10-18;
Matthew 2:13-15, 19-23

The Gospel lesson for this Sunday narrates the story of the holy family's flight to Egypt to escape the wrath of Herod, and then their settlement in Nazareth. The Old Testament lesson, although addressing an earlier situation, speaks of a Savior as well as a protecting angel and thus shows analogies to the Gospel reading. The psalm offers thanksgiving to God while the epistle reading focuses on the descendants of Abraham who, like the patriarch himself, went down to and came out of Egypt.

Isaiah 63:7-9

Read out of context, these three verses from Isaiah 63 appear to parallel the responsorial psalm for the day. Psalm 111 is a hymn of praise that extols God by recounting the history of his saving events on behalf of his people, and that is what we find in Isaiah 63:7-9 as well. Read with the other texts for the First Sunday After Christmas, the links with the Gospel lesson become obvious. Both mention angels or divine messengers (Isa. 63:9; Matt. 2:13, 19), and Matthew's account of the flight of the holy family to Egypt and their return parallels the Old Testament reading's allusions to the Israelite Exodus from Egypt.

Understood in this way, the main theme of Isaiah 63:7-9 is the saving, redemptive activity of God in history, particularly on behalf of the elect. Such an understanding of the passage from Isaiah is not only legitimate, especially in the framework of Christian worship, but accurate if the verses are read alone. However, our interpretation and proclama-

74

tion of the text can be both broadened and deepened by considering its literary and historical context.

Although it is not immediately obvious, Isaiah 63:7-9 is the first part of a prayer, an act of worship, that is not concluded until Isaiah 64:12. It is not immediately obvious because the prayer language—that is, direct address to God—is not explicit until 63:14. The first part of the prayer instead refers to Yahweh in the third person. Nevertheless, the structure, contents, and purpose of the prayer closely parallel a particular type found in the book of Psalms (e.g., Ps. 44; 74; 79) and the book of Lamentations, the complaint song or lament by the community.

All the major elements of such complaint psalms are present. (1) Affirmations of God's capacity to respond. Here, as elsewhere, that takes the form of praise of God in terms of his actions in the past. Psalm 89, which like our text begins with an announcement of the intention to praise, is a close parallel. (2) Confession of sin. (Some individual complaints have instead a confession of innocence; cf. Ps. 17.) In this case the confession is part of the historical recital (63:10 ff., 16; 64.5 ff.), the rebellion of the people contrasting with Yahweh's saving acts. (3) Account of the trouble or distress. The community reminds the Lord of their present difficulties (63:18-19; 64:7, 10-11), in this case the destruction of the city of Jerusalem and the temple. (4) Complaints against God and petitions for his help. The community asks the Lord to intervene on their behalf (63:15, 17; 64:1 ff., 9, 12).

In this framework, praise of God for his historical activity on behalf of the people undergirds petition. The God addressed by a people in trouble is one who has saved the people in the past and is capable of doing it again. Moreover, God's disposition to act in mercy is revealed by history. There is yet another point to this recital as a part of prayer: When the history of salvation is told as part of petition, it quickly leads to confession of sin. If complaint and petition are in view, then praise and confession must go hand-in-hand. Part of penitence is to recall what God has done on one's behalf.

Historically, most of the materials in Isaiah 56–66 stem from the postexilic period. They are not the work of a single author, but amount to a collection of prophetic and liturgical units from the era. The song (Isa. 63:7–64:12) of which our reading is a part appears to be an exception, in that it presumes the situation of the Exile. It must have originated in worship services among either the exiles in Babylon or those who remained in the ruined land of Judah. Like many of the Psalms, it would have found its place in the liturgical life of the community far beyond the time of its origin.

The text is rich in the language of the history of Israel's election and of the covenant. "Steadfast love" (from *hesed*, verse 7) characterizes the ideal relationship of both parties in a covenant, and may be interpreted if not translated as "covenant loyalty." In this verse, however, it is plural and in parallel to "praises" in the next line. Thus a more accurate translation would be: "I will recount the loyal deeds of Yahweh, and Yahweh's praiseworthy actions." Verse 8 contains a paraphrase of the fundamental formula for the conclusion of the covenant between God and people, "Surely they are my people." The full formulation contains two parts, "You shall be my people and I will be your God" (cf. Exod. 6:2-8; 19:3-6; Lev. 26:12; Hos. 1:8-9). The address to the people as "sons" recalls the language of Hosea 11:1 ff. and Isaiah 1:2. Although there are textual problems, verse 9 certainly alludes to the Exodus from Egypt (cf. Exod. 12:1-32). The problem of text and translation concerns "in all their affliction he was afflicted, and the angel of his presence saved them" (RSV), which follows the Hebrew text closely. The New English Bible, following the Greek and reading the last line of verse 8 with the beginning of verse 9, gives a very different meaning: "And he became their deliverer in all their troubles. It was no envoy, no angel, but he himself that delivered them."

Isaiah 63:7-9, containing words of praise that recall saving events parallel to those in the Gospel lesson for the day, enables us to confess our faith in the God who does such things. But also, as part of a prayer of complaint and petition they may enable us to confess our corporate sins as well.

Psalm 111

Although the other readings for the First Sunday After Christmas vary during the three years of the cycles, the psalm selection remains the same. This psalm, also the reading for the Fourth Sunday After Epiphany, Year B, is shot through with optimism about the present and the future. To this extent, it perhaps reflects the sentiments of the early post-Christmas Season—a sense of happiness, contentment, and well-being.

Three general matters should be noted about the psalm. (1) Although a thanksgiving psalm (note verse 1b), the text, unlike most thanksgiving psalms, does not recall any past calamity or period of distress from which the worshiper has been rescued. Thus the psalm contains no indications about the trouble from which the worshiper suffered. This might suggest that the occasion for thanksgiving was one of well-being. In ancient Israel, certain sacrifices (called in the RSV "peace offerings"; Lev. 3) were made when life was okay, when things were good. Perhaps this is the background to this psalm. (2) The psalm contains no direct address to the Deity. The audience is thus not God but humans. The psalm is therefore not prayer but proclamation, preaching, the sharing of a faith perspective. (3) The psalm is an acrostic or alphabetic poem composed of lines running through the Hebrew alphabet. (The opening phrase "Praise the Lord!" or "Hallelujah" stands outside the acrostic.)

One possible way of getting into this psalm is to notice the fivefold repetition of the term or idea "for ever" (verses 3b, 5b, 8a, 9b, and 10c). This phenomenon is further explored in the treatment of this psalm in Year C.

One can also imagine this psalm as a worshiper's sermonette delivered to an audience whom the speaker is trying to convince (or affirm) of God's accessibility and fidelity. God is accessible through his works; this is a theme that runs throughout the psalm. Verse 2b, a text difficult to translate, is read as "within reach of all who desire them" by the NJPSV. Such a reading affirms the accessibility of the Divine through his works, which range for expelling the inhabitants of the land of promise to providing food for his followers to providing the law and its precepts. The fidelity of God is reflected in the remembrance of his works, his commitment to the covenant, and the trustworthiness of his precepts. To fear (worship) such a God is the beginning (or the essence) of wisdom.

Hebrews 2:10-18

The latter part of this text (2:14-18) also serves as the epistolary lection for the special day of Presentation (February 2) in all three years. The reader may wish to consult our remarks on this passage in connection with the Day of Presentation later in this volume, as well as in the other volumes of *Advent, Christmas, Epiphany* for Years B and C.

It is fully appropriate on this First Sunday After Christmas to concentrate on how Christ in the Incarnation fully identified with us—wholly, unexceptionally, unreservedly. Few New Testament texts press this point more forcefully than today's text from the Epistle to the Hebrews where we are assured that Christ has been "made like his brethren in every respect" (verse 17). Our text suggests that Christians have not always found it easy to believe that the Son of God actually became "flesh and blood" (verse 14) in a fully human sense. Knowing ourselves as we do, we find it hard to conceive of Christ looking at life through our eyes. When we look inward we see frailty, flaws, and gross imperfection and know only too well that flesh and blood humanity carries with it limitations far too great, far too severe to befit the Son of God.

Today's text responds to this resistance of ours, this reluctance to believe in a Christ who was and is one of us. First, we are assured that God willed it this way. It is the God "for whom and by whom all things exist" (verse 10) who thought it fitting for Christ to be perfected through suffering. Christians confess God as the source, means, and object of all things, the one from whom, through whom, and for whom all things exist (cf. Rom. 11:36; I Cor. 8:6; also Col. 1:16-17). However much we may see the Incarnation as a mystery, the God we confess is surely able to turn the mystery into reality. To wonder whether Incarnation is possible is to doubt God's preeminent power.

Second, our text stresses the common origin we have with Christ. The one "who sanctifies [Christ] and those who are sanctified [us] have all one origin" (verse 11). Literally, the text reads that the sanctifier and the sanctified are "all of one" *(ex henos pantes)*. Most likely this means that both we and

78

Christ are "of God," perhaps even "of the one God"and hence "of the same family" (NIV), "of the same stock" (JB), or "form a single whole" (JB, note). The emphasis here is not that Christ owes his origin to God in the sense that we do, for this would suggest that Christ was created, and thus that "there was a time when he was not." The emphasis is rather that just as Christ cannot be understood apart from God, neither can we. In this sense, we are his "brethren," members of God's family.

Third, our text extends this point further by stressing Christ's solidarity with us as "brethren" or "children of God." This is achieved by several Old Testament quotations attributed to Christ. The first is Psalm 22:22, in which the psalmist praises God and proclaims the divine name to his brethren, or fellow worshipers. We have no record in the Gospel tradition where Christ quotes this particular passage, although Christ on the cross utters the more famous opening line, "My God, my God, why hast thou forsaken me?" (Ps. 22:1; Mark 15:34). Perhaps through this association, the entire psalm was read as a prayer of Christ, in which case its use here would make sense. We may hear an echo of this sentiment in John 17:6: "I have manifested thy name to the men whom thou gavest me." We should also recall the other times when Christ is closely identified with his "brethren" (Matt. 12:48-49; 25:40; 28:10; Rom. 8:29).

The other Old Testament quotation is Isaiah 8:17-18, where the prophet confesses his trust in God (verse 13; also Isa. 12:12; II Sam. 22:3), and acknowledges the "children" God has given him. Here again these words are understood as an utterance of Christ who, like the prophet, had implicit trust in God and finds himself before God with a company of fellow believers.

Both of these texts have the force of identifying Christ with us as his "brethren," the fellowship of those who belong to God and are at God's disposal. Accordingly, Christ entered fully into the human family, sharing "in flesh and blood" (verse 14; cf. Rom. 8:3). That he did so completely is signified by plunging into the ultimate act of humanity—death (verse 14). This is the suffering of which our text speaks (verse 10; cf. 9:13-14; 13:12). Yet his death was unique in that it overcame death. By dying, he killed death (cf. II Tim. 1:10; I Cor. 15:55; Rev. 12:10).

This was another respect in which Christ differed from angels (verse 16). His ultimate concern was with the "descendants of Abraham," his own family, the children of God. This was where his full identity lay. Consequently, his priestly work was concentrated with the human family, with whom he became completely identified as the great high priest (3:1; 4:14; 5:5, 10; 6:20; 7:26; 8:1; 9:11; 10:21). In this capacity, he demonstrated absolute fidelity as God's priest (cf. I Sam. 2:35), making expiation for the people (5:1; I John 2:2).

He achieved full identification through suffering and temptation (verse 18; cf. 4:15; also Matt. 4:1-11; 26:41; Luke 22:18; Rom. 8:3). Consequently, he can be fully sympathetic with us in our own human struggles.

It may seem that the heavy emphasis on Christ's suffering in today's text carries us too quickly to Good Friday. As a result, the homilist may struggle to relate it to the time immediately following Christmas. But surely the post-Christmas period is the time for us to think of the implications of the Incarnation: our commonality with Christ in God's family, his full identification with us in the human arena where praise and suffering go hand-in-hand, our common fidelity to the task set before us.

Matthew 2:13-15, 19-23

It is appropriate, after reading and hearing again Luke's nativity story, to return to Matthew, not simply because Matthew is the Gospel for this year but because Matthew has stories about the child Jesus. One clearly gets the impression that Matthew's accounts concern a child but not necessarily an infant as in Luke. The flight to Egypt (verses 13-15) and Herod's slaughter of children "two years old or younger" (verse 16) imply that we are here dealing with "post-Christmas" stories. We begin at verse 13 because the account of the visit of the Magi (2:1-12) is always the Gospel reading for Epiphany. Verses 16-18 are omitted, not because they tell a horror story but because they interrupt the account of the holy family's move from Bethlehem to Egypt to Nazareth. In the reader's move from verse 15 to verse 19 there is no break in thought or in the texture of the material.

First, let us locate our lection for today. The reader knows at 2:1-2 that the record to follow will be one of threat and clash. "In the days of Herod the king, behold, wise men from the East came to Jerusalem, saying, 'Where is he who has been born *king* of the Jews?' " (italics added). One does not ask a king the address of the new king, nor does one country comfortably accommodate two kings. The sky darkens and lowers. That which follows is a cycle of Herod stories as one would find among a suppressed minority who looked to the new king for relief from the old. These Herod stories are typically anti-institutional, charting the almost comical frustration and fall of a tyrant upon the occasion of the birth of a deliverer from tyrants. The stories are as follows:

Herod the king	verses 1-2
Herod the troubled king	verses 3-6
Herod the deceptive king	verses 7-8
Herod the deceived king	verses 9-15
Herod the vengeful king	verses 16-18
Herod the dead king	verses 19-23

The narrative of Matthew 2:13-15, 19-23 is carried along by the use of easily discernible Old Testament materials. One hears the clear echos of two stories involving Old Testament heroes, and there is the clear and direct use of the promise/fulfillment motif. The revelations from God by means of dreams, especially to Joseph (1:20; 2:12, 13, 19, 22), recall the stories of Joseph as dreamer and as interpreter of dreams (Gen. 37–41), and the rescue of the favored child from the murderous designs of a wicked and threatened ruler brings to mind the beautiful stories about the young Moses (Exod. 1:1–2:10). The more direct use of the Old Testament occurs in the common Matthean formula, "to fulfil what . . . [was] spoken by the prophet," which occurs at verse 15 and at verse 23. "Out of Egypt have I called my son" has a clear source (Hos. 11:1; also Exod. 4:22), but "he shall be called a Nazarene" has an uncertain origin. A corruption of the word

"Nazirite" (Judg. 13:7) is a possibility. The commentaries will argue the issue.

But Matthew has more in mind than telling Herod-versus-Jesus stories or tracing the early itineraries of Joseph, the Child, and his mother. Matthew is concerned here as in the geneaology (1:1-17) and the birth narrative (1:18-25) to tell the reader who Jesus is. And what does today's lection supply in answer to the question, Who is Jesus? Several affirmations can be made.

One, Jesus of Nazareth is indeed Jesus of Bethlehem, but he came to be the Nazarene by the clear guidance and providence of God who makes even wicked rulers such as Archelaus serve the divine purpose.

Two, Jesus fulfills the role and purpose of Israel in that, like Israel, he was called of God out of Egypt. This theme of being God's obedient and faithful Israel will continue through the experience of baptism and the wrestling with temptation in the wilderness (3:13–4:11).

Three, Jesus' escape from the wrath of a wicked ruler not only recalls the story of Moses, but prepares the reader to hear Jesus as one like Moses whom God has raised up (Deut. 18:18). This Moses likeness will reappear strongly when Jesus speaks with authority from the mountain (chapters 5–7).

Four, Jesus appears here as a providentially favored child in a cycle of Herod stories, but the fact is, his identity is clearly stated: Jesus is God's son (verse 15). Matthew makes room for this declaration throughout the narrative in the way he refers to the holy family: Joseph is addressed by the dream angel and Joseph is the obedient servant but the subject is "the child and his mother" (2:11, 13, 14, 20, 21). "The child and his mother" is a clear and beautiful way to make reference, in a very human story, to One who is beyond all doubt, even in infancy, the Son of God.

January 1 (When Observed as New Year's Eve or Day)

Deuteronomy 8:1-10; Psalm 117; Revelation 21:1-6a; Matthew 25:31-46

The Old Testament reading has Moses addressing the people, describing their past, and anticipating their future in the land beyond the river. The text like the New Year teases us to reflect backward and to contemplate forward. The psalm calls forth praise apropos of a new beginning. The epistle reading envisions a new and eternal heaven and earth and a new and eternal Jerusalem. The newness of a New Year that gives us the taste of beginning again, of leaving behind, also raises the yearning for the totally and permanently new. The Gospel text preserves for us the association, so common in Judaism, of the New Year with judgment.

Deuteronomy 8:1-10

The book of Deuteronomy (from the title of the Greek translation, "second law") is so called because it includes the report of Moses' second presentation of the law to the people of Israel. It is concerned throughout with the faithful obedience of the law, but the book is hardly a law code. In its structure as a whole there is a narrative framework setting the scene on the plains of Moab, in the wilderness, before Israel's entrance into Canaan. Thus the book is an account of the last words and deeds of Moses, followed by the concluding narrative of his death. Virtually everything is framed in the form of direct address, with Moses speaking to the people. Both in style and contents, the great majority of the individual units are sermons. Where law or individual laws appear, they are preached, that is, explained, interpreted, reinterpreted, and laid upon the hearts of the hearers.

The goal is to make the law effective, to evoke obedience. When the book contains references to the history of God's actions on behalf of the people, these two are preached, with the awareness of a congregation of hearers who stand generations after those saving events. The people are reminded of what the Lord has done and urged to remember and respond accordingly.

Deuteronomy 8:1-10 is typical of the other sermons in the book. It is not the proclamation of a single law, as in Deuteronomy 15:1-11 and elsewhere, but a more general and thematic address. At least the first six verses concern the point stated at the outset: "All the commandment which I command you this day you shall be careful to do." Everything else serves the purpose of stimulating obedience to the law as a whole. People should obey, for obedience results in the abundant life, including the gifts of progeny ("multiply") and the promised land (verse 1).

Verses 2-6 bring remembrance of the past into the service of obedience. Specifically, the preacher reminds the congregation of Israel's wandering in the wilderness and interprets God's intentions behind some of the important events of that era. By knowing and remembering such things they are enabled to keep the commandments (verse 6). They are told variously that the forty years of difficulty were to "humble" them (verses 2, 3), to test them to see if they would be obedient or not (verse 2), to teach them that "man does not live by bread alone" (verse 3), and to discipline them "as a man disciplines his son" (verse 5). The difficulties in the wilderness, then, the congregation is told, were "to do you good in the end" (Deut. 8:16).

In the older traditions in Exodus 16 the miracle of the manna was God's positive response to the people's complaints. Here the original purpose of the miracle and the memory of it are used more theologically. The meaning of the lesson of the manna is not obvious on the surface: "make you know that man does not live by bread alone, but that man lives by everything that proceeds out of the mouth of the Lord" (verse 3). Certainly what proceeds out of the mouth of the Lord is the divine word. In Deuteronomy, that word can correspond to the revealed law (Deut. 30:14; 32:46), which leads to life in the fullest sense (Deut. 30:15-16). More generally, what proceeds out of the mouth of the Lord is the creative and giving word. All the gifts of creation—and not just the miraculous manna—come from God.

That is the theme addressed in verses 7-10 as the preacher turns from the past to the future, from the memory of the wilderness to the promise of the land. There is the sharp contrast between the difficult environment of the wilderness to the "good land, a land of brooks of water, of fountains and springs" (verse 7). The speaker describes the land of Canaan as well-watered (verse 7), rich in the produce of the ground (verse 8), capable of providing food for the people (9a), and full of valuable minerals (9b). The natural response to such abundance—it is not a command—will be to "bless the Lord your God for the good land he has given you" (verse 10).

Like most of the other passages in the book of Deuteronomy, this one is a model for preaching, both in form and contents. In terms of form, the deuteronomic preachers begin—as contemporary ones do—with sacred traditions concerning revelation and history; they treat them with respect, but at the same time attempt to bring them into ever-new situations, reinterpreting them and showing how they address their congregations in a time distant from those events.

In terms of contents, the themes of this passage include: (1) The importance of obeying the commandments, the laws, given in the covenant between God and people, is stressed. In no case is the law seen as oppressive, or impossible to follow; rather, it is a gift that leads to life. (2) The preacher urges the congregation to remember God's saving acts. Remembrance is active, not just cognitive: bring to mind and let the memory guide your actions. (3) Everything the people have, particularly from the land, is a gift of God, and the appropriate response is to enjoy and be grateful. There is no room for arrogance or pride in one's own accomplishments, but only humility and gratitude. (4) Then there is the persistent view of retribution: obey and be blessed and—implicit here but explicit elsewhere—disobey and be cursed. That theology has its limitations, especially when applied to individuals. Experience teaches us what the Book of Job argues, that the righteous also suffer. However, in Deuteronomy the view is a corporate rather than an individualistic one. It is the people, the nation, that will live long in the land if they are faithful and suffer if they are not. In what ways does this view apply to groups, churches, or to nations?

New Year's Day is an appropriate time to consider the last things, the final judgment, and the new heavens and earth. That is what the New Testament readings call for. It is also a good time to reflect on past, present, and future, in history, on our gifts and our response to them. That is what Deuteronomy 8:1-10 bids us do.

Psalm 117

This, the shortest of all the psalms, was frequently treated in antiquity as if it were not an independent composition. Some ancient Hebrew manuscripts treated it as the end of Psalm 116 while others placed it at the beginning of Psalm 118.

In spite of the psalm's brevity, it contains the basic components of a hymn of praise. The following are the component parts: (1) an opening call to praise (verse 1), (2) the reasons or motivations for praise (verse 2*ab*), and (3) a concluding call to praise (verse 2*c*).

Those called to praise are the nations (the *goyim*; the Gentiles) and the people of the world. The universalism of this text, its call to the citizens of the world to praise God, makes it appropriate for the Christmas New Year season. This universalism was found appealing to Paul who quotes Psalm 117:1 in Romans 15:11 where he argues that the inclusion of the Gentiles into the people of God was always part of the purpose of God.

The background for this universalism is probably to be seen in the ritual and worship of the Jerusalem temple. Here the Judean Deity (Yahweh) was worshiped as creator of the world and as the Lord of the universe. Such a view led naturally to the view that all of creation (see Pss. 104; 148), including non-Judeans, should praise God. The move from claiming Gentile praise for God to inclusion of the Gentiles in the people of Yahweh was a logical step for Paul once he had drawn out the implications of being Christian.

The motivations for praise in the psalm are God's "steadfast love" and "faithfulness." The first is the translation of the Hebrew word *hesed* used to express commitment and loyalty to (even passion for) a person, obligation, or agreement. Thus the use of the adjective "steadfast" in the translation. The term translated "faithfulness" is the Hebrew *ameth* which basically means truth or truthfulness. The fidelity to promise or divine truthfulness is what is being emphasized. Paul picks up on this point in the New Testament in his argument that inclusion of the Gentiles was an expression of God's truthfulness or righteousness, his commitment to a promise made long ago.

Revelation 21:1-6*a*

This text also serves as the First Lesson for All Saints Day in Year B, and the reader may wish to consult our remarks on the passage in that setting in *After Pentecost, Year B*. It is used as the epistolary reading for the Fifth Sunday of Easter in Year C. Additional comments may be found in *Lent, Holy Week, Easter, Year C*.

The use of this text in such varied liturgical settings provides an excellent example of how a single passage will be read and heard differently in different contexts. On All Saints Day it serves as a reminder of the heavenly hope to which God's people aspire and for which they have lived and died. In the post-Easter season of Year C, it functions as one of several semicontinuous readings from the Apocalypse. Bracketed by texts from the same canonical writing on preceding and succeeding Sundays, it will be heard as part of the continuous revelation of John. In its post-Easter setting, its triumphant note will be especially apparent. But heard in the context of New Year's Eve or New Year's Day, the same text is bound to evoke yet another set of responses.

What strikes us first is the recurrent refrain of the new: new heaven, new earth, new Jerusalem, all finally culminating in the bold declaration by the enthroned God, "Behold, I make all things new" (verse 5). We are hearing again the voice of Yahweh who spoke to the disconsolate exiles, urging them to "remember not the former things, nor consider the things of old," declaring, "Behold, I am doing a new thing" (Isa.

43:18-19a). If they felt locked into the slavery of exile and alienation, they are now reminded that God can break through the old and inaugurate the new. Things need not remain as they have been. Dramatic change is possible when God decides to let "new" shatter "old."

Similar sentiments are echoed by Paul's declaration of Christ as the arena of new creation (II Cor. 5:17). He too calls attention to this new reality, inviting us to open our eyes: "Behold! Look! The old has passed away, the new has come." If Yahweh had broken through Israel's fixation on the past by reminding them of the divine capacity for renewing, Christ now becomes for Paul (and for us) the agent of divine renewal. Through him the old era gives way to the new era. In this new age, moral renewal is possible: we can now walk in "newness of life" (Rom. 6:4). Conforming our will to the divine will results in a "renewal of the mind," which doubtless entails both a renewal of our intellect as well as our will. How we think changes along with why we act. What ultimately matters is not how well religious acts are performed but whether they are indicative of genuinely moral and spiritual renewal—whether they are expressive of the "new creation" (Gal. 6:15).

To be sure, the vision of the Seer in today's text is an eschatological vision, one of several visions with which the book of Revelation closes. The collapse of the old order is seen in the passing of heaven and earth, or the world as we know it (verse 1). The vanishing of the earthly order is often depicted in apocalyptic thought as earth, mountains, and sky fleeing away (cf. 6:14; 16:20; 20:11; II Pet. 3:7; also Ps. 114:3, 7). Into this cosmic vacuum there descends a new order, the heavenly city of Jerusalem (cf. 3:12; Gal. 4:26; Heb. 11:16; 12:22). With its descent comes the presence of God, radically new in the way it redefines the people of God. The new presence enables the new relationship of which the prophets spoke (Jer. 31:1; Isa. 8:8, 10). To dwell with God is to know God in a radically different way. The pressures, anxieties, and pains of the old order are no more (verse 4).

Even if the vision is eschatological, should it be any less compelling? Isn't it usually the vision of what can be that forces us to question what is and what has been? It was the

future that beckoned the exiles to forget the old and look to
the new. It was the Christ-event that shattered the old with
the utterly new. It is the hope of a future totally defined by
God that shatters our reliance on the past and moves us along
toward a new time, a new day.

Matthew 25:31-46

The Gospel reading for today prompts the observance of
New Year by reflecting on rather than forgetting the past.
The "new" in our text is the new age, the time of final reward
and punishment, launched by the coming of the Son of man
who pronounces judgment entirely on the basis of past
behavior toward persons in need.

Before looking at this lection, let us locate it in the scheme
of Matthew's Gospel. Jesus' apocalyptic speech delivered
from the Mount of Olives details the end of the temple,
Jerusalem, and this present age, and envisions the coming of
the Son of man (24:1-36). This discourse is followed by a stern
call to vigilance in view of the uncertain time of that certain
event (verses 37-44). The call to vigilance is followed by three
parables concerning behavior during a possible delay in the
Lord's coming: the parable of the slave supervisor (24:45-51,
"My master is delayed"), the parable of the ten maidens
(25:1-13, "As the bridegroom was delayed"), and the parable
of the talents (25:14-30, "Now after a long time"). At this
point Matthew places our reading, as if to say, "But when the
Lord does come, late or soon, it will be as follows." With
25:31-46, an account without parallel in the other Gospels,
Matthew concludes the public ministry of Jesus.

Matthew 25:31-46 is not a parable but a prophetic vision not
unlike the throne scene of Revelation 20:11-15 in which the
final judgment occurs. The enthronement of the Son of man
occurs elsewhere in Matthew 19:28 but the uses of Psalm
110:1 (the Lord seated at the right hand of God) are many and
varied in the New Testament. In fact, the image in Psalm
110:1 lies at the base of the early Christian confession, "Jesus
is Lord" (Rom. 10:9; Phil. 2:11), which replaced "Jesus is the
Messiah" as the church moved into cultures where a messiah
was not expected.

There is no question but that for Matthew the one enthroned in power and glory is Jesus, but the passage draws upon titles from Jewish literature that Christians applied to Jesus. Daniel 7:13-14 provides a scene of one like a son of man coming with the clouds of heaven to be presented before the Ancient of Days who grants to this one dominion, glory, and kingdom. The image is, as in Matthew, that of a cosmic ruler. The term "Son of man" shifts to "King" (Zech. 9:9; Ps. 89:18, 27) at verse 34 as well as to "son of God" (implied in "my Father," verse 34). In addition there is a variation of the picture of the shepherd dividing sheep and goats from Ezekiel 34. But regardless of the various sources for the imagery, for Matthew the scene is that of the Parousia, the coming of Jesus as Lord and judge of all people, Jews and Gentiles, church and non-church alike.

Several features of the judgment are most striking. First, there is the Lord's identifications with the poor, lonely, hungry, sick, and imprisoned (verses 35-36, 40, 42-43, 45). At Matthew 10:40-42 and 18:5 in the instructions about giving the cup of water and practicing hospitality, Jesus says such activity is ultimately toward himself and toward God. But there is nothing there or elsewhere in the gospels which approaches the complete identification expressed in "I was hungry. . . , I was thirsty. . . . , I was a stranger." Nor is there any indication that the text refers only to the poor and neglected within the church; before him are gathered "all the nations" (verse 32).

A second striking feature of the vision is that judgment is not based on heroic deeds or extraordinary feats but on the simple duties, the occasions for expressing care for other persons which present themselves every day. In fact, some students of Matthew have expressed concern over the absence of major Christian themes such as faith, grace, mercy, and forgiveness. That those matters are important to Jesus and to Matthew is beyond question; they are well documented elsewhere, as in 20:1-16, but not every parable or vision emphasizes every truth. To do so would blur all truth. However, it should be said that the Christian's concern for faith and grace should not replace attention to fundamental human obligations which, as this vision reminds us, are a primary concern of him who is Lord of all people of the earth. One does not cease to be a member of the human race once one joins the church.

A third and final unusual feature of the judgment is that both the blessed and the damned are surprised. Those banished to eternal punishment apparently miscalculated on what it takes to gain eternal bliss. And those rewarded had attended to the needs of others with such naturalness and grace that they were surprised that their behavior received heaven's attention. Saints are always surprised to hear their deeds recounted.

Second Sunday After Christmas

Jeremiah 31:7-14 or *Ecclesiasticus 24:1-4, 12-16; Psalm 147:12-20; Ephesians 1:3-6, 15-18; John 1:1-18*

The early church proclaimed that, in the coming of the Christ, the Old Testament prophecies and predictions were fulfilled. The Old Testament lesson for today speaks of the redemption to come when the scattered of Israel would be gathered from the farthest corners of the earth and when merriment, gladness, and feasting would signal the status of the new affairs. The reading from Ecclesiasticus describes the Divine Wisdom, which like the Word in the prologue to the Gospel of John, is said to have existed with God from the beginning and to have become implanted like a tree in Israel. The psalm praises God for his great gifts but above all for the fact that God has not dealt with any other nation as with his own people. The epistle contributes its melody to the theme of the Incarnation and the dwelling of God among humans.

Jeremiah 31:7-14

Jeremiah 31:7-14, which has few direct links with the other lessons for the day, is appropriate for the occasion because it expresses the mood and spirit of the celebration of Christmas. The passage is filled with announcements of salvation, that the Lord has saved, gathered, consoled, and ransomed a people from sorrow to joy.

Because it is so similar to the perspective of Isaiah 40–55 and Isaiah 35 (see phe comment for the Third Sunday of Advent in this volume), many commentators have taken this passage, along with most of the other materials in Jeremiah 30–31, the so-called Book of Consolation, as additions to the book from the time of the Babylonian Exile. In that case, the song of gladness anticipates release from Babylon and return to Judah. However, the references to "Jacob," "Israel," "Ephraim," and the "remnant of Israel" could very well mean the inhabitants of the Northern Kingdom who had been carried off by the Assyrians. In that case, Jeremiah here announces the return of those captives, and "the north country" (verse 8) would have been the far reaches of the Assyrian Empire in the seventh century B.C.

Although the passage is hymnic in tone and some of its contents, it is part of a prophetic announcement. The call to sing and praise (verse 7) is like the beginning of many hymns, and there are allusions to a ceremony of praise and thanksgiving (verses 12, 13), but the unit is framed by messenger formulas and oracle formulas that mark it as prophetic address. Throughout the prophet quotes the words of Yahweh concerning the future. Thus the text is a prophetic announcement of salvation concerning the return of exiles. It is good news of the ransom and redemption (verse 11) of people from captivity.

The context of this text contains both joy and sorrow concerning the Northern Kingdom. The immediately preceding section (Jer. 31:1-6) is a distinct unit of prophetic announcement of salvation. The prophet announces not only the return of the exiles from Samaria, but also the reunification of all the tribes at Zion. The passage that follows (Jer. 31:15-22) is the poignant lament of Rachel, mother of Benjamin and Joseph, for her children, that is for the tribes descended from them.

The passage consists of two parts that likely arose as two separate prophetic speeches, verses 7-9 and verses 10-14. The addressees of the first part are not specified, but the prophet hears God announcing that those who are scattered will be returned. Even those least able to travel, the blind, the lame, pregnant women, and women in labor (verse 8) will make the journey. The language of care and concern is particularly strong, as seen in Yahweh's affirmation that he is Israel's "father" (verse 9; see also Deut. 32:6 and Hos. 11).

In verses 10-14 the prophet addresses the nations with a summons to hear. What they are to hear is the news that the one who scattered Israel will gather them, and they will come and sing in Zion (verse 12). Mourning will be turned into joy (verse 13), and celebrations will break out. Faces will shine in the presence of the Lord's goodness, and there will be abundant food (verse 12). The prophet's point of view is Jerusalem, and even the temple on Mount Zion. He seems to envision a reunion of the long-divided people in the Holy City.

The central motif of our reading is the redemption of a lost people. In verse 11 redemption and ransom are used as synonymous expressions. Both refer to the practice of reclaiming a possession or a person left in pledge for a debt or from slavery. The people are assumed to be owned by another, a foreign nation. Only Yahweh can ransom or redeem them, although there is no reference to a price paid. Yahweh, like a loving father (verse 9) will reclaim his son. The view is a corporate one, with the son standing for the people. What is their response? They are only to return when released and join in the joyful celebration of their reunion.

Ecclesiasticus 24:1-4, 12-16

Few biblical books give us more information about its author than the book of Ecclesiasticus, also called "The Wisdom of Jesus the Son of Sirach." The author, Jesus Ben Sirach, was a wisdom teacher who conducted a school in Jerusalem in the early second century B.C. On the basis of information that he gives us, as well as the report by his grandson who translated the book into Greek (see the Prologue), the original composition of the book can be dated shortly before 180 B.C. This places the author and his audience in the Hellenistic period, before the Maccabean wars, but in a time when there must have been conflict between Jewish and Greek ideas and religious practices. The somewhat polemical tone at points, insisting that divine wisdom belongs to his people in Jerusalem (24:8-12), should be read in the light of that conflict.

Ecclesiasticus is wisdom literature, similar both in style and point of view to the book of Proverbs. It includes a great many sayings like those in Proverbs 10–31, and a number of more extended discourses similar to the ones in Proverbs 1–9,

Ecclesiastes, and Job. While sayings and discourses on similar topics are grouped together, attempts to discern the organization of the composition have been less than satisfactory. The author considers wisdom in many different ways, as practical knowledge gained from experience and tradition, and as an abstract and universal phenomenon. The reading for the day is selected from an extended discourse on the nature of wisdom that includes 24:1–25:11. The immediate context is Ecclesiasticus 24:1-22, in which personified wisdom herself is the speaker.

Wisdom's speech, rich in allusions to Old Testament traditions, gives an account of the relationship between wisdom and the world in general and Israel in particular. It combines history of salvation motifs with attention to nature and creation, as Ben Sirach frequently does throughout the book.

Verses 1-2 introduce the speech itself and the speaker, personified Wisdom. Such personification of wisdom, always as a female figure, is well-known in both earlier and later literature (Prov. 8:22-36; Wisd. of Sol. 6:12-20; 8:1 ff.). Her intention here is to praise herself. She is pictured as standing before and addressing two audiences at once, "her people," that is, Israel, and "the assembly of the Most High." That assembly is mentioned elsewhere in the Old Testament as well as in other ancient Near Eastern literature. The scene pictured is the divine throne room, with the lesser deities or messengers in the presence of God (Isa. 6; Ps. 89:6-7; I Kings 22:19-23).

Wisdom's speech itself recalls her cosmic origins (verses 3-6), her special relationship to Israel (verses 7-12), her growth like every good plant (verses 13-17), and concludes with an appeal to follow her (verses 18-22).

Particularly important when this passage is considered along with the Prologue to John is the language of verse 3. That wisdom "came forth from the mouth of the Most High" suggests a parallel to the word (Greek *logos*) of God present before creation. Elsewhere in the book God is said to have accomplished by his words what is attributed here to wisdom (42:15). The background of this passage certainly is to be found in the accounts of creation in both Genesis 1 and 2, where God creates by word. The "mist" is an allusion to Genesis 2:6. A more fully developed view of personified wisdom as God's activity in the world is found in Wisdom of Solomon 7:22–8:1. In that same book the identification of wisdom and the word of God is quite explicit (9:1-2).

Verses 13-17 give a virtual catalog of good plants as analogies for the growth and development of wisdom in the good soil of the people of Israel. This series of metaphors picks up on the motif of planting in verse 12 and sets the stage for wisdom's call to eat "of my produce" in verse 19.

Whereas verses 3-6 emphasize the cosmic presence of wisdom, verses 7-12 affirm that she found her true home among a particular people, Israel, and in a specific place, Jerusalem. The point of that claim is not reached until after wisdom's speech is concluded: "All this is the book of the covenant of the Most High God, the law which Moses commanded us" (24:23). That is, wisdom and the law amount to the same. Thus the major concern of the passage is divine revelation. How is God present and known in the world by human beings? God is known in and through wisdom present in creation, and specifically through the revealed law. Through faithfulness to the law of Moses one knows God.

Psalm 147:12-20

Psalm 147 is comprised of three units which give the impression of being distinct units (verses 1-6, 7-11, and 12-20). In fact, the ancient Greek translation treats the psalm as two compositions (verses 1-11 = Ps. 146; verses 12-20 = Ps. 147). The themes of the return to and restoration of Jerusalem are so persuasive in the psalm that the Greek translators associated it (or both) with the prophets of the return, namely, Haggai and Zechariah.

The blessing and restoration of Zion (Jerusalem) or the creation of a new Jerusalem run as themes throughout most of the reading for this Sunday. A second theme is God's sending of the word (or wisdom) into the world. We can analyze Psalm 147:12-20 around these two themes.

1. Verses 12-14 call upon Zion to praise God (verse 12) and

then offer reasons for that praise (verses 13-14). The city is divinely protected (verse 13a) and amid her streets the children play (verse 13b). Although these two ideas may not seem to go together, they do since security for the present provides assurance for the future, for the children to have a chance to grow to maturity. Verse 14a parallels 13a and 14b does the same for 13b. God provides peace throughout Jerusalem's realm (as well as protection for the city) and fills the land with wheat (so that its children may eat and grow).

2. Verses 15-20 speak of the word, its sending forth, and its residency with Jacob. God's word (or command/utterance) is described as an active agent. Along with the snow, the frost, the ice, the cold, God gives his word which has the power to melt the frozen; he sends his breath (he breathes) and the waters flow. The world of nature is at the mercy, is the active respondent, to the divine word.

But to Israel, God has acted in a way unique: to Jacob/Israel he has given his statutes and ordinances, the embodiment of the word. One of the psalm's fragments found among the Qumran (Dead Sea) Scrolls has the following reading for verse 20 a-b: "He has not dealt thus with any other nation; nor made known to them the ordinances." In the word, God came unto his own.

Ephesians 1:3-6, 15-18

Since this passage serves as the epistolary lesson for the Second Sunday After Christmas in all three years, the reader may wish to consult our remarks in *Advent, Christmas, Epiphany* for Years B and C. It also overlaps with passages used elsewhere in the *Common Lectionary:* 1:1-10 serves as the epistolary lesson for Proper 10 in Year B; 1:11-23 as the epistolary lesson for All Saints Day in Year C; 1:15-23 as the epistolary lesson for Ascension in all three years.

Even though the Gospel and epistle differ in many respects, they agree in one fundamental respect: the story of Christ began before the world began. If John's Prologue focuses on the person of Christ "in the beginning," this epistolary prayer sees the saving work of God as having begun before time. We are told that even "before the world was made, [God] chose us, . . . in Christ" (verse 4, JB). This can easily be understood as a further development of Paul's theology of election (Rom. 8:29; cf. II Thess. 2:13). Here our own calling, or election, by God becomes an extension of Christ's own vocation. Elsewhere in John's Gospel, Christ claims to have been given God's glory even before the world was founded (John 17:24). It is a theme later echoed in the early Christian confession that Christ was "destined before the foundation of the world but was made manifest at the end of the times" (I Pet. 1:20).

In an important sense, then, the Epistle to the Ephesians pushes beyond the Johannine Prologue to insist not only that the story of Christ began before the world began, but the story of our own salvation as well. How we experienced this blessing from heaven is spelled out through the use of several images and metaphors.

First, as already noted, our salvation is viewed as divine election. Naturally the notion of election is thoroughly grounded in Old Testament thought, but here it is not the election of a people on earth but of a people in heaven before the beginning of time.

Second, our salvation is viewed as sacrificial purification: God chose us to be "holy and blameless" (verse 4; cf. 5:27; Col. 1:22).

Third, our salvation is viewed as sonship. We were destined even from the beginning to be the children of God (verse 5; cf. John 1:12; Gal. 3:26; I John 3:1). To be sure, ours is an adopted status (verse 5, NIV, JB). It is a status made possible "through Jesus Christ," God's beloved Son through whom God lavishly bestowed divine grace.

These are all viewed as "blessings in the heavenly places," and thus God "has blessed us with all the spiritual blessings of heaven in Christ" (verse 3, JB). Everything that was theoretically possible in heaven became actually possible in and through Christ. For this reason, God is the object of our prayers of thanksgiving. Hence the prayer opens with a prayer of blessing: "Blessed be God" (verse 3, JB). It is a form of prayer deeply rooted in Jewish thought and practice, reminiscent of prayers offered by David (I Chron. 29:10-19), the psalmist (Ps. 144:1), Azariah (Dan. 3:26), Tobit (Tob. 8:5;

13:1), Sarah (Tob. 3:11): Raguel (Tob. 8:17-19), and later of Zechariah (Luke 1:68). It becomes a standard form of epistolary prayer (II Cor. 1:3; I Pet. 1:3).

As the first part of today's epistolary lection serves as a reflection on God's saving work in the heavens before the foundation of the world, the second part turns to the here and now. It is prayer offered on behalf of the readers because of their faith and love (verse 15; cf. Col. 1:3-4, 9; Philem. 4-5; Rom. 1:8-9). Their steadfastness has become known and their love for fellow Christians has been demonstrated, and both have become an occasion of ceaseless thanksgiving (verse 16).

The prayer is offered for their (and our) benefit. It is a prayer for spiritual illumination. God is regarded as the Source and Giver of true wisdom, revelation, and knowledge. It is a sentiment reminiscent of Isaiah 11:2 where the messianic king is said to be imbued with the Spirit of the Lord who bestows wisdom and understanding. In similar fashion, Wisdom 7:7 portrays Solomon as calling on God and thereby receiving the "spirit of wisdom." We are further told that wisdom of this sort is to be preferred to scepters, thrones, and wealth. Indeed, in our text divinely given wisdom is precisely that which enables us to know that our true wealth consists in the inheritance we share as saints (verse 18).

If we compare the two parts of today's lection, we might say that the first part underscores our heavenly salvation as part of God's divine plan, whereas the second part shows us how this is worked out in the life of faith and love. The second part is a prayer that what was begun in the mind of God before the world began might come to fruition as we discern the heritage that is truly ours.

John 1:1-18

The Gospel lesson for Christmas, Third Proper (second additional lesson) was John 1:1-14 and the preacher is referred to those comments for use here, especially if that lection was not treated in a Christmas service. All of today's readings proclaim God's visiting us with favor, but the

Prologue to John's Gospel is of central importance to Christian history, Christian doctrine, and the understanding of the life of faith.

We will here add to the earlier discussion only comments on verses 14-18 that constitute a unit that concludes the Prologue as a literary piece distinct from the narrative beginning at verse 19.

Verses 14-18 make the following three statements:

1. "And the Word *became flesh*'" is a christological affirmation of a radical nature with far-reaching implications for our thinking about God, life in the world, and what it means to be Christian. Analogies about changing clothes, as in the stories of a king who wears peasant clothing in order to move among his subjects freely, are not adequate for clarifying John 1:14. The church has always had members who wanted to protect their Christ from John 1:14 with phrases such as "seemed to be," "appeared," and "in many ways was like" flesh. Whatever else John 1:14 means, it does state without question the depth, the intensity, and the pursuit of God's love for the world.

2. John 1:14-18 is a confessional statement. Notice the use of "us" and "we." The eyes of faith have seen God's glory in Jesus of Nazareth, but not everyone has. At the time of this Gospel the Baptist sect (verse 15) and the synagogue (verse 17) were viable religious groups and they did not see the glory. Faith hears, sees, and testifies, but faith is not arrogant or imperialistic as though its view were so obvious as to be embraced by all but the very obstinate. Faith involves a searching (Rabbi, where do you live? 1:38), a response to an offer (Come and see. 1:39), a hunger (14:8), a willingness to obey (7:17). Nothing about Jesus Christ is so publicly apparent as to rob faith of its risk, its choice, and its courage. Faith exists among alternatives.

3. The observation above in no way means that faith must be tentative and quiet about its central affirmation that the God whom no one has seen (verse 18) is both known and available in Jesus Christ. Jesus reveals God (verse 18) and makes God available to us (verse 14) in gracious ways (verse 16). Believing in Jesus is not simply adding another belief to one's belief in God; it is also having one's belief in God

modified, clarified, and informed by what is seen in the person and work of Jesus. Jesus' statement, "He who has seen me has seen the Father" (14:9), does not simply tell us what Jesus is like but what God is like, and to know God is life eternal (17:4).

Epiphany

Isaiah 60:1-6; Psalm 72:1-14; Ephesians 3:1-12;
Matthew 2:1-12

Epiphany themes dominate these classic texts that have come to be used for this day. Images of light, glory, and brightness are introduced in the Old Testament reading from Isaiah, and they are counterbalanced by the double reference to darkness in verse 2. Universal manifestation of God's glorious light is also indicated by the reference to the nations who would come to see the light. In the psalm it is the universal recognition of the righteous king's dominion that especially commends the text for this day. The manifestation of God's revelation to the Gentiles is the key theme sounded in the epistolary reading. The Gospel lesson, which records the visit of the Magi, has become the Gospel reading most closely associated with the Epiphany. In narrative form we see the impact of the Christ Child reaching to the distant East, thus symbolizing his manifestation to the Gentiles.

Isaiah 60:1-6

Our reading begins a major section in the collection of prophetic and liturgical materials commonly identified as Third Isaiah. Chapters 60–62 contain a series of promises and announcements of Jerusalem's salvation and restoration. They are addressed to or concern the inhabitants of Judah and Jerusalem, and probably stem from early in the postexilic period, not long after exiles began to return from Babylon. The temple is either under construction or recently completed. As Haggai 2:1-9 indicates, the community that began to reestablish itself on the ruins of Jerusalem soon became discouraged that the restoration was not all they expected, especially given the dramatic vision of Second Isaiah. Isaiah 60 seems to be addressed to that discouragement, proclaiming the future glory of Jerusalem.

The entire passage, indeed, virtually all of chapter 60, is addressed to Jerusalem. The verbs of the initial verse, "arise," "shine," are feminine singular, appropriate for addressing the city personified as a woman. Thus the "you" throughout is Zion, standing also for its inhabitants. It is not so easy to identify the speaker of the lines. In verses 7, 10, 15-18 the one who says "I" surely is Yahweh. However, in verses 1, 6, and 9 Yahweh is mentioned in the third person, suggesting a prophetic speaker. This alternation of speaker probably is not evidence for multiple authorship, but rather the free movement from direct to indirect account of Yahweh's message for the people.

In terms of literary genre, the poem is a particular kind of announcement of salvation, one with strong eschatological overtones and contents. It does not concern the last things in the narrow sense, but does anticipate a dramatic transformation in historical circumstances. Attention does not focus upon a particular event, as in Second Isaiah's announcement of the end of the Exile and the return of the captives, but on a new set of circumstances.

The two parts of the passage correspond generally to the two major themes associated in Christian liturgical tradition with Epiphany. Verses 1-3 proclaim the manifestation of God's presence, the appearance of God at a particular time and place in history, thus contributing to reflection on the Incarnation. Verses 4-6—the original unit goes at least through verse 7 and more likely through verse 9—picks up and develops the motif already introduced in verse 3, the pilgrimage of the Gentiles to see the appearance of the Lord. Epiphany came to be associated with the visit of the Magi, and then in some traditions with the proclamation of the gospel to the nations.

Images of light and darkness dominate the first three verses. "Light" symbolizes life, salvation, and joy, while darkness represents death (see Isa. 9:2; Ps. 23:4). The theme of the arrival of light is stated in verse 1 and repeated in verse 2, against the background of darkness. In verse 3 nations now come to Jerusalem's light. The appearance of the light is the same as the arrival of "the glory of the Lord." Unusual here is that this glory, or the Lord himself (verse 2), "has risen," "will arise." More typically, in the accounts of the appearance of the Lord the imagery speaks of his coming down. The metaphor clearly is that of the rising sun. But, lest one identify Yahweh with any heavenly body, the concluding part of the poem is quite explicit in insisting that Yahweh—and not the sun or moon—will be "your everlasting light" (60:19).

The light of God's presence will shine on Jerusalem, and it will then be the light that attracts nations from their darkness (verse 3). This picture seems indebted to Second Isaiah's proclamation that the servant Israel will become a "light to the nations" (Isa. 42:6).

In verses 4-6 Jerusalem is called to behold all those streaming to her. The nations are coming, and they are bringing her children back. She will rejoice like a mother reunited with her sons and daughters. Moreover, the nations will bring their material wealth to Jerusalem. "Abundance of the sea" (verse 5) doubtless means goods brought by ship. Verses 6 and 7 concern goods brought by land, especially from Arabia. Midian and Ephah would have been traders from northern Arabia. Sheba was farther to the south. All this reference to material wealth is hyperbole, to be sure, but it is quite specific. Many of the items mentioned were important to the temple, either for decoration (gold), for rituals (frankincense), or for offerings (flocks, rams). Jerusalem becomes a world center, not just for religious observances, but for economic and political reasons as well.

Epiphany is a time of light, the light of the Lord's presence. This text suggests two directions for meditation on the appearance of that light in the darkness. One is simply to celebrate and give thanks. The other is to consider how those upon whom the light has shined are to enlighten the darkness in the world around them.

Psalm 72:1-14

A portion of this psalm was the responsorial psalm for the Second Sunday of Advent (see pages 25-26). Today's verses are also the psalm selection for Epiphany during all three years of the lectionary cycle.

Epiphany, in the Western tradition, commemorates several themes: the visit of the Magi, the first manifestation of Jesus to the non-Jewish, Gentile world represented by the Magi, and the church's missionary work in the modern world. Psalm 72 shares in this universal perspective and in seeing an interrelationship of the Jewish people with non-Jewish nations.

Psalm 72 was no doubt written as the community's intercessory prayer offered on behalf of the Davidic king at his coronation and/or the annual celebration of the king's rule. Perhaps no other text in the Old Testament gives such an elevated and yet humane portrayal of (or perhaps longing for) the ideal Davidic ruler. The monarch is depicted in this text as the embodiment of justice and compassion, as the inaugurator of a new era.

As an intercession, the psalm requests and petitions the Deity for many things, all mediated through the monarch. One of these, and thus the psalm's use on Epiphany Sunday, is the request for a universal rule, for a dominion that extends throughout the inhabited world (verses 8-11). A number of geographical expressions are employed to speak of this dominion: "from sea to sea," "from the River to the ends of the earth," "Tarshish and of the isles," and "Sheba and Seba." The first two expressions are mythological in background and are used metaphorically to denote the entire world. The last two refer to the regions to the distant west of Palestine and to the distant lands to the east, respectively. The basis for such cosmic claims on behalf of the Judean monarch was the belief in God as creator. As creator of the world, God could make his earthly representative ruler of the world. Thus the doctrine of creation undergirded the extravagant claims of the Davidic monarch and gave birth to the hope of a universal rule for the Messiah.

Three actions by the nations are requested in the prayer, all expressing and demonstrating subordination to the Davidic ruler. Although all three are practically synonymous, one may detect a difference in the sources of the imagery. One (verse 9) is drawn from the area of warfare and denotes the surrender of a foe and the submission of an enemy. The one representation we possess of an Israelite king appears on the Black Obelisk of the Assyrian king Shalmaneser III (set up about 841 B.C.). On this inscription, the Israelite king Jehu is shown kissing the ground ("licking the dust") at Shalmaneser's feet. We know from the accompanying inscription that Jehu surrendered to the Assyrians. The second image (in verse 10) is that of paying tribute and bringing gifts to remain on peaceful terms. Throughout history, subordination to a superior state was always shown in the Middle East by the (generally annual) giving of gifts by the inferior. Finally, verse 11 draws on the practice of common protocol at the royal court. Bowing was the appropriate posture to greet the appearance of the king.

Ephesians 3:1-12

Epiphany is a time when we celebrate the manifestation of the gospel to the nations. Indeed, the word "epiphany" means "manifestation." It suggests that something becomes manifest that was previously not manifest, apparent that was not otherwise apparent. What was veiled is now unveiled. What was hidden is now revealed. Ignorance gives way to knowledge, darkness to light, hiddenness to openness.

It may be obvious to us that Gentiles should be a part of the people of God. After all, we are Gentiles, most of us. But this was not always obvious. Nor was it inevitable that the church would include both Jews and Gentiles as equals. It only looks obvious and inevitable to us now because we view history from afar. The controversy has come and gone, the agonizing conflict is over. It is difficult for us to believe that it ever occurred.

Such complacency is foreign to our text for today. True, the inclusion of the Gentiles is viewed from a distance. It is an event that has already occurred, a conflict the church has already absorbed into its history. But rather than being a matter of course, it is seen as a matter of wonderment. How the Gentiles came to be a part of the people of God is viewed here as nothing less than a miracle of cosmic proportion.

We should note, first, that the only language appropriate

to capture its true significance is the language of mystery. It is "the mystery hidden for ages in God" (verse 9). Here we have the language of apocalyptic in which the true mind and will of God is seen as that which has been enshrouded in a veil of hiddenness, locked up as it were, until the appropriate time for unveiling occurs. Consequently, previous generations were unaware of it (verse 5). It has been hidden from human eyes for generations (cf. Rom. 16:25; I Cor. 2:7; Col. 1:26).

But the mystery has now been unveiled. What was once hidden and unknown "has now been revealed to [God's] holy apostles and prophets by the Spirit" (verse 5). The time has come in the divine economy (*oikonomia*, verses 2 and 9) for God to uncover what has been hidden. The use of the term *oikonomia* should be noted. It is an expression difficult to render in English: "plan" (RSV), "administration" (NIV). It suggests a planned order, an organized scheme for accomplishing a specific purpose (cf. 1:9-10; Col. 1:25; I Cor. 9:17; also 4:1). The point is that God's decision to include the Gentiles in the plan of salvation was not an afterthought. It was part of God's overall purpose and scheme from the very beginning. It was "exactly according to the plan which [God] had had from all eternity in Christ Jesus our Lord" (verse 11, JB).

We should also note Paul's relationship to this mystery. He is, after all, imprisoned for Christ on behalf of the Gentiles (verse 1). His special vocation was to preach the gospel to the Gentiles (verse 8; cf. Gal. 1:16; 2:7; I Tim. 2:7; Acts 9:15).This task had been given him, the least likely candidate, given his previous record as the church's archenemy. Accordingly, he was the "very least of all the saints" (verse 8), the "least of the apostles" (I Cor. 15:9-10; I Tim. 1:15). Yet he had received an unusually generous measure of God's grace in being selected as a minister of the gospel (verse 7; cf. Rom. 1:5; 12:3, 6; 15:15-16; I Cor. 3:10; Gal. 2:9; Col. 1:25). It was grace bestowed "by the working of his power" (verse 7). For this task he strove "with all the energy which [God] mightily inspires within [him]" (Col. 1:29; also Phil. 4:13).

All this suggests that Paul was seized by the power of God to make known the mystery of salvation for the Gentiles. For him it was not volunteer work. He did not come to the task as a seeker. Rather God had sought him out, and he had responded involuntarily. It was not a matter of choice, but of compulsion (I Cor. 9:16–17). His insight into this mystery came as the result of revelation (verse 3; Gal. 1:12). In this respect, he stands in the succession of his predecessors, the "holy apostles and prophets" (verse 5; cf. 2:20).

The essence of the mystery was that the Gentiles now had a full share in God's blessing. Along with the Jews, they were now full heirs of the divine promise (Gal. 3:29). They were no longer stepchildren, but children with all the privileges of heirs (Rom. 8:17). No longer were they outside the body, but were now organically related to the body of Christ (2:16-18). No longer aliens, they were citizens with all the rights and privileges of full membership.

With this new-found status as full members of the people of God comes full access to God's promises (verse 12; 2:18; also John 14:6; I John 3:21). This makes it possible to come to God with "boldness and confidence" (verse 12; cf. Heb. 3:6; 4:16; 19:19, 35).

In retrospect, we can hardly believe that it should have been otherwise. What was once hardly imaginable now appears obvious. In commenting on a theory that had received the Nobel Prize, one observer noted the true test of a brilliant theory: "What first is thought to be wrong is later shown to be obvious." That pagans should be included in God's plan was first thought by some to be impossible, indeed morally wrong. Now it appears to be obvious. Through the church we have come to see "how comprehensive God's wisdom really is" (verse 10, JB). Here we have seen the emergence of a new humanity, a form of fellowship that knows no inequities or barriers. For many it remains an unfulfilled promise, which is why Epiphany still needs to be celebrated. We need to be reminded of the profound impact the gospel has had in and on the world—that the message of Christ continues to have manifest witness among all peoples.

Matthew 2:1-12

The Season of Epiphany is the time of the church's proclamation of the appearance or manifestation of Christ to

Israel and to the nations. The word "epiphany" transliterates a Greek verb meaning "to be manifest, to appear openly" (Titus 2:11). Antiochus, a pre-Christian Syrian ruler, impressed with his own power, assumed the name Antiochus Epiphanes as a declaration that he was the appearance of a god on earth. During this season the church proclaims Christ Epiphanes, and appropriately enough, the Gospel lesson to launch this season each year is Matthew 2:1-12. In this text Matthew says that even in infancy the Christ child stirred a capital city, disturbed a reigning king, and attracted foreigners to come and worship.

It is clear that Matthew intends 2:1 to begin a new cycle of stories (ending at verse 23) rather than continue the birth story of 1:18-25. Literarily speaking, the birth story has its own conclusion (verse 25) and the account of the visit of the wise men (RSV; "astrologers" in NEB) has its own introduction (2:1). This separation of the two stories is important lest there be frustrating and futile attempts to interweave and harmonize Luke's nativity (2:1-20) and Matthew's story of the Magi. Chronologically speaking, Matthew 2:1-12 carries clues that this is not a nativity but a childhood story. The NEB has "after his birth" instead of the more vague "now when Jesus was born" (RSV). Add to this the time needed for traveling from the East, the fact that Mary and the child were in a house (verse 11), and the age of children to be killed in Herod's attempt to destroy the child (verse 16), and one gets the clear sense that Matthew's Magi and Luke's shepherds do not arrive in Bethlehem at the same time. The Eastern church has long stressed the Feast of Three Kings and Epiphany as distinct from Christmas. In fact, Epiphany is the greater festival, to which Christmas is prelude. Such a distinction between the festivals sets the church and the preacher free to attend to the different emphases in Luke and Matthew, to leave now Luke's stable and shepherds and to see the Christ Child among the powerful and rich. One cannot miss the echoes of the Moses story, the child who found himself among the powerful and rich of Egypt (Exod. 2) and who later became the deliverer of God's people.

Matthew 2:1-12 carries within it more echoes than simply

those from Exodus 2. The general culture, religious and secular, contained many stories to the effect that the birth of a great ruler would be accompanied by celestial signs. In the Old Testament, a strange seer from the East, Balaam, spoke of a star arising out of Jacob (Num. 24:17). Isaiah 60:1-6 announced the coming of kings from distant lands with gifts of gold and frankincense, paying homage to Israel's God. All this is to say that Matthew had available the threads with which to weave the rich tapestry of this much-loved story.

But Matthew is not simply telling a beautiful story; he is making several theological statements. First, by the use of his familiar quotation formula, "so it is written by the prophet" (verse 5), Matthew shows that Jesus qualifies as the Davidic ruler to be born in David's city of Bethlehem (Mic. 5:2). Jesus is the one who fulfills God's promise to Israel.

Second, Jesus not only is the one to "govern my people Israel" but he also is the one to draw all nations to Israel's God. Some readers of Matthew are so struck by the use of Matthew's promise/fulfillment pattern that they forget that the promise in the Old Testament included Gentiles as well as Jews. Ruth, Jonah, Isaiah (2:1-3; 9:1-2), and other texts declare this plainly, and Matthew picks up on this theme of the mission to the nations (4:14-16; 28:18-20). In today's reading, the coming of the wise men to worship the Christ Child symbolizes the coming of the nations. This story functions for Matthew as the story of the coming of the Greeks does for the Fourth Evangelist (John 12:20-32); that is, as a symbolic announcement of the mission to the nations.

A third theological statement made by Matthew in this story is that these events are providentially guided. We are not here reading of good fortune, happy coincidences, and historical accidents. Jesus is the son of God, king of the Jews, and Davidic ruler. It is no surprise, then, that his life is not only divinely begun (1:18-25), but announced with extraordinary signs and preserved providentially from the threats of a jealous tyrant. Matthew thereby creates in the reader a sense of praise and gratitude, along with high expectation for the story that will now unfold.

Baptism of the Lord (First Sunday After Epiphany)

Isaiah 42:1-9; Psalm 29; Acts 10:34-43; Matthew 3:13-17

The Old Testament reading is provided by the first Servant Song from Isaiah, which has long been recognized as informing the Synoptic account of the baptism of Jesus. Its emphasis on the bestowal of the Spirit on God's chosen one is clearly echoed in Matthew's account of Jesus' baptism, which serves as the Gospel lesson for today. Compared with the parallel accounts in Mark and Luke, the Matthean account is quite distinctive with its more extended dialogue between John and Jesus. Psalm 29 is used for this day in all three years because of its repeated emphasis on the voice of the Lord and the various ways it breaks through the natural order to be heard. It provides an excellent background against which to interpret the heavenly voice confirming the identity of Jesus as God's chosen one at his baptism. The second lesson for this day is provided from the book of Acts in all three years. Today's selection is Peter's sermon to the household of Cornelius, remarkable as a rare mention of the baptism of Jesus outside the Gospels.

Isaiah 42:1-9

This text is also the Old Testament reading for Monday of Holy Week. At that point in the Christian Year it serves to characterize the obedience of Jesus as God's servant, and to set the events of that week in an eschatological context, the ultimate reign of God. On this day in the year, celebrating the baptism of the Lord, the emphasis will be upon the designation and confirmation of the servant of God.

111

Isaiah 42:1-9 consists of two originally independent units, the first of the Servant Songs in verses 1-4 and a distinct prophetic speech in verses 5-9. Both parts were composed by Second Isaiah shortly before the end of the Exile in 538 B.C. The combination of the two units addresses one of the perennial problems in the interpretation of the Servant Songs, namely, the identity of the servant. While the answer to that question is unclear within the song, the following verses interpret the servant as the people of Israel (verses 6-7).

The Servant Song in verses 1-4 is the first of four such poetic passages in Second Isaiah; the others are Isaiah 49:1-6; 50:4-11; 52:13–53:12. It has the form of a public proclamation in which Yahweh is the speaker, introducing the servant. The audience is not identified; it may have been Israel as a whole, the nations, or the heavenly council presumed in Isaiah 40:1-8. The answer depends to some extent upon the identification of the servant. The proclamation has the force of ordination, indicating first that God has chosen this particular one, and second, the purpose for which he was chosen. Thus, the form as well as the contents make it explicit that the servant's role is an extension or embodiment of the divine intention. Designation by conferring God's spirit applies to leaders, including kings, and to prophets. What the servant does and how he accomplishes it have the divine blessing, authority, and power to accomplish God's purposes.

This servant has a particularly intimate relationship to the one who has chosen him. The only reason given for the election of this servant is God's love: "in whom my soul delights" (verse 1). The Hebrew word for "soul" here refers simply to the self, so NEB accurately translates, "in whom I delight." He is characterized as gentle, perhaps in contrast to the ancient prophets or the kings of Israel and Judah, and persistent in the pursuit of his responsibilities.

While debate about the identity of the servant is likely to continue, there is no doubt about his role. It is stated three times that he is to "bring forth justice" (verses 1, 3, 4). "Justice" *(mishpat)* is one of the most fundamental categories in the prophetic tradition. It characterizes the fair and equitable behavior of human beings in society, established with due process in law, administered without discrimination, and based on the just will of Yahweh. To establish justice is to establish the reign of God. The word in the present context refers primarily to the administration of justice, the promulgation of a just order in society. The NJPSV translates in all three instances "true way."

Another key term for understanding the role of the servant is "law" (verse 4), the traditional translation of the Hebrew *torah*. The concept was deeply ingrained in Israel's view of its relationship to its God. In one sense it is the instruction in covenant responsibilities given by the priests. Thus the NEB and NJPSV read here "teaching." Eventually it came to mean the whole body of divine revelation, embodied in the first five books of the Bible. Instruction in and the interpretation of the covenant stipulations is necessary for the establishment of justice. Consequently, while the servant's role is similar in some ways to both priests who were responsible for instruction and to prophets who proclaimed God's word, the role is most like that of a king who administers the law.

The ordination of the servant looks to a time when all people will live in the same just order. The song does not seem to envision a dramatic day when all things will be transformed suddenly, but a gradual promulgation of justice until it includes the world.

The second unit (verses 5-9) is introduced by a prophetic messenger formula ("Thus says God, the Lord"), elaborated by means of a series of participial clauses characterizing the Lord (verse 5), who then speaks (verses 6-9). Yahweh speaks directly to an audience in the second person. That audience is the people of Israel, shown here to have roles and responsibilities quite like those given to the servant of the Lord in the previous unit. The style of the passage is both hymnic and persuasive, even somewhat argumentative at the end. There are points to be made, and it is assumed that the hearers need to be convinced.

These verses organize the main theological themes of Second Isaiah almost systematically. Yahweh is introduced as the creator of the earth and all who dwell in it, giver of the breath of life (verse 1). Then there is the election and

redemption of Israel (verse 6*a*), with allusions to both the past
and the coming release from Babylonian captivity. Next, the
chosen people are reminded of their role and responsibility
toward the rest of the world (verses 6*b*-7). Belief in creation by
a single God and belief in the election of a particular people
lead our prophet to the obvious conclusion that these chosen
people are called to be "a light to the nations." Israel's call is
not laid out as duty, but the response to gifts received. Then
the prophet returns to the initial concern with the authority
of Yahweh, with polemical asides against "graven images"
(verse 8). The section concludes with the reminder that this
God is doing new things, and one can believe in them
because in the past he had announced the future through his
prophets, and it happened as he said it would.

One of the most critical expressions in the passage is also
enigmatic. What does it mean that Israel is given as "a
covenant to the people" (verse 6)? The words may be read
"covenant-people" (NJPSV). The term (*berit*) could refer to
the stipulations of the covenant, that is, the laws that specify
the right human behavior. Thus the role of Israel would
parallel that of the servant in verse 4, the establishment of
justice based on the law. It could indicate that through Israel
God establishes a world-wide covenant, including all
humankind. Given the fact that "covenant to the people"
parallels "light to the nations," it seems likely that both of
these meanings are intended. Israel, teaching the will of God
and thereby bringing all peoples into a covenant with the one
creator, enlightens the world.

Psalm 29

The open heavens, the voice of God, and the imagery of
water are all features in the narrative of Jesus' baptism and
play roles in this event depicted as the affirmation of his
messiahship. A similar set of images is found in Psalm 29 and
explains the choice of this psalm for this Sunday throughout
the three years of the cycle. (It is also the psalm reading for
Trinity Year B.)

When the ancient rabbis read this psalm, they noticed the
eighteen occurrences of the divine name Yahweh ("the

Lord" in the RSV) and saw these as paralleling and even providing the basis for their eighteen benedictions used in synagogue worship and private devotions.

The repetitive quality of the psalm is further evidenced in the sevenfold repetition of the term "voice" (of the Lord). Such repetitions indicate an artistic effort and a desire to overwhelm the hearer with a certain emotional impact, an emotion focused on God and his voice.

The hearer of this psalm, like the listener to the account of Jesus' baptism, is not asked to become a part of the scene or a participant in the account. The significance of the action asks that the worshiper simply affirm what has been said and then live in the certainty of what has been affirmed.

Acts 10:34-43

Originally Epiphany was a celebration focusing on the baptism of Christ. This was especially the case in the Eastern church from the third century onward. It eventually came to rank with Easter and Pentecost as one of the three major feasts of the church. In the West, Epiphany came to be associated less with the baptism of Christ and more with Christ's manifestation to the Gentiles, as symbolized in the visit of the Magi. Consequently, the observance of Epiphany in the West saw the disappearance of the consecration of the baptismal water that characterized the celebration of Epiphany in the East.

The *Common Lectionary* now clearly acknowledges this historical development in which the celebration of the Epiphany has become split from the celebration of the Lord's baptism. Today's texts concentrate exclusively on the latter. In each of the three liturgical years, the second lesson is taken from the book of Acts and relates to a significant conversion from the early church: Cornelius (Year A), the twelve disciples from Ephesus (Year B), and the Samaritans (Year C).

Today's second lesson consists of the summary of Peter's sermon to Cornelius. This same text serves as the first option for Lesson 1 or the second option for Lesson 2 for Easter Sunday in all three years. The reader may wish to consult our remarks in that connection in the volumes *Lent, Holy Week, Easter* for Years A, B, and C.

What makes today's text especially appropriate in the context of celebrating the Lord's baptism is its explicit reference to the "baptism which John preached" (verse 37). Though it does not specifically say that Jesus was baptized by John, this is implied in the following phrase: "how God anointed Jesus of Nazareth with the Holy Spirit and with power" (verse 38). This is one of the few references outside the Gospels to Jesus' baptism (cf. Acts 1:21). The baptism of Jesus was regarded as the moment when God's Spirit was bestowed on him, as the narrative accounts of this event in the Gospels make clear (cf. Matt. 3:13-17; Mark 1:9-11; Luke 3:21-22). It was an anointing in the sense that Jesus received a measure of God's Spirit as a chrism that was poured out (cf. 4:27). As such, it was a bestowal of power.

It is common for the receiving of God's Spirit to be understood as an anointing. When Samuel anointed David with oil, he received a powerful infusion of the Lord's Spirit (I Sam. 16:13). Similarly, at his Nazareth inaugural Jesus applies Isaiah 61:1-2 to himself as he claims that the Lord's Spirit has anointed him to launch his prophetic mission (Luke 4:18). The Lord's baptism, then, is regarded as a singular moment of divine anointing, when God acknowledges Jesus as the beloved Son and signifies this by bestowing the Spirit.

This sermon summary, attributed to Peter, conforms to the story line of the Synoptic Gospels in seeing Jesus' baptism as the inauguration of his ministry. Even though it was widely recognized that the story of Jesus was a continuation of the Old Testament story and could be told as another chapter in the saga of significant figures, such as Abraham and Moses, here the first peg to be driven down is his baptism by John the Baptist. It is after this that Jesus embarks on his ministry of "doing good and healing" (verse 38). It is truly the inaugural event of his life and ministry, and for this reason was often seen in the early church as the moment when he really became the Son of God.

Today's text invites us to ask about the significance of the Lord's baptism. We see that it was above all an inaugural event, a time of beginning, which not only sets Jesus' ministry apart from the work of John the Baptist but also marks a beginning in its own right. It launched his ministry of good works and healing through which the power of God was manifested: it became clear that "God was with him" (verse 38). It was the beginning of the era in which the "good news of peace" was proclaimed (verse 36). Its essence was his universal Lordship: "He is Lord of all" (verse 36). It also inaugurated a new era in which forgiveness of sins was made possible through his name (verse 43).

Matthew 3:13-17

One of the accounts of Jesus' baptism serves each year as the Gospel lesson for the First Sunday After Epiphany. Matthew's record of the event (3:13-17) is especially appropriate as an Epiphany text since in this Gospel the voice from heaven publicly proclaims Jesus as the son of God (verse 17).

Both Matthew and Luke (3:21-22) follow Mark (1:9-11) but each has its own accents. Matthew is most concerned to explain or to clarify matters open to misunderstanding in Mark who seems unconcerned that questions would arise as to the reason for Jesus' baptism. That Jesus was baptized is an historical certainty; the church would never have created such a story. After all, why would Jesus go for baptism by a preacher who called for repentance and forgiveness of sin? This puzzle occupied many in the early church. Jerome cited a certain gospel according to the Hebrews in which Jesus responds to his mother's suggestion that they be baptized by saying, "In what have I sinned that I should go and be baptized by him? Unless, perhaps, what I have just said is a sin of ignorance." Matthew enlarges upon Mark to deal with this problem as well as address the issue of Jesus' relation to John the Baptist.

On the question of why Jesus was baptized, Matthew makes three statements. First, he says Jesus went to the Jordan "to be baptized" by John (verse 13). In other words, his act was intentional; he was not simply caught up in John's preaching and his movement. Second, John recognized that

Jesus did not fit the image of those coming in repentance, seeking forgiveness. Jesus transcended John's baptism (verse 14). And third, Jesus states his reason for being baptized: "to fulfil all righteousness" (verse 15). This is to say, it is what God wills, it is an act of fidelity to the commands of God (as in 5:20).

As stated earlier, this passage also addresses the question of Jesus' relation to John. Since John had disciples (Luke 11:1) and a movement arose around him (John 1:6-8, 15; Acts 18:24–19:7), that John baptized Jesus could have been (and probably was) used by John's disciples to argue his superiority over Jesus. All the Gospel writers deal with John and his movement. Matthew inserts in the baptismal scene a polemic to the effect that John himself recognized Jesus' superiority and was hesitant to baptize him. In fact, said John, Jesus should be the one baptizing (verses 14-15).

In addition to these two concerns of Matthew, the account is offered as a prototype of Christian baptism, an act of the church that carried the authority of Jesus' own example. It is especially important to notice in this regard that the writer offers not a word about Jesus' feelings, his internal state, or any messianic self-consciousness, if such a condition were present. On the contrary, the focus of attention is upon what God announced at Jesus' baptism.

That Jesus' baptism was an epiphany event has in all three Synoptics triple attestation: the heavens were opened, a sign associated with divine revelation (verse 16; Ezek. 1:1); the Holy Spirit descended upon Jesus, empowering him for the ministry before him (verse 16; 4:17); and the voice from heaven declared, "This is my beloved Son, with whom I am well pleased" (verse 17; Ps. 2:7; Isa. 42:1). It is not, then, with the baptism itself that Matthew is most concerned but with the divine proclamation that immediately followed. Since Matthew has earlier offered the virgin birth as a statement that Jesus is son of God (1:18-25), it is not appropriate to use Matthew in support of the adoptionist Christology which holds that Jesus became son of God at his baptism.

Two words about the voice from heaven: (1) the expression "this is" rather than "thou art" (Mark 1:11; Luke 3:22) means that for Matthew the declaration was not to Jesus but to John and perhaps the others present; in other words, it was a public announcement; and (2) the voice joins Psalm 2:7 and Isaiah 42:1, the former being a coronation proclamation (the king is God's son) and the latter a reference to God's suffering servant. Sovereignty is joined to sacrificial service, a theme which was to characterize both Jesus' teaching and his life.

Second Sunday After Epiphany

Isaiah 49:1-7; Psalm 40:1-11; I Corinthians 1:1-9; John 1:29-34

The Old Testament lesson for today is provided by the Second Servant Song from Isaiah, a fitting complement to last week's Old Testament reading. Its special emphasis on the calling of the servant and his special vocation as a "light to the nations" makes its especially appropriate in this Epiphany setting. The psalm and the epistolary reading are similar in that both contain prayers of thanksgiving. In the psalm, thanksgiving finally prompts the psalmist to tell abroad the good news of deliverance. Of course, the epistolary reading has not been selected to relate thematically to the other readings since it is the first of several semicontinuous readings from I Corinthians 1–4 that continue for seven weeks. The gospel lesson consists of the Johannine account of the baptism of Jesus. Since John's account of this event is not used in any of the three years for the baptism of the Lord, it occurs here. Actually it is not an account of the event in the strict sense, but more or less presupposes it. In the context of the Epiphany, its emphasis on John's role as one who bore witness should be noted.

Isaiah 49:1-7

This same reading, including the second of the Servant Songs, is also assigned for use on Tuesday in Holy Week. There, as here, the passage from Second Isaiah is seen in the context of Christian worship as a prophecy fulfilled by Jesus. On the Second Sunday of Epiphany the call and designation of the servant is linked with the baptism of Jesus by the Holy Spirit (John 1:32 ff.). However, the text requires to be heard in other ways as well, including in its own literary and historical

120

context. It may turn out that Second Isaiah's servant is not only a type of Jesus, but may also be a model for understanding the vocation of the church.

The Servant Song ends with verse 6. Verse 7 begins a new unit, an announcement of salvation to Israel, that runs through verse 12.

In the first Servant Song (Isa. 42:1-4; see the commentary on last week's Old Testament lesson) Yahweh was the speaker, designating his servant. Here the servant himself speaks. The song has many of the features of a typical prophetic address, including a summons to attention at the outset, and direct quotation of the words of God (verses 3, 6), and there is a very expansive messenger formula in verse 5. It also has some of the features of a thanksgiving psalm, with an account of trouble and the report of deliverance from it.

However, in important ways the passage is like prophetic vocation reports found in other prophetic books (Isa. 6; Jer. 1:10-17; Ezek. 1-3; cf. Isa. 40:1-11). The basic issue is the call of the servant and his response to that call. There is a dialogue on the subject between the prophet and the one who has called him. Like Jeremiah, the servant reports (verses 1, 5) that he was designated "from the womb" (Jer. 1:5), and like Jeremiah (Jer. 1:16), Isaiah (Isa. 6:5), and Moses (Exod. 3-4), he responded with a sense of unworthiness (verse 4). In this passage the note of inadequacy seems to stem from frustration with the results of work already in progress. Likewise, as with others, the Lord reacted with reassurance. As in other vocation reports, the task of the servant is spelled out, and it concerns his "mouth" (verse 2).

Thus, while the emphasis in the first Servant Song was upon the royal, administrative responsibility of the servant, here the role is more prophetic. The servant was given powerful words to speak, but held back until the appropriate time. That is the meaning of the metaphors of the weapons in verse 2, and it seems to stand in contrast with the gentle servant of Isaiah 42:2-3, at least until one sees the way these weapons are to be used.

In short, the servant reports that he has been called to a task that involves words, that he came to believe that his work was in vain (verse 4), but then was confident of God's approval. Whether this reflects stages in his work or ambivalence is not clear. The call is reiterated and the duties spelled out (verses 5-6). The servant is to "bring Jacob back to him." This responsibility corresponds to the central message of Second Isaiah, that is, that Yahweh will set the captives in Babylon free and bring them back to Jerusalem. Then there is a second role. In addition to raising up the tribes of Jacob, the servant is to be "a light to the nations," toward the end that the Lord's "salvation may reach to the ends of the earth" (verse 6).

Thus the servant has both a national and a world-wide vocation. As in Isaiah 42:5-9, the redemption of Israel by the one God is a step toward making the glory of that God known to all humankind. In our passage that concern was indicated from the very outset, for the addressees of the speech are "the coastlands," the "peoples from afar" (verse 1). This probably does not anticipate what we would call missionary activity to the Gentiles, but rather the display of the glory of God and the establishment of the universal reign of the Lord of Israel.

While the roles of the servant are clear, identification of the servant is difficult. Verse 3 states explicitly that the servant is Israel. But how can the servant then have a role *toward* Israel? Moreover, the language is highly individualistic. Some commentators, stressing the parallels to the vocation accounts of the prophets, see the servant as Second Isaiah himself. It is possible that the ambiguity here and in the other songs is intentional.

Modern hearers of this passage may find it possible to identify with any or all of the human parties. As individuals and as a church, we experience vocations, and may experience unworthiness or frustration. For such there is the divine reassurance in verses 4b and 5b. As servants of God we may hear a call to set captives free and to make the reign of God visible throughout the world. We may recognize ourselves in captive Israel, and then for us there is the proclamation of the message of release, the good news that God intends restoration (verses 5-6a). Or we may even be able to see ourselves in those other nations, to whom the good news comes.

Psalm 40:1-11

Psalm 40, portions of which are used as reading for the Annunciation, is a thanksgiving psalm but a thanksgiving psalm that moves into petition and lament (following verse 10). Today's reading picks up the plea or appeal in verse 11. The thanksgiving portion of the psalm is completed in verse 10.

The structural components of the thanksgiving ritual can be seen in this psalm if one pays attention to the contents and to the changes in the person being addressed. Verses 1-3 have the worshiper, who is celebrating some event that produced well-being, address a human audience offering testimony to God's saving action. The impersonal statement of verse 4, which sounds like a beatitude, probably represents the priest's affirmation of the worshiper and his/her confessional thanksgiving. With verse five, the worshiper turns to direct address to the Deity and continues this, except in verse 17*a*, throughout the psalm.

From what we can deduce about thanksgiving services, it is clear that the liturgy was divided in two distinct phases. One was oriented to a human audience (friends, family, the congregation). In this phase, the worshiper gave testimony to the new status that God had created, reiterated the conditions of trouble from which he/she had been rescued, and sought to convince the hearers to have a similar type of faith in God's ability to redeem. This part of the service probably occurred before the direct thanksgiving to God. The latter was the central focus of the second phase of the worship service.

Verses 1-3 describe briefly the worshiper's earlier sentiments at the time of trouble (1*a*) and testify to the fact that God responded (1*b*). Much of this section, however, is devoted to the consequences, to the new status the person has, to the new condition of life. The imagery is well reflected in the NJPSV's rendering of verse 2 (verse 3 in the Hebrew):

He lifted me out of the miry pit,
    the slimy clay,
    and set my feet on a rock,
    steadied my legs.

123

The new status is declared to produce a new song, a song of praise, a turn from lament to hymn, from petition to praise (3*a*). Verse 3*b* suggests the public character and the public benefit to be derived from the worshiper's (the king's?) testimony. Others will see, stand in awe, and participate in a similar faith and trust.

The priestly blessing in verse 4 in itself contains some preaching and proclamation. While affirming the experience of the worshiper, it simultaneously invites others to test the proposition that "blessed is the one who . . . ."

The opening word by the worshiper to the Deity (verse 5) repeats, in direct address and with different words, the sentiments of verses 1-3. In verses 1-3, the before and after conditions of the individual worshiper were stressed. In verse 5, two slightly different slants are given to the thanksgiving: (1) the material is less personalized and is presented in general terms—"wondrous deeds," "thy thoughts," "them"; and (2) the public quality of the sentiments receives attention. Along with personal pronouns referring to the speaker (seven times in verse 1-3, twice in verse 5), the worshiper now speaks of an "us" that is the recipient of God's actions and thoughts. (This could suggest that the speaker was either the king or some other leader.) This shift to the more general produces a reduction in the passion but simultaneously incorporates the audience in the ritual.

Verses 6-10 comprise the worshiper's statement of fidelity to God and a rehearsal of what the person believes, feels, and does as response to the Divine.

Verse 6 suggests that conventional, habitual religious practices—four different kinds of sacrifices are referred to—are not seen as the only or the necessary components in religion. The writer gives expression to the commitment of one's self in what must have been a popular saying indicating one's hearing of and submission to another—"You have dug ears for me." For the worshiper, what God desires and requires is first of all, a faithful hearing—receptivity.

The hearing response leads to voluntary obedience (verses 7-8). In terms somewhat reminiscent of the prophet Isaiah (see Isa. 6), the person volunteers—"I come" ("Here am I").

The second half of verse 7 with its reference to the book could denote that (1) in the book of his life it is written (and preordained) that the psalmist will make the will of God the delight of living, (2) the record of the person's life kept in the divine world demonstrates that the psalmist is one delighting in obedience, (3) the book of the law, the Torah (the Pentateuch?) was written as if speaking of the psalmist, or (4) to say "it's in the book" was a way of affirming something's and someone's truthfulness. However one understands the particulars, the affirmation is clear. The psalmist claims a complete submission to and obedience to God. "Thy law is within my inward parts" is an affirmation of the internalization of the law—inward being, the conscience, the heart, the ultimate commitments are devoted to the will of God.

Verses 9-10 affirm the public testimony of the commitment. This affirmation is stated twice positively and three times negatively. "I have told," "I have spoken," "I have not restrained my lips," "I have not hid," and "I have not concealed."

The psalmist thus delineates an action sequence pattern—sincere hearing leads to responsive commitment which leads to public exuberance, the testimony in the congregation.

Verse 11, in the RSV, appears as an appeal. It is possible to translate the verse as an affirmation as is done in the NJPSV: "O Lord, You will not withhold from me Your compassion; Your steadfast love will protect me always."

I Corinthians 1:1-9

On the Sundays immediately following Epiphany, the epistolary reading for all three years is taken from First Corinthians. In Year A, I Corinthians 1-4 provides the reading for the second through the eighth Sunday after Epiphany. In Year B, I Corinthians 6-9 provides the reading for the second through the sixth Sunday, with Second Corinthians providing the epistolary reading for the following Sundays after Epiphany. In Year C, I Corinthians 12-15 provides the reading for the second through the eighth Sunday after Epiphany.

We should also note that today's text overlaps with the

epistolary reading for the First Sunday of Advent in Year B (1:3-9). The reader may wish to consult our remarks in *Advent, Christmas, Epiphany, Year B* for additional comments.

Today's epistolary reading marks the beginning of the semicontinuous reading of I Corinthians 1–4 that occurs over these seven Sundays. Accordingly, some words of introduction to this epistle are in order here.

The epistle divides into three sections. After the initial greeting and prayer of thanksgiving, chapters 1–4 contain an extended exhortation. Here Paul urges the church to be unified in its mission and outlook as it lives out the message of the cross in its midst. They are to embody the unity of purpose exemplified in the work of Paul and Apollos. Chapters 5–6 treat two topics primarily: the proper response to sexual immorality within the church and the proper response to internal conflicts. In each case, the Corinthians had been lamentably deficient in their conduct, in spite of the fact that some were claiming to have superior wisdom. Here Paul is reminding them that there are a number of things they still do not know. Chapters 7–16 may be regarded as instructional. They contain what appear to be Paul's answers to a list of questions that the Corinthians submitted to him. In serial fashion, he treats a variety of topics, including marriage (chapter 7), eating meat offered to idols (chapters 8–10), worship (chapter 11), spiritual gifts (chapters 12–14), resurrection (chapter 15), the collection and miscellaneous matters (chapter 16).

As to the situation prompting the letter, it appears that some within the church had pretensions to wisdom that posed a threat to the church. In some cases they exhibited arrogant behavior that was insensitive to the needs of other members in the church. Rather than developing a sense of corporate solidarity in which individual preferences gave way to the common good, there was emerging a kind of robust individualism that pushed freedom over responsibility.

In response to this situation, Paul urges the Corinthians to become more united in their fellowship. He calls on individuals to seek the common good rather than their own personal good, to be willing to make concessions in the interest of others. The letter also imposes limits on spiritual enthusiasm. While recognizing the power of the Spirit in energizing the church and its ministries, Paul also sees the excesses of spiritualism. If spiritual pursuits threaten domestic stability, they should be curbed. If they threaten to undermine meaningful worship, they should be balanced with more edifying spiritual behavior. On the whole, what emerges is a set of exhortations and instructions designed to make congregational life a meaningful form of fellowship.

Today's epistolary lection consists of two parts: the opening greeting (verses 1-3) and the opening prayer of thanksgiving offered on behalf of the Corinthians (verses 4-9).

The Greeting (verses 1-3). The greeting is typical in many respects of other Pauline greetings (cf. Rom. 1:1; II Cor. 1:1; Eph. 1:1; Col. 1:1; II Tim. 1:1). Paul identifies himself as an apostle called through the will of God (verse 1). Not only is he called, however, but the Corinthians themselves are "called to be saints" (verse 2; Rom. 1:7). As such, they stand solidly with Christians everywhere who "call on the name of the Lord Jesus Christ" (verse 2), that is, with those everywhere who confess Christ as Lord and pray to God through Christ (Acts 2:21; 9:14, 21; 22:16; Rom. 10:12-13; cf. Ps. 99:6; Joel 2:32; II Tim. 2:22).

We should note that the letter is addressed quite specifically to the congregation at Corinth—a single, local church (verse 2). This reminds us that the letter was first addressed to someone else before we became its readers. In one sense, we are reading someone else's mail. We are overhearing a conversation between Paul and his church. But even if we stand outside the circle of the original conversation, because we have been sanctified in Christ and call upon the name of the Lord as they did, their conversation enlightens us as well. As a result of the canonical process, the church decided that the letter was instructive to later readers as well.

The Prayer of Thanksgiving (verses 4-9). Typically, Paul's opening prayers set the mood of the letter as well as telegraph some of its central concerns. This one is no exception. The mood is above all reassuring. The readers are reminded that they are "not lacking in any spiritual gift" (verse 7). If some of the church members were claiming superiority in these matters, it is not difficult to see how other members would come to feel deficient. It is a common concern in all churches: the strong get stronger and the weak get weaker. To combat this debilitating tendency, Paul reminds them (and us) that each of us has been endowed by the Spirit in some way, with some gift. We should not allow the heroic spiritualists to intimidate us and leave us feeling spiritually depressed.

Not only does the prayer reassure us about our own spiritual endowments, it reaffirms the Lord's fidelity: "God is faithful" (verse 9; cf. 10:13; II Cor. 1:18; I Thess. 5:24; II Thess. 3:3; also Heb. 10:23; 11:11; I John 1:9; Rev. 1:5). The God who promises delivers. The One who called us into fellowship will make good on the promises offered. We are promised that the Lord Jesus Christ will sustain us to the end (verse 8). It is not as if Christ has left us orphaned, with no direction and sustenance for the interim, much less that he will leave us stranded as we gaze into the future. No, instead he will present us "guiltless" before God in the final day, the "day of the Lord" (verse 8; II Cor. 1:14; Phil. 1:6, 10; 2:16; also Acts 2:20).

Besides this generally reassuring tone, the prayer signals themes later developed in the letter: the proper role of wisdom and rhetorical ability (chapters 1–2), the right attitude toward spiritual gifts (chapters 12–14), the proper view of the end-time (chapter 15).

John 1:29-34

John 1:29-34 is very much an Epiphany text for in it Jesus is declared publicly to be the Lamb of God, the one who baptizes with the Holy Spirit, and the Son of God.

The one who makes this proclamation about Jesus is John the Baptist. In this Gospel, the role of John is that of a witness to Jesus Christ. He has been so portrayed in the Prologue (1:6-8) and so he is subsequently described (1:19, 32; 5:33). This identification of Jesus as God's Christ and Son of God is unparalleled in the Synoptic accounts of John's ministry. In those Gospels John preached about one coming, a stronger one, who would baptize with the Holy Spirit (Matt. 3:11-12; Mark 1:7-8; Luke 3:15-18), but John has no direct association with Jesus and does not identify Jesus as this messianic figure. Matthew (3:13-17), as we saw in last Sunday's lesson, does say that John recognized Jesus as greater and heard the voice from heaven declare him God's beloved Son. Both Matthew (11:2-6) and Luke (7:18-23) report that the imprisoned John sent to Jesus asking, "Are you he or shall we look for another?" but in none of these Synoptic references to John is he characterized as a witness to Christ in the manner of the text before us.

The first section of the Gospel of John immediately following the Prologue (1:1-18) begins with an expression which could serve as a title for what follows: "And this is the testimony [witness] of John" (verse 19). John's testimony consists of two parts: his witness about himself (1:19-28) and his witness about Christ (1:29-34). To this second part we give our attention here.

The first question is, How did John know who Jesus was? John says that the point of his own ministry of baptism was that Christ would be revealed to Israel (verse 31), but first Christ had to be revealed to John. Already John had said to the Jews, "Among you stands one whom you do not know" (verse 26); now he acknowledges, "I myself did not know him" (verses 31, 33). John can therefore witness only after he has received the revelation about Jesus. This perspective is supported elsewhere in the New Testament. Knowing the Son is by revelation (Matt. 11:27); God, not flesh and blood, has made him known (Matt. 16:17); only by the Holy Spirit can anyone say Jesus is Lord (I Cor. 12:3).

John the Baptist says the revelation occurred in this way: "He who sent me to baptize with water said to me, 'He on whom you see the Spirit descend and remain, this is he who baptizes with the Holy Spirit' " (verse 33). John saw the Spirit descend as a dove (verse 32; agreeing with Matthew who says John witnessed heaven's attestation to Jesus, 3:16-17), and he knew. We assume the Evangelist is reporting on an occurrence at Jesus' baptism, but no account of Jesus' baptism is actually given. This event, awkward for Matthew and Luke, is simply omitted by the Fourth Evangelist except for this reference to what John saw.

Although it may seem minor at this point, it is important to notice that twice the Evangelist says the Holy Spirit "remained" (verses 32-33) on Jesus. To remain or to abide is a favorite expression of the Fourth Gospel to express the relationship between Christ and God and between Christ and his followers (e.g., 15:1-11). Here the point is that Jesus and the Holy Spirit have no "come and go" relationship as though he were a charismatic prophet. He is the permanent bearer of the Spirit and his life carries the quality, knowledge, and power which that implies. And Jesus gives the Holy Spirit to his followers (1:33; 20:22). According to this Gospel, true Christian spirituality is not an alternative to the life of obedient discipleship; it does not distance one from Jesus of Nazareth but rather ties one inseparably to him.

A final word: John the Baptist hails Jesus as "the Lamb of God, who takes away the sin of the world" (verse 29). The preacher will want to resist being drawn immediately to all the lamb images in the Jewish sacrificial system. The allusions are plentiful: the sin-offering lamb, the Passover lamb, the warrior lamb of apocalyptic literature, but which is in the writer's mind? In what sense does Jesus take away the sin of the world? More atonement doctrines are found in Paul and Hebrews than in the Fourth Gospel. For this Evangelist, Jesus lays down his life for the sheep (10:15) and dies as the true Passover Lamb (19:31-37). Whether 1:29 relates to either of those interpretations of Jesus' death or adds a third is not clear. Sermons that focus on this statement can share with the congregation the rich plentitude of symbolism and Old Testament associations without seeming to be certain about the writer's specific focus. Churches appreciate honest caution.

Third Sunday After Epiphany

Isaiah 9:1-4; Psalm 27:1-6; I Corinthians 1:10-17;
Matthew 4:12-23

Light shining in darkness is the central theme of the Old Testament reading from Isaiah. Its depiction of the messianic king has become a symbol of hope. The image of light is also the note on which the psalm opens, with its declaration, "The Lord is my light and my salvation." In the epistolary reading we hear Paul exhorting the Corinthians to realize the unity that has eluded them. The Gospel reading from Matthew begins the semicontinuous reading of this Gospel which runs through the next five weeks. Even so, Epiphany themes are dominant in the prophetic announcement taken from Isaiah 9:1-4, the Old Testament reading for today.

Isaiah 9:1-4

Except for the first verse this passage is included in the Old Testament lesson for Christmas, First Proper. For a commentary, see pages 49-51 in this volume. Isaiah 9:1-2 has been assigned for this occasion because the first two verses are cited in the Gospel lection, as a particular prophecy that Jesus fulfills.

The lesson includes two parts: a narrative introduction (verse 1) that locates and dates the events, and the initial parts of a prophetic announcement concerning the rule of God through the designation of a new descendant in the line of David. Thus the reading is incomplete. The proclamation that light has shined upon those in darkness (verse 2) is followed by an account of celebration (verse 3). Then the reasons for celebration are given, with our lesson including only the first of the three reasons. Ending the text with verse

131

4 puts the emphasis upon the dramatic contrasts between light and darkness, the joyful celebration, and God's intervention to release the people from oppression (verse 4).

Psalm 27:1-6

The first six verses of this psalm only represent a portion of the entire composition. The structure of the overall psalm is as follows: (1) an affirmation of confidence addressed to a human audience (verse 1-6); (2) a petition addressed to God requesting help (verses 7-12); (3) a confessional statement by the worshiper to a human audience (verse 13); and (4) a response by the priest (or other cultic official) to the worshiper (verse 14). (A full treatment of the entire psalm is found in Propers 20–21, Year B.)

The psalm lection for this Sunday contains the worshiper's opening statement of confidence addressed not to God but to a human audience, perhaps the official in charge of the sacrificial service or maybe friends and family or even opponents assembled at the sanctuary for religious services or perhaps for some ordeal.

The psalm opens with a statement of great confidence. Three metaphors are used to describe God the source of confidence: light, salvation, and stronghold. The two affirmations in verse 1 are followed, however, by two rhetorical questions: "Whom shall I fear?" "Of whom shall I be afraid?" The rhetorical questions help raise the question of fear in such a way that the worshiper can answer "no one." Their function, of course, is to reinforce courage. Whoever wrote this psalm (and we should think of some cultic official associated with the temple) knew that courage is a fragile vessel lightly floating upon an abyss of fear. Thus every effort is made to sustain courage.

Verses 2-3 require (or allow) the worshiper to speak even more concretely about one's opponents. Note the heavy imagery of the verbs—"assail, eat my flesh [a pictorial designation for slander], stumble, fall, encamp, arise." The nouns too are loaded and graphic terms—"evildoers, adversaries, foes, host, war." What one fears is here embodied in graphic terminology so that the collected confidence and courage of the psalmist can assert themselves. (Even the ancients knew the power of positive thinking!)

Verse 4 has the worshiper say that the one thing desired is to live in the temple "all the days of my life." In ancient Israel, those who lived in the temple precincts were fugitives fleeing from opponents or persons given to the temple. (One should beware of spiritualizing such an expression as "dwell in the house of the Lord all the days of my life" to mean "go to heaven" or "be with God.") That a fugitive could take refuge in the sanctuary is evident in Deuteronomy 16:1-13, and I Samuel 1 tells how Samuel was given to the temple to abide there forever. Whether refuge in the temple is what the psalm has in mind is not certain but seems probable (note the references to witnesses in verse 12).

Verses 5-6 reaffirm the worshiper's confidence and contain the vow to offer sacrifice and worship after God has aided the supplicant. Three images of shelter are used in verse 5: a shelter (in Hebrew a *sukkah*, a lean-to which offered shade and cool in the fields), a tent, and a rock. The worshiper's confidence of God's favor leads to a boast in verse 6a. The supplicant claims not only escape from the adversary but triumph over all enemies round about! This sections closes with a vow, publicly announced, that sacrifices and songs would be offered in the temple. Courage and confidence would culminate in celebration.

I Corinthians 1:10-17

The opening exhortation of the Epistle of First Corinthians is an appeal for unity (verse 10). Paul had received a report from "Chloe's people" that there was quarreling among the Corinthian brethren (verse 11). The word used here (*eris*) suggests attitudinal divisions and interpersonal bickering rather than doctrinal or ideological schisms. It is often closely associated with jealousy and petty strife (cf. 3:3; Gal. 5:19-20). His hope, of course, is that these would not develop into full-scale "dissensions" (*schismata*, verse 10), which is always the danger. Petty disagreements become the occasion for more serious doctrinal cleavages, and often the latter become the justification for the former.

It is difficult to ascertain clearly the nature of the internal differences or strife within the church. Paul elaborates in verse 12 that the members were defining their loyalties around various personalities, such as himself, Apollos, Cephas (Peter), and even Christ. What did it mean for them to claim to belong to each of these figures? Most likely these were the figures being suggested as the ultimate poles of authority and sources of guidance for Christian life and practice. Thus, some preferred Paul since he was their founding missionary (2:1-5), even though he was now living across the Aegean carrying on his apostolic work in Ephesus (16:8). Others preferred Apollos, the minister who had been there most recently and whose intellectual ability, rhetorical eloquence, and knowledge of the Scriptures especially commended him (3:4-6, 22; 4:6; 16:12; Acts 18:24; 19:1; also Titus 3:13). Still others preferred to look to one of the original apostles for guidance, and thus offered Cephas as their polestar (9:5). And still others, eschewing all human teachers, looked only to Christ for guidance, realizing that they were "of Christ" (3:23; II Cor. 10:7; cf. Mark 9:41) and remembering perhaps that the risen Lord had promised to be with them and instruct them in the ways of truth (Matt. 28:20; cf. Luke 12:11).

As admirable as each of these might have been, the underlying assumption had a debilitating effect on the life of the church. It meant that the unity they all shared in Christ was being dissolved in favor of human loyalties. What should have been holding them together—their common life in Christ—was evaporating before their very eyes.

What was at stake, according to Paul, was the nature of existence in Christ. Thus, he asks rhetorically, "Is Christ divided?" (verse 13). How can Christ's body be dismembered? A divided Christ is no Christ at all. Yet this is what happens when we define Christian existence in terms of human loyalties. Paul insists that he was neither crucified for them nor were they baptized in his name (verse 13). Since no human being fills this role, they can belong to no one in the sense they are claiming.

The exegetical question, of course, is in what sense some were claiming to be "of Christ" (verse 12), and why this would be objectionable, if indeed it is. The gist of Paul's remarks suggests that all four groups are being reprimanded for false loyalties, or for identifying their loyalties wrongly. Those claiming to belong to Christ are perhaps being censured because they are as divisive and exclusive in their claims as the rest, in which case they would be party to dismembering the Body of Christ. Even the right title, or the right cliché, is meaningless if it becomes the occasion for arrogant and exclusive claims.

Paul is aware that such loyalties are often the result of our relationship with the one who baptized us, or introduced us into the faith. It is understandable why we should feel such strong attachment to the pastor or minister who baptized us. Even Paul recognized his special relationship to those whom he baptized or taught personally (4:17; Philem. 10, 19). Yet he also recognized the inherent danger that those whom he baptized could mistakenly construe their relationship with Christ as essentially a relationship with Paul (verse 15). Accordingly, he stresses how few people he actually baptized—Crispus (Acts 18:8), Gaius (Rom. 16:23; cf. Acts 19:29), and the household of Stephanas (16:15, 17).

It was after all Paul's primary task to preach the gospel, not to perform acts of baptism (verse 17; cf. Rom. 15:15-16; Gal. 1:16). Even when his task was defined this way, there were hazards, because the effectiveness of his preaching could be laid to his rhetorical ability. He is all too aware that preaching could be packaged in such a way that it derived its power not from the message itself but from the messenger, and the messenger's way with words. Paul saw this as emptying the cross of its power (verse 17).

The overall appeal is for Christian unity—for the congregation to be one in its mind, or outlook, its purpose, and its life (verse 10; cf. Rom. 12:16; 15:5; II Cor. 13:11; Phil. 2:2; 4:2; I Pet. 3:8). We should not confuse unity with uniformity. To agree and to be of the same mind and judgment does not require us to formulate our theology in identical terms. Indeed, the true test of Christian unity is the ability to disagree in our formulation of the truth, even in our convictions about the truth, without compromising our ultimate loyalty to Christ—and to each other.

Homiletically, today's text has served historically as a crucial text on Christian unity. Even though the focus of the passage is congregational and the divisions that were occurring pitted individuals against individuals, its scope is naturally much broader. As such, it speaks to all situations where the Body of Christ is being dismembered, whether the nature of the division is congregational, confessional, denominational, or religious in the broadest sense.

One of the most fundamental insights worth exploring is that our unity in Christ exists at a basic, substructural level. As such, it is something already there by virtue of our incorporation into Christ through baptism. It is already there waiting to be realized or actualized rather than being out there, unrealized and waiting to be created. It is something we have and make real rather than something we do not have and thus must create. In mediating church squabbles, or even denominational differences, it is often much more constructive to begin with what we already have in common in Christ, the unity we already share, rather than assuming that our experience of Christ—either our personal experience or our church's experience—is wholly ours and radically different from that which others claim to be true Christian experience.

Matthew 4:12-23

Today's lesson is appropriate for the Season of Epiphany not only in the general sense of relating the beginning of Jesus' public ministry but in the particular sense of providing an announcement to the nations, "the people who sat in darkness/have seen a great light,/and for those who sat in the region and shadow of death/light has dawned" (verse 16).

There are in Matthew 4:12-23 four discernible parts: the beginning of Jesus' public ministry in Galilee (verses 12-16); a summary statement of Jesus' message (verse 17); the call of the first four disciples (verses 18-22); a summary of Jesus' travels and the nature of his ministry (verse 23).

In the first unit Matthew follows Mark (1:14-15) both in locating the account immediately after the temptation story (Matt. 3:1-11; Mark 1:12-13) and in the description of Jesus launching his ministry. (Luke 3:14-15 has the same order but abbreviates the account to introduce the rejection in Nazareth, 4:16-30.) The record as Matthew provides it says that Jesus withdrew into Galilee upon hearing of John's imprisonment (verse 12). Whether the withdrawal from Judea was prompted by concern for his own safety, or to avoid having his ministry construed as merely a continuation of that of the now silenced John, or to use John's imprisonment as a natural turning point providing opportunity to begin his own separate work, we do not know. Once in Galilee, Jesus moved from Nazareth to Capernaum (verse 13; implied in Luke 4:23). Whatever may have been the practical considerations prompting such a move, Matthew interprets it as the fulfillment of the prophecy in Isaiah 9:1-2. This fulfillment formula, familiar in Matthew, has no parallel in the other Gospels. Luke refers to Jesus' work in Capernaum (1:21-28), but no connections are made to prophecy. Mark's account of Jesus' message says, "The time is fulfilled" (1:15), but for Matthew the *place* is fulfilled, "Galilee of the Gentiles" (verse 15). Attention to the Gentile mission continues this theme from the visit of the wise men from the East (2:1-12). In its own context Isaiah 9:1-2 refers to the march of the army of Assyria westward to the Mediterranean and the promise of a deliverer to free the besieged people. Matthew (or his source) applies the passage to the Sea of Galilee and to the coming of Jesus as Messiah.

As for Jesus' message (verse 17), it was essentially a continuation of John's preaching. Here Matthew reworks Mark 1:15, changing "kingdom of God" to his more characteristic "kingdom of heaven" and omitting "and believe in the gospel." The phrase "is at hand" is a translation of the perfect tense which may also be translated "is near," or "is here." The whole of Jesus' message is needed to determine if he announced the approaching end of this age and the soon arrival of the age to come (this age and the age to come is a distinction provided by Jewish apocalyptic eschatology) or if Jesus was saying that his arrival marked the presence ("is here") of the reign of God. Scholars are divided on the matter but generally tend to speak of God's reign being both present and future in the work and words of Jesus. Jesus announces, then, both a hope and a warning: in view of God's new activity, the people must prepare through repentance.

The third unit, the call of the first four disciples (verses 18-22), follows closely Mark 1:16-20 (Luke's account is somewhat different, and later, 5:1-11. In John, Jesus calls his first disciples in Judea from among the followers of John, 1:35-43). There is no evidence here of an earlier meeting, nor any basis to discuss the psychology of conversion. The suddenness of the call prompted E. Lohmeyer to call this an epiphany story. The metaphor "fishers of men" is more familiar than clear. When pressed to yield details descriptive of the church's mission, the image becomes rather unattractive. Even though the image has continued to live in the church, it did not fare so well in New Testament writings. The shepherd analogy became more popular.

And finally, verse 23 provides a summary of Jesus' travels (all Galilee; for some strange reason, Luke has Judea, 4:44) and his activity: teaching in the synagogues, preaching, and healing. Mark has preaching and exorcising demons (1:39). Matthew follows verse 23 with an elaboration of Jesus' fame (throughout all Syria, verse 24), his healings (verse 24), and his gathering of crowds from Galilee, Decapolis, Jerusalem, Judea, and beyond the Jordan (verse 25). Very likely, verses 23-25 are Matthew's preparation for the Sermon on the Mount which is delivered not only to "the crowds" but to people gathered from everywhere. In other words, Jesus' teaching is for everyone.

Fourth Sunday After Epiphany

Micah 6:1-8; Psalm 37:1-11; I Corinthians 1:18-31; Matthew 5:1-12

One of the most famous Old Testament passages supplies the first lesson for today: the text from Micah that speaks of justice, kindness, and humility as the essence of doing God's will. Psalm 37 is well known for its firm stance against the wicked and the assurance that wrongs will be righted and that the unrighteous will get their just desserts. The epistolary reading is Paul's classic statement of his theology of the cross, in which he pits God's foolishness against human wisdom. In the Gospel reading, we have the most familiar version of the Beatitudes in which we have sketched a profile of life in the kingdom of God. This collection of passages combines four classic biblical texts, each in its own way has earned its rightful place as memorable and compelling.

Micah 6:1-8

This reading, which includes some of the best-known lines of prophetic literature, consists of two distinct units of speech, verses 1-5 and 6-8. As the Book of Micah has come down to us, the two are meant to be heard as part of a larger collection, but since each unit is in a different genre and conveys its own message they are best analyzed individually.

Micah 6:1-5 is the beginning of a prophetic lawsuit against Israel. First the prophet speaks (verses 1-2), and then Yahweh addresses the people directly (verses 3-5). In formal legal language similar to that found in Micah 1, the prophet utters on behalf of Yahweh a series of summons to the people of Israel (verses 1-2). They are called to present their case

139

before the mountains and hills, and then commanded to hear Yahweh's "controversy" (better, "suit," or "lawsuit"). The prophetic speeches of judgment generally resemble the pattern of the legal process, with accusation and then pronouncement of punishment. Here, however, the specifically convenantal background is more obvious, reflected in the formal legal terminology and in the call to natural phenomena, such as mountains and hills or, elsewhere, heavens and earth. The contents and form of this section are familiar from other prophetic literature (Isa. 1:2-2; 3:13-15; Hos. 4:1-6; Jer. 2:4-13). The unit is a prophetic covenant lawsuit.

It is different, however, from others in that a specific accusation or indictment does not follow the summons. Instead, Yahweh begins with self-defense, asking what he has done to weary Israel, and then recites the history of his saving actions on behalf of the chosen people (verses 3-5). These actions are familar from the first six books of the Bible: the Exodus from Egypt, the designation of leaders—the reference to Miriam with Moses and Aaron is remarkable—the preservation in the wilderness, and the entrance into the promised land (Shittim and Gilgal).

Such a recitation of the history of salvation frequently serves as the basis for prophetic accusations against Israel. Here, however, the purpose is summarized in the last line of verse 5: "that you may know the saving acts of the Lord." If an indictment is implied it is that Israel has forgotten what Yahweh has done and that she belongs to Yahweh.

Micah 6:6-8 is in the form of a question and answer, with a worshiper speaking in verses 6-7 and another voice responding in verse 8. The form borrows from priestly and liturgical practice. When a layperson wished to enter the temple for worship or proposed to offer a sacrifice, there was a ritual of inquiry and instruction. A religious specialist, generally a priest, answered the questions about appropriate worship or sacrifice. Our text is thus a priestly or prophetic torah or instruction (see Pss. 15; 24; Isa. 1:10-17; Amos 5:21-24; Hos. 6:1-6). As in the other prophetic uses of the instruction, Micah has changed the contents of both the question and the answer. Specifically, cultic inquiry has been turned into the question of what the Lord "requires," that is, what it takes to restore and maintain one's relationship with God, given the acknowledgment of sin (verse 7*b*). Moreover, a cultic pattern has been used to reject reliance upon cultic activity.

The worshiper's question concerns sacrifices and offerings. With the use of hyperbole it moves from the normal practice ("burnt offerings," "calves a year old") to exaggerated proposals ("thousands of rams," "ten thousands of rivers of oil") to climax with the possibility of child sacrifice ("my first-born"). There is irony in the tone, suggesting already that what is not possible is not necessary or right. If one relies upon sacrifices, how many does it take? There is, at least theoretically, no end. Israel knew that its neighbors practiced or had practiced child sacrifice, but the prophet considers it ridiculous to think that Yahweh would require it (cf. Gen. 22).

The answer ignores the question; the prophet does not even bother to reject these proposals, as Amos did (5:21-24). Instead, he states what God does require (verse 8). It is clear that no new expectations are introduced. The Lord has already shown what is "good" and what he requires. The three "requirements" summarize the responsibilities of the nation and of individuals in the covenant relationship; all have to do with human activity in society and under God. "To do justice" (*mishpat*) concerns the establishment of law in the courts, the care for equity in all human relationships. "To love kindness" (or "mercy," "steadfast love," *hesed*) is to be faithful in covenant relationships, to maintain solidarity with others, including those in need or trouble. "To walk humbly with your God" is not an additional expectation, but a summary of the others. It means to acknowledge the Lordship of God, to submit one's will to the will of God. Genuine piety is seen in doing justice and loving mercy.

Psalm 37:1-11

This lection, also the reading for the Seventh Sunday After Epiphany, Year C, is a portion of a psalm that reads in many ways like a miniature book of Proverbs. Similarly, it shares terminology and outlook with parts of the Sermon on the Mount.

The content of this psalm speaks to the situation in which the wicked and evil are prospering and the meek and faithful are going unrewarded. The author, and one should here imagine a priest offering pastoral advice in a teaching situation, offers what may be summarized in three principles.

1. The unrewarded, the unprosperous should not become distressed over their predicament. Two conditions are warned against. *(a)* Fretting (verses 1, 7*b*, 8*b*) should not be resorted to since it only produces greater evil. Although the author does not spell out the implications, one could say that fretting (from an old English word meaning "to devour") is self-destructive, dissipating the self, wasting energy, encouraging self-pity. Fretting is frustrating, ungoal-oriented; it is to life as flailing is to a drowning person. *(b)* Anger and wrath, that is, frustration directed outward, are simply another form of expressing distress and should be avoided (verse 8*a*). Envy is simply anger in a different package (verse 1*b*).

2. The righteous should endure, trusting in God (verses 3, 5, 7); not merely enduring passively but actively doing good (verse 3*a*). As in other psalms and biblical texts, a positive attitude is encouraged.

3. Finally, the psalmist promises, people are properly rewarded; the evil are cut off, the wicked fade and disappear, and the good, the meek enjoy security, receive the desires of their heart, are vindicated, and delight in prosperity. Perhaps the story seems to end too well; but surely the Bible teaches that virtue brings reward even if it is only itself.

The ancient rabbis wrestled with the problem of this psalm and transferred the final rectification to the world to come. Hear how they described it in a parable: "The Holy One, blessed be He, said to David: When thou seest that I do good to the wicked, let not thy heart grieve. But go on doing good. If I do good to the wicked who vex Me and profit Me not, if I do good to them, then for thee who trustest in Me, who art diligent in the study of Torah, who dost justice and righteousness—for thee how much more and more shall I do if thou continuest to trust in Me.

"With whom may David be compared? With a laborer who worked all his days for the king. When the king did not give him his hire, the laborer was troubled and said: 'Am I to go forth with nothing in my hands?' Then the king hired another laborer who worked for the king but one day, and the king laid meat before him, gave him drink, and paid him his hire in full. The laborer who had worked all his days for the king said: 'Such reward for this one who did no more than work but one day for the king? For me who have been working for the king all the days of my life, how much more and more my reward!' The other laborer went away, and now the one who had been working all his days for the king was glad in his heart. So David said, 'Thou has put gladness in my heart, from the time their corn and their wine increased (Ps. 4:8). That is to say, when is there gladness in my heart? When I see what Thou hast done for the wicked.'

"From the prosperity of the wicked in this world, you can tell the reward of the righteous in the world-to-come. If so much for the wicked [in this world], how much more and more for the righteous [in the world to come]!"

I Corinthians 1:18-31

The vital importance of this text is seen in its frequent use in the *Common Lectionary*. It serves as the epistolary reading for Tuesday in Holy Week in all three years (cf. our comments in *Lent, Holy Week, Easter* in Years A, B, and C). The middle section of this text (1:22-25) provides the epistolary lection for the Third Sunday of Lent in Year B (cf. our comments in *Lent, Holy Week, Easter, Year B*). Yet another portion of this text (1:18-24) serves as the epistolary lection for the celebration of Holy Cross (September 14) in all three years (cf. our comments in *After Pentecost* in Years A, B, and C).

Since it occurs today as part of the semicontinuous reading of First Corinthians, we will pay special attention to how it relates to its immediate context (chapters 1–4). Last week's lesson concludes on the note that Paul's primary task was to preach rather than baptize. As a clarifying remark, he insists that he does not preach "with eloquent wisdom," fearing that this will somehow empty the cross of its power. This mention of his preaching the cross prompts today's text, a rather extended treatment of "the word of the cross" (verse 18). In fact, verse 17 may perhaps be understood best as introducing this section rather than concluding the former section (JB). Our text begins, then, with Paul's insistence that the cross can be compromised by rhetorical display. Preaching the cross can actually be robbed of its true power if it derives its force from "eloquent wisdom," the preacher's ability as a wordsmith.

Here we see Paul already beginning to respond to a way of thinking in the church that he regards as not only unproductive but sinister. It looks as if some of the members had an inflated view of wisdom and knowledge, so much so that it became the sole measuring rod of all things, even things religious. Later Paul must remind the Corinthians that knowledge must be counterbalanced with love (8:1). Knowledge tends to be inflating whereas love tends to be upbuilding. Knowledge thinks of self, love thinks of others.

It may have been that some were beginning to measure the Christian message by the standards of human reason. Why did God choose to work through a crucified Messiah? How can an event of desperation—the crucifixion—become an event of salvation? How can a moment of powerlessness be a display of divine power? These are the questions human reason puts to God. Before we know it, humans have put God in the dock, as if God must be defended in the court of human wisdom! Paul sees this as the beginning of unbridled arrogance. Today's text is his response.

First, he recognizes that the "word of the cross" (verse 18) has a radically polarizing effect. Its preaching inevitably creates two groups: "those on their way to ruin" and "those on their way to salvation" (verse 18, NEB). The former, "those who are perishing" (RSV) are those for whom Christ is "a deadly fume that kills" (II Cor. 2:16, NEB; cf. II Cor. 4:4; II Thess. 2:10). The latter, "us who are being saved" (RSV) are those for whom Christ is "a vital fragrance that brings life" (II Cor. 2:16, NEB; cf. Acts 2:47; Luke 13:23). Later, Paul concedes that it is "those who have heard [God's] call" (verse 24, NEB) who are able to see in the cross divine power and divine wisdom.

To understand the cross rightly is a matter of proper perception. But it is perception that stems from our experience of salvation. In one sense, Paul is quite willing to concede that being able to see the cross as saving event is a subjective experience. First we must have experienced the divine summons, the call of God, and in responding have experienced salvation. Then we are able to see the event as an insider. From inside the event we can see divine power at work, primarily because it has had a transforming effect on us.

Second, we should note the way in which Paul pits divine wisdom and power against human presumption. His response is thoroughly informed by Old Testament thought, not only the direct quotation from Isaiah 29:14 (verse 19) but other reminiscences as well (Ps. 33:10; Isa. 19:12; 40:13; 44:24; Job 12:17). The preacher would do well to run these various references, for each in its own way relates to a common theme: God cannot and will not be judged in the court of human wisdom. The history of God's dealings with Israel and other peoples has shown that Yahweh has often made a mockery of human wisdom. Humans have often prided themselves on their wisdom while remaining oblivious to God's true purposes. To presume that God needs our advice and counsel is not only the mark of arrogance but illusion. It reflects a profound misunderstanding of God as well as ourselves. Elsewhere Paul insists that human reasoning left to itself results in darkened hearts rather than enlightened minds (Rom. 1:21).

Paul recognizes that one of the best ways to cut through this rational misunderstanding is with irony. Thus he asserts that God has really chosen to save us through folly (verse 21). In a similar vein, Jesus reminded his disciples that God had hidden certain things from the wise and revealed them instead to babes (Matt. 11:25; Luke 10:21). As it turns out, the ways of God are ultimately inscrutable (Rom. 11:33-34). At its worst, divine folly is superior to human wisdom; divine weakness exceeds human strength (verse 25). To pit ourselves as God is a mismatch from the start.

Third, the cross is God's way of communicating with us, and as such breaks the usual horns of the dilemma.

Ordinarily, there are two ways of authenticating divine presence and activity: signs and wisdom. Here Paul classifies humanity into two broad groups: Jews and Greeks (verse 22). The one looks for signs, dramatic demonstrations of the presence of God (cf. Matt. 12:38; 16:1-4; Luke 11:16, 29-32; Luke 23:8; John 2:23; 4:48; 6:30; 7:31; 11:47; 12:37; 20:30-31). The other looks for logical explanations (cf. Acts 17:18). Miracles and wisdom—these become the major ways of determining whether God is speaking or acting in the world.

Paul insists that neither gets at the proper way of understanding God. Rather it is the cross through which we find the true nature of God being revealed to us. Unlike miracles, it is not a grand display of power and strength. It is in fact raw powerlessness. Unlike wisdom, it does not conform to our ways of thinking and reasoning. It rather runs against the grain of the way we think. In both respects, it radically calls into question the way we ordinarily define God. For this reason, it tends to be a stumbling block rather than a stepping-stone (verse 23; Gal. 5:11; Rom. 9:32-33; I Pet. 2:8; also Matt. 16:23; Isa. 8:14).

Fourth, our text lays stress on the primacy of God—on who God is and what God has done. Against this, human presumption collapses. In the second section (verses 26-31), Paul insists that it is God who is finally responsible for Christian existence. The Corinthians had little to commend themselves (verse 26). Note the threefold refrain: "God chose . . . God chose . . . God chose" (verses 27-28). They are living proof of God's being at work in them, not of their being at work in themselves. Ultimately, "no human being [can] boast in the presence of God" (verse 29). We should note the force of verse 30. Even though it is christologically rich, with all its claims about Christ, it is fundamentally a statement about God. The opening words may be paraphrased as follows: "It is of and from God that you are what you are in Christ Jesus; it was after all as a result of God's action that Christ became our wisdom, justification." If we must boast, we can only boast of what God has done (verse 31; cf. Jer. 9:23-24; II Cor. 10:7; Gal. 6:14; Phil. 3:3).

Matthew 5:1-12

Today is the first of five consecutive Sundays which have as the Gospel lesson a portion of Matthew, chapter five. In fact, the five Sundays provide the occasion for treating that entire chapter in the sequence of its own material. Since Matthew 5 is a portion of the Sermon on the Mount (Chapters 5–7), we should take time now to introduce ourselves anew to that body of teaching.

The Sermon on the Mount is the first of five major sections of Jesus' teachings provided by Matthew. All five sections conclude with the same formula (7:28; 11:1; 13:53; 19:1; 26:1), giving the impression of careful structuring. Some scholars consider the choice of five to be a deliberate paralleling of the five books of Moses. That Matthew draws on the Moses story to tell about Jesus has already been seen in the child's rescue from the wicked tyrant (2:13-23), and appears again in today's reading: like Moses, Jesus brings God's instruction from the mountain. However, the depth and breadth of subject matter in the Sermon on the Mount, plus the fact that portions of it have parallels scattered rather than gathered in Mark and Luke, persuade one to believe the "Sermon" is really a compilation of teachings of Jesus delivered at different times and places during his ministry. Such a view does not rob any of the sayings of their meaning or authority, but it does free the interpreter from trying to discover or having to construct a single audience for all the material. Were a subject or title to be given to this collection of sayings, it could well be "Life Under the Reign of God" or "The Law of Christian Society."

It is not altogether clear to whom Matthew has Jesus address these teachings. In 4:23-25, a crowd gathers from all the regions of the land to hear Jesus, and at 5:1, "Seeing the crowds, he went up on the mountain." Likewise, at 7:28 the section concludes with the observation that "the crowds were astonished at his teaching." However, Matthew says at 5:1, "And when he sat down *his disciples* came to him" (italics added). Does this mean he taught those from the crowd who were his disciples or that he taught the crowds? Luke, who places the sermon "on a level place" (6:17) and provides a

147

partially different and greatly abbreviated version, helps us here very little. He says there was with Jesus "a great crowd of his disciples and a great multitude of people" (6:17). Luke concludes by saying that Jesus had spoken "in the hearing of the people" (7:1). Luke's version of the Beatitudes is given specifically to his disciples (6:20). The question of audience is very important, however inconclusive the evidence. Perhaps it would be safe to say that the Sermon on the Mount was not offered as a way of ordering society as a whole regardless of faith or relationship to Jesus. Rather, these teachings are for the community of his disciples, but not first for his immediate disciples during his ministry. The presence of the crowds keeps the invitation open; "whosoever will" is still true. And speaking to his followers in the presence of the crowds keeps all of them honest about who they are and where their commitments lie. The church is a community but not a ghetto; meetings are open to, and aware of, the world.

The Sermon on the Mount begins with blessings or beatitudes. To preface instruction with blessing is as appropriate here as prefacing the Ten Commandments with the recital of God's deliverance of Israel from Egypt (Exod. 20:1-2). In other words, God's imperative is couched in and surrounded by grace. The obedience demanded by the Sermon on the Mount must be understood as response to, not an effort to gain, God's favor. The beatitude says, "Blessed are those who"; that is, it gives its blessing, it is not an urging or an exhortation to be this or that. The preacher will want to be careful not to give the impression that Jesus said, "We ought to be poor in spirit," or "Let us be meek." He pronounces his blessing and the language is performative, conferring its blessing in the saying of it.

The preacher cannot possibly give in one sermon detailed word studies and exegetical analyses of each beatitude. There will be occasions for that task. In this sermon, however, it would be helpful to give attention to the background of the blessing in Judaism (Ps. 84:5-6, 12; 128:1; Ecclus. 25:7-10) and to call attention to the powerful dynamic of saying the blessing and receiving the blessing. Second, notice that these blessings completely reverse the values of most societies, including our own. No doubt many in Jesus' audience, zealous to take the kingdom in their own hands, were infuriated by these beatitudes and the behavior called for in the teachings that followed. Third, attention needs to be given to the types of persons who receive Christ's blessing. Commentaries will help with words such as meek, poor in spirit, peacemakers, and those who mourn, but it will be important to get an overview. These blessings elaborate upon the description of those to be visited with God's favor in Isaiah 61:1-3. And finally, the preacher would do well to distinguish between Jesus extending his blessing upon the victims in society and Jesus calling persons to be victims. The former he does; the latter he does not do. Even victims do not have to have a victim mentality. Victims hear Christ's beatitude and then take the initiative to claim a life appropriate to that beatitude. Those who give the coat, love the enemy, turn the cheek, and go the second mile are no longer victims. They are kingdom people.

Fifth Sunday After Epiphany

Isaiah 58:3-9a; Psalm 112:4-9; I Corinthians 2:1-11; Matthew 5:13-16

In today's Old Testament reading we hear a compelling cry for justice and kindness—a helpful reminder that God's light shines no more brightly than when we serve humanity. Epiphany is the form of service. Similar themes are echoed in today's psalm in its insistence that light shines through the lives of the righteous. Here too righteous living is living committed to others. In the epistolary reading, we hear Paul clarifying the nature and essence of his missionary preaching and congregational teaching, insisting that both derive their power from God and not from human sources. The Gospel lesson is provided by the Matthean version of Jesus' teaching concerning the salt of the earth and the light of the world. The second image carries through themes from the Old Testament reading and the psalm as it presents disciples as the means of God's manifestation.

Isaiah 58:3-9*a*

This reading continues the major theme of Micah 6:6-8 from last week's lesson, the definition of genuine piety, and the relationship between religious practices and the moral life. Micah 6:6-8 addressed the question of sacrifices and offerings. Isaiah 58 considers fasts and fast days.

Our passage is part of the so-called Third Isaiah (Isa. 56–66), and very likely stems from the years soon after the return of the exiles from Babylon. The reading reflects some of the religious practices that developed during the Exile and afterward, and also indicates some of the divisions that were emerging in the newly reconstituted community of faith in

150

Judah. The mood of disappointment and frustration with the new life in Jerusalem is similar to that reported in Haggai 2:1-9 and Zechariah 7.

The reading is part of a composite unit of literature (Isa. 58) concerned with the general topic of cultic activity. Verses 1-12 concern fasts; verses 13-15 turn to the issue of proper observance of the sabbath.

In some ways the form of the passage is similar to the prophetic torah or instruction in Micah 6:6-8 (see also Amos 5:21-24 and Isa. 1:10-17), with a question from the laity answered by a religious specialist. But the dialogue here is more like a dispute than a request and an answer. It is clear that the addressees are the people in general, but the role of the speaker is not so obvious. Generally, he speaks with prophetic authority, on behalf of God. It is quite possible that the setting for such a discourse was the sort of community of worship and teaching that later became the synagogue.

First (verse 3*ab*) our speaker quotes the words of the people. They complain to God because their fasts have not been effective. The assumption is that fasts are a form of prayer, probably of penitence. Fasts in ancient Israel, along with the use of sackcloth and ashes (verse 5), generally were associated with rituals of mourning, but they were also used as part of petition and intercession (II Sam. 12:16, 22). Public fasts became important in the exilic and postexilic periods, and several such days were known (Zech. 7). The rituals for the Day of Atonement must have included fasts (Lev. 16:29-31; 23:27-32; Num. 29:7).

Next (verses 3*c*-4) our speaker responds with an indictment of the people for their attitudes and their behavior on fast days. Business as usual, and oppressive business at that, continues on such days (verse 3*c*, reading with the RSV footnote and the NJPSV). People are contentious when—verse 4 implies—the public fast should be a reverent expression of solidarity before God.

To this point the author has said, in effect, that fasts are not effective because the participants do not take them seriously. In verses 5-7, however, he begins to question the very idea of fasts (verse 5), and then to state what kind of "fast" would evoke the desired response from God (verses 6-7). In a series of rhetorical questions, each expecting the answer yes, an answer is spelled out in four points: "loose the bonds of wickedness," "undo the thongs of the yoke," "let the oppressed go free," "break every yoke" (verse 6).

It turns out that these four metaphors refer to one activity, to care for the poor, to set them free from oppression, from the bonds of their poverty. Verse 7 states the point in very practical terms. Those complaining should see that those in need have food ("share your bread"), housing ("bring the homeless poor into your house"), and clothing ("when you see the naked, to cover him"). The final line of the verse is best read, "And not to ignore your own kin" (NJPSV), that is, your fellow Judeans. This catalog of social responsibilities is similar to that in Zechariah 7:8-10, and is an echo of Isaiah 1:10-17, which advocates justice and righteousness, especially for widows and orphans, as the necessary prerequisite for genuine worship.

Verses 8-9a promise that when these conditions are fulfilled, the people will live in the light of God's presence, and he will hear their prayers. It is possible to take this promise as a form of works righteousness, that good works will earn salvation. Good works would then only replace fasting as means of earning God's favor. Doubtless many heard—and many will continue to hear—these words in that way. However, the more fundamental meaning is that those who attend to justice and righteousness thereby live in the presence of the just and righteous God, they are part of God's people. Moreover, when the people attend to the needs of the hungry, the homeless, and the naked, they have their own reward: the solidarity of the community is strengthened, their "light" breaks forth, their "healing" springs up, and their "righteousness" is active.

Psalm 112:4-9

Like Psalm 37, last Sunday's lection, Psalm 112 is human-to-human address which seeks to instruct and offer advice about the art of living. Like Psalm 37, this text is also an alphabetic psalm having twenty-two lines (omitting the opening, "Praise the Lord"), each beginning with a successive letter of the alphabet.

The symmetry and order of the psalm, reflected in its alphabetic structure, are also characteristic of its thought. It assumes a morally oriented and governed world in which the righteous and blessed enjoy well-being and in which the wicked (noted only in verse 10) receive the opposite.

In the central section of the psalm, today's portion, the righteous (see verse 1) are described. Three characteristics of the righteous are expounded. (Verse 4 as is noted in the RSV marginal reading is difficult to translate. It could read: "He [the righteous] rises in darkness like a light for the upright ones, gracious, merciful, and righteous.")

1. The righteous deals equitably and generously, lending his money and giving to the poor (verses 5, 9). In ancient Israel, it was forbidden to charge interest on a loan to one's countryman. This prohibition against lending money at interest is found in all sections of the Hebrew Scriptures (Exod. 22:25; Lev. 25:35-38; Ps. 15:5; Ezek. 18:8). One should not make a profit by trafficking on the misery of others' problems. At the same time, goodness is relational; it is what one does to and with others.

2. The righteous life can withstand adversity and can confront existence with serenity (verses 6-8). The righteous is not shaken (not a reed blown back and forth by every wind), can withstand evil tidings or bad news, is stronghearted and firmly planted, unafraid. Constancy in life is the principle advocated and the personality trait being praised.

3. The righteous are remembered (verses 6b). Not only the person but the acts of righteousness are lasting. Verse 9b can be translated "his act of charity endures for ever" since the word for righteousness also meant charity.

I Corinthians 2:1-11

Today's lection consists of two parts. In the first section (verses 1-5) Paul recalls the circumstances of his original visit among them when he founded the church. The focus here is on his own work and preaching, as seen by his use of the first person singular. In the second section (verses 6-11) there is a shift in both tense and person. With the present tense dominating, these remarks appear to deal less with past missionary preaching and more with his typical practice of providing instruction. They also depict what "we" do, perhaps a reference to Paul and Apollos as the teachers of the Corinthian church (cf. 3:4-9; 4:6), or even to Christian teachers, apostles, and prophets generally.

We might note at the outset that the train of thought continues through verse 13 (RSV), even through verse 16. Ending the lection with verse 11 is somewhat unusual, since it falls in the middle of the second section. One natural breaking point is with verse 10a (NEB, NIV; cf. JB). Naturally the preacher will have to reach an independent decision.

Paul's missionary preaching (verses 1-5). In this opening section, Paul develops themes introduced earlier in last week's reading. Having noted that the Corinthians could not account for their own existence apart from the mighty work of God, he now makes a similar observation about his own preaching. Ultimately he wants to emphasize that the power of his preaching derived not from his facility with words but from God's power (verse 5). Neither their existence as a church nor his message as a preacher could be attributed to human generation or ingenuity. They both serve as living proof of divine power. The gospel Paul preached was the power of God (1:18, 24; Rom. 1:16; 15:19; II Cor. 12:9; I Thess. 1:5).

The heart of his preaching was "Jesus Christ and him crucified" (verse 2). This was the "word of the cross" (1:18), the message whose content was the proclamation of Christ's crucifixion (Gal. 6:14). In these verses Paul insists that his manner of preaching conformed to the message he preached. In his ministerial life-style, he came to them as one who was "weak, nervous, and shaking with fear" (verse 3, NEB; II Cor. 10:10; 11:30; Gal. 4:13). He made no attempt to package the gospel in "plausible words of wisdom" (verse 4, RSV); he did not "sway . . . with subtle arguments" (NEB). His own testimony here squares with the charges of his opponents that his manner of speaking was not especially impressive (II Cor. 10:10).

Rather than deriving its power from well-turned phrases,

Paul's preaching convicted because of its "spiritual power" (verse 4, NEB). The preached word was nothing if not an occasion through which God's Spirit bore testimony (II Cor. 6:7; cf. Matt. 10:20; John 14:26; Acts 4:8). As Paul insists elsewhere, preaching is not a matter of mere words. Done properly, it becomes a sacramental act through which God's power is mediated through the Spirit (I Thess. 1:5).

Wisdom for the mature (verses 6-11). In his earlier remarks, Paul has given wisdom a diminished role in the work of God. At this point, he changes tactics and concedes that there is in fact a form of Christian wisdom reserved for those who are suitably mature to appropriate it. It looks as if he envisions a two-tiered form of Christian teaching, a lower wisdom for the young and inexperienced, a higher wisdom for the more advanced Christian. This distinction became much more full blown in later Christian thought, especially in Alexandrian thinkers such as Clement and Origen. The Gnostics drew the line even more sharply.

Paul's distinction here has a particular point. He wants to assure the Corinthian "gnostics" that there is a form of higher wisdom. It is reserved for the mature (*teleioi*, cf. 14:20; Phil. 3:15; Col. 1:28), and hence has eluded them because of their conspicuous lack of spiritual maturity (3:1, 18). What characterizes it is its secrecy and hiddenness. According to the Synoptic tradition, Jesus had stressed to his disciples that God's revelation was "hidden from the wise and revealed to babes" (Matt. 13:35; Luke 10:21; cf. Ps. 78:2; Col. 1:26).

Especially blind to this hidden wisdom were the "rulers of this age" (verse 6), likely a reference to the heavenly powers inimical to the purposes of God (Eph. 1:21; 2:2; 3:10; 6:12; also Rom. 8:38; I Cor. 15:24; Col. 1:13, 16; 2:10, 15; I Pet. 3:22). They are the minions of *the* ruler of this age, Satan (John 12:31; 14:30; 16:11; II Cor. 4:4), whose work is carried out through such earthly rulers as Pilate and Herod. Had these figures perceived this hidden wisdom, they would not have acted to thwart the purposes of God by crucifying Christ (verse 8).

As it is, God's purposes are enshrouded in a mystery, oblivious to human eye, ear, and mind (verse 9; cf. Isa. 52:15; 64:3; 65:16; Jer. 3:16). They are available to those who love

God (verse 9*b*). Note: God's wisdom is not for those who *know* God, but those who *love* God (cf. I Cor. 8:1). Being privy to this is a matter of God's revelation through the Spirit (verse 10; cf. Matt. 11:25; Dan. 2:22). It is after all the spirit of a person who knows the interior of the person (verse 11; cf. Prov. 20:27; Zech. 12:1). By analogy, it is God's Spirit who probes the depths of God (verse 10; Rom. 11:33; Job 11:7-8). Once again, we are reminded that as human beings, we are not privy to the innermost thoughts of God, as if we could discern the mind of God and serve as a counselor. Rather, we receive God's revelation as a gift.

The latter part of this passage, which is not covered in today's lection, further stresses that access to the mind of God does not occur through human wisdom (verse 13). It is rather a matter of spiritual discernment (verse 14). The real irony, of course, was that the Corinthians against whom Paul is arguing were apparently insisting that they had achieved the status of "spiritual persons" (3:1). But their childish behavior showed the contrary.

Among the several homiletical possibilities presented by this passage, one of the most intriguing is to explore what Paul means by the "wisdom for the mature." One way of proceeding might be to note that the ordinary route to wisdom is through knowledge, whereas Paul insists that the point of entry is love (verse 9). How then does love become the qualifying norm for Christian wisdom?

Another possibility is to explore the way in which divine wisdom normally eludes this age and the rulers of this age (verse 6). Here it might be worthwhile to contrast the ways in which "human wisdom" construes reality with the way in which "divine wisdom" construes reality.

Matthew 5:13-16

This is the second of five consecutive Sundays which draw upon Matthew 5 for the Gospel lesson. Since this is the first chapter of the Sermon on the Mount, the reader may wish to review the introductory comments on Matthew 5–7 in the commentary for last week.

Verses 13-16 are here taken to be a distinct unit deserving

comment without any sense of breaking into a thought in the verses which precede or follow. And such may quite well be the case. These verses take up the subject of discipleship by means of two metaphors, salt and light: those two images govern the text. However, before proceeding with the discussion, the preacher might entertain the suggestion that the unit begins at verse 11. It is at verse 11 that the Beatitudes in the third person shift to the second person. Verses 11-12 address the reader (listener) directly: blessed are you, revile you, persecute you, against you, your reward, before you. This direct address continues into verses 13-16. If a natural break occurs at verse 11, what difference would be made in the interpretation of verses 13-16? One major difference: the theme of persecution (verses 11-12) would serve as a backdrop for understanding the salt and light sayings. To be more specific, if the pressure of persecution causes you to lose your saltiness, you are of no more value to anyone. Or, if persecution causes you to hide or to put your witness under a bushel, you become an absurd denial of your purpose. Or, by your good works the persecutors may be silenced and caused to glorify God. The possibility of this perspective should certainly be considered. Now to verses 13-16, our lesson for today.

Disciples of Jesus are not urged to be salt and light: they are defined as being salt and light. The urging or the imperative comes in being shown the absurdity of denying that role or trying to deny it. What could be more useless or meaningless than saltless salt and hidden lamps? Nor should the interpreter lose sight of the common and basic elements involved here. Salt, light, bread, water, flesh, blood, and breath; these essentials and not exotic options provide Christ and the early church with descriptions of the life of discipleship.

The salt saying (verse 13) has parallels at Mark 9:50 and Luke 14:34-35 and is, judging by its different contexts, a floating saying. The metaphor of salt carries not only its common and plain sense drawing upon the basic functions of salt in all societies, but also religious and symbolic meaning. Salt was involved in Israel's covenants with God (Lev. 2:13; Num. 18:19) and in the purification of sacrifices (Exod. 30:35;

Ezek. 16:4). "Sharing the salt" also came to be a way of referring to table fellowship (Acts 1:4, translated "staying with them" in the RSV). Whether any or all of these associated meanings were stirred in the minds of Jesus' hearers is only conjecture. It is also conjecture to assume Jesus meant for the salt metaphor to emphasize some particular quality of salt, such as preserving, or flavoring, or purifying. But one thing is not conjecture: the quality of saltiness gives salt its identity and purpose. Likewise, the quality of following and obeying Jesus, even under hardship, gives a disciple identity and purpose. Remove that and such phrases as, "was once a disciple," or "still has the appearance of a disciple," are of no more value than saying "but it was once salty," or "but it still looks like salt."

The metaphor of light is carried in three sayings (verses 14-16). The first, using the analogy of a city on a hill, has no parallel in the other Gospels even though light is a metaphor common to many religions. For Christians, Christ's claim, "I am the light of the world" (John 8:12), is so central that the use of the image of light to describe the disciples is understood only in a derived and dependent sense. Still the obligation, implications for mission, the exposure and vulnerability in a hostile world are no less present in this definitive image of who we are in the world (Phil. 2:15). The second saying (verse 15) has parallels in Mark (4:21) and Luke (8:16; 11:33) but in other contexts, again indicating a saying for which we cannot recover an original setting. Variations in the saying occur: under a bushel, under a bowl, in the cellar. There may be some significance to the difference between Matthew's "light to all the house" (verse 15, all the church) and Luke's "that those who enter may see the light" (8:16; 11:33, guidance for new members). But why would anyone hide a light? Persecution perhaps; fear of the lamp going out, perhaps; pride and embarrassment because of the cross, perhaps; making the church into a secret sect of the elite (Gnostics), perhaps.

The last saying (verse 16) is in Matthew alone and makes an extraordinary demand upon disciples. Their life and work is for all the world to see, but to be offered with such humility and grace that not they but God will be praised. That is a most difficult assignment.

Sixth Sunday After Epiphany (Proper 1)

Deuteronomy 30:15-20 or *Ecclesiasticus 15:15-20; Psalm 119:1-8; I Corinthians 3:1-9; Matthew 5:17-26*

Here as always during the liturgical year, the Gospel is primary, gathering to itself the other readings. Matthew's Jesus is the new Moses, giving the authoritative teaching for his followers. Foundational for Matthew is the Mosaic law. The reading from Deuteronomy as well as the alternate lection recalls that Moses' word was God's word, which to obey was life, to neglect was death. Psalm 119 pronounces a blessing on those whose obedience to the law draws them near to God. The epistolary text is Paul's explanation why he could not offer the strong word of the Lord to the Corinthians; their immaturity was such that milk not meat was called for. Throughout today's texts the word of God is central.

Deuteronomy 30:15-20

This passage is itself a powerful sermon, and appropriately so, for both in terms of its location in the book and its substance it is a summary statement of the message of the book of Deuteronomy. It contains the final words of a lengthy speech attributed to Moses on the plains of Moab (Deut. 29:1–30:20), introduced as "the words of the covenant which the Lord commanded Moses to make with the people of Israel" (29:1). Immediately following this paragraph, the narrative resumes, leading finally to the report of the death of Moses. In substance, these six verses state the major points of the book: obedience to the law, establishment of the covenant, the conditions for life in the promised land, and responsibility laid upon the hearts of the people.

Opinions vary considerably concerning the antiquity of this paragraph. As it now stands, it has been incorporated into the edition of the book prepared by the deuteronomistic historian who wrote the account of Israel's past from the time of Moses to the Babylonian Exile (Deut. through II Kings). When that work was written about 560 B.C., Israel no longer lived in the land, so words such as these provided interpretation of the disaster of the Exile and guidance for a future return. But the lines are characteristic in every respect of the heart of the book of Deuteronomy, from the seventh century B.C., before the Exile, but centuries after the time of Moses. In that context, the words were addressed to a people who had experienced the fulfillment of the promise of the land. Moreover, there are elements of the most ancient covenant tradition itself, going back to Israel's earliest days. Centuries of use and reinterpretation underscore the grave importance of the matters addressed in this text.

The context of the passage is the conclusion of the covenant between Yahweh and Israel. The reference to "heaven and earth" (verse 19) as witnesses reflects the background of this covenant in the ancient Near Eastern treaty tradition, in which the gods were called upon to witness the agreement and its stipulations and to verify violations (cf. Isa. 1:2 and the comments on Mic. 6:1-5 on pages 139-41). This covenantal context means that the speech is addressed to the people of Israel, that the focus of attention is corporate, not only for the sake of the present group, but also for the community that extends through time (verse 19).

Obedience to the law is a matter of life and death: that is the central point of the address. In language that is repetitious and hortatory, this point is urged upon the audience, laid upon the hearts of the hearers (on the style and perspective of Deuteronomy, see the comments on Deut. 8:1-10 on pages 83-86). The law is not perceived as a burden, but a gift, for it leads to life, the good life that the Lord wishes for his people. "Life" means the long and abundant life in the good land. "Good" and "evil" (verse 15) are not used here as moral categories; they mean well-being or prosperity and trouble or misfortune.

"Commandments" and "statutes" are used together in Deuteronomy to signify the law as a whole, the stipulations of the covenant (Deut. 4:1; 5:31; 6:1). We should not be misled by the repeated reference to such requirements in the plural, for although there are many laws they all rest upon and amount to one prohibition and one commandment. That one prohibition is not "to worship other gods and serve them" (verse 17); the commandment is to obey the first commandment (Deut. 5:7). During the centuries when the book of Deuteronomy was developed, that was not an abstract or vague possibility, but a concrete and practical temptation. In the land there were the deities of the Canaanites; in Babylon there were the gods of the dominant culture, including the heavenly powers (cf. Deut. 4:19). We may appropriately see this issue as the conflict between faith and culture. To what extent can one acknowledge the authority of the forces the culture considers as "gods," or make use of the culture's symbols of faith? Deuteronomy is clear: Do not bow down to them at all.

The single commandment on which all the individual laws rests is the positive side of the prohibition: Love the Lord your God, and cleave to him (verse 20). This love is parallel to that of a child for a parent, entailing respect and obedience (Deut. 6:5; 8:5). It amounts to devotion to a single God (Josh. 22:5; 23:6-8). How can one command an attitude, a feeling? It can only be in response to God's love (Deut. 7:7, 13; cf. Hos. 11:1 ff.), expressed in the history of election and salvation.

If there is but one requirement, with a negative and a positive side, then why are there so many statutes and ordinance and laws? Ancient Israel knew, as we do, that in practice the meaning and application of that loyalty to God are complex. Precisely what does it mean to avoid the worship of other gods and to love God in various circumstances? The multitude of laws, and their frequent reinterpretation through time, testify to the understanding that those who intend to obey the command to love only one God must work at learning and applying the meaning of that love. The rabbinical tradition developed a practical criterion for applying the law that stems from the theology of this passage. The law leads to life. If one interprets the law and finds that it leads to death, then the interpretation is wrong.

Ecclesiasticus 15:15-20

For a discussion of the book of Ecclesiasticus as a whole see the comments on pages 94-96.

Our reading is part of a discrete unit that begins in verse 11 and concludes with verse 20. The passage is a disputation in the wisdom style, a debate concerning a fundamental theological issue. The teacher begins by quoting the point of view of his opponents (verse 11), but he does not give the arguments for their side. He makes his case through the use of logic (would God act contrary to his nature? verses 11-12), by alluding to Scripture (verses 14, 17), by stating commonly accepted doctrine (verse 18), and even by reducing the alternative to the absurd (verse 16). He concludes with a summary statement of his answer to the question at issue (verse 20).

The question at stake is the subject of one of the most persistent of all theological debates, the existence of free will. However, in Ben Sirach's time the debate was not quite an argument over free will and predestination. Rather, it had a particular, limited focus on the question of the source—and hence the responsibility for—human sin. It was recognized that there was an evil impulse (Hebrew *yeṣer*) in human beings. If God created that impulse, then some could say, "Because of the Lord I left the right way" (verse 11), "It was he who led me astray" (verse 12).

Ben Sirah's answer is unequivocal. God does not act contrary to his nature. He did indeed leave human beings with their own inclinations (verse 14)—here he uses the term *yeṣer* to mean freedom of the will—and he set choices before them (verse 15). Though God made both fire and water he is not to be blamed if you decide to put your hand into the fire (verse 16). He reminds the hearers of the ancient choice between life and death, alluding to Deuteronomy 30:19 (see above). God does indeed have the power and wisdom to see every human act, and will hold individuals responsible (verses 18-19; cf. also 21:27-28). Not only has he not commanded anyone to be ungodly, neither has he given anyone permission to sin (verse 20).

That would seem to settle the matter, but the other side of the argument must not be written off too quickly. Ben Sirach's vigorous rhetoric itself indicates that the controversy was a real one, with two sides. Do not the Scriptures more than once report that Yahweh "hardened the heart" of someone to do evil (e.g., Exod. 14:4)? Moreover, since God created human beings, he must be responsible for all that they are. Elsewhere Ben Sirah himself seems to take a different point of view. He bewails the creation—by whom?—of the "evil imagination" (33:3), and suggests that good and evil, the sinner and the godly are created by God (33:14-15). Later rabbinic reflection will conclude that the evil impulse *(yeṣer)* was created by God, and the Torah was given as a means to overcome it (Babylonian Talmud *Kiddushin* 30*b*).

However, the disputation in Ecclesiasticus 15:11-20 does not mean to consider all aspects of the problem of the freedom of the will and evil impulses. In effect, it addresses the question of responsibility for sin. Here the answer is consistent with the Hebrew Scriptures in general. God, who indeed gave human beings freedom of choice, is not responsible for the wrong choices. Whatever the ultimate source of the possibility of sin, human beings are held accountable for their decisions. In short, theological reflection cannot be the excuse for irresponsibility.

Psalm 119:1-8

Portions of Psalm 119, the longest of the Psalms, are treated in each of the years in the lectionary cycle (Propers 18 and 26, Year B, Proper 24, Year C, and the Eighth Sunday After Epiphany, Year A in addition to this Sunday). The 176 verses of this psalm divide into twenty-two stanzas of eight lines each. In each individual stanza, all eight lines begin with the same Hebrew letter, working through the alphabet in order. In each of the stanzas there is a play on a series of synonyms for the law or the will of Deity. Generally, there are eight such synonyms per stanza and generally the same eight are used throughout the entire psalm. In verses 1-8, the eight terms referring to the Torah are: law, testimonies, ways, precepts, statutes, commandments, ordinances, and statutes (repeated).

The Old Testament readings (Deut. 30:15-20 and Ecclus. 15:15-20) speak of two ways—life and death, good and evil, fire and water, obedience and disobedience (to the commandments)—and challenge the hearer to choose the one over the other. Psalm 119 is praise of the law and praise of the one who has chosen the path of obedience, the way of law-piety. As such, it revels in the law and rejoices in the commandments.

Verses 1-8 reflect a rather interesting pattern insofar as speaker-audience is concerned. Verses 1-3 contain two benedictions pronouncing blessedness upon the obedient. The benedictions are thus composed to be addressed to a general human audience. Verses 4-8 are a prayer addressed directly to the Deity. The prayer, running throughout the remainder of the psalm, is thus the response to the benedictions.

In the prayer of verses 1-8, the worshiper asks to be obedient and observant of God's Torah. Running through these verses are both negative and positive strands. The positive aspects are reflected in references such as "be steadfast," "keep," "eyes fixed," "praise," "learn," and "observe." The negative aspects, that is, the inability to keep the law and obey the commandments, is also present. The worshiper prays "not to be put to shame" and that God "forsake me not utterly." On the human level, the fear is that of failure; on the divine-human level it is the fear of being forsaken by the Divine.

Shame, which is noted frequently in the Bible, is a common human emotion. It is often, as here, associated with the failure not to measure up, the failure to be what one aspires to be, the failure to achieve one's goal. Shame is, however, an emotion that does not necessarily arise from public awareness or disclosure. One doesn't have to be found out in order to suffer shame. The ancient rabbis noted that "it is the heart which puts a person to shame because the heart knows what it has done and is ashamed of itself."

I Corinthians 3:1-9

Clearly, the Corinthians placed a high premium on spiritual pursuits. Paul later devotes three chapters (12–14) to the question of "spiritual gifts" (*pneumatika*, 12:1), or perhaps "spiritual persons." That the Spirit and the things of the Spirit set the Corinthian agenda is seen by the sheer frequency with which these terms occur in the letter. Doubtless many of them were claiming to be "spiritual persons" (3:1). In the Second Epistle to the Corinthians Paul refers to his readers as a "letter . . . written not with ink but with the Spirit of the living God" (3:3).

Wanting to be a spiritual person is a worthwhile aim, of course, but something had gone awry in the Corinthian church. Some saw themselves as spiritual persons, but this seems to have translated into a form of spiritual superiority. It expressed itself as arrogant behavior (4:6-7, 19; 5:2), so that Paul had to issue warnings against human boasting (1:29-30; 3:18; 4:7). One of the forms it took was insensitivity to other members of the church, especially those who were not as advanced spiritually (cf. chapters 8–10). Paul has to remind them that even though certain forms of behavior are permissible they may not be edifying (6:12-13; 8:7-13; 10:23-30).

What emerges in this letter is an extended critique of those with spiritual pretensions. It is the "strong" who are reminded to be mindful of the "weak" (8:7-13). Those who claimed that they were already filled, rich, and reigning are reminded that true spiritual existence is life that is deprived, poor, and humiliating (4:8-13).

Today's text provides an important part of this critique because it points up the self-deceiving character of spiritual pursuits. We think we are spiritual, we see ourselves as spiritual, we may even call ourselves spiritual when in reality we are grossly, if not comically unspiritual. Paul's critique of them is that in spite of their pretensions to being spiritual they were in fact persons "of the flesh" (verse 1). The term "flesh" in the New Testament almost uniformly has a negative connotation, signifying an outlook that is essentially centered on the self and pursues our own self-interest. It is essentially human in its orientation in that it is driven by the desire to fulfill human wants and human needs. Though he uses a different word in verse 14 *(psychikos)*, Paul insists that the "unspiritual" person is the one who is unable to discern spiritual things. The "unspiritual" person is a two-dimensional figure living in a three-dimensional world.

Paul follows up on this in verse 4, when he insists that those who define themselves and their religious life by human loyalties, even in relation to prominent religious leaders such as Paul or Apollos, are behaving as "merely men" (verse 4), or "ordinary people" (JB). This is a sure sign that they are "all too human" (verse 4, NEB).

Our text warns us that being spiritual may result in illusion. Our practice may not measure up to our pretensions. We may pretend to maturity when we are actually spiritual infants (verses 1-2; cf. Heb. 5:12-13; also I Cor. 13:11).

And what is the sure sign of unspiritual behavior? Jealousy and strife (verse 3; cf. 1:10-11; Gal. 5:19-20; James 3:14). One mark of spiritual immaturity is the inability to get along with one another. No matter what we claim, we are not spiritual if our behavior toward other members of the fellowship is marked by petty jealousies and strife.

In the second part of our text (verses 5-9), Paul goes ahead to clarify the true nature and status of Christian leaders, in this case himself and Apollos. Do they deserve to be the defining points of Christian existence? No. They are "servants" through whom the Corinthians had come to faith (cf. Acts 18:4, 11, 24). The proper way of viewing God's messengers is as instruments in the hands of God, doing work the Lord had assigned them (cf. II Cor. 4:5).

In this discussion, we hear again a theme Paul mentioned earlier: the primacy of God in the work of salvation. True, Paul planted and Apollos watered, but the growth was God's (verses 6-7). Consequently, the only proper way for defining ourselves is in terms that relate us to God: God's fellow workers . . . God's field, God's building." We should not overlook this heavy emphasis on the role of God. It is Paul's remedy for human presumption. We finally must recognize that church growth, even spiritual growth, occurs at God's initiative: "*only* God . . . gives the growth" (verse 7, italics added).

We might also note in passing Paul's emphasis on his solidarity with Apollos: "he who plants and he who waters are equal" (verse 8). Their work together "as a team" (verse 8, NEB) should be exemplary to the Corinthians who seem bent on strife.

The true mark of spirituality is to recognize that we only identify ourselves properly when we identify ourselves by God and with God. Becoming fixated on human leaders, however prominent or dear to us, misdirects us and finally causes us to operate on a purely human level.

Today's text holds numerous possibilities for sermons. It may serve as a way to explore the true nature of spirituality—the illusion, the pretension and the reality, the signs. Or, today's text may be read as a commentary on the opening description of the Corinthians as the "church *of* God" (1:2, italics added). Then again, the graphic metaphors employed in verse 9 have their own possibilities. What does it mean for us to be "fellow workers for God" or "co-workers of God" (cf. II Cor. 1:24; 6:1; I Thess. 3:2; also III John 8). The church as God's field, or more literally as God's farm, calls up images from Jesus' parable of the sower (Matt. 13:3-9, 18-23), as well as the various parables of growth. The image of God's building also has rich connotations (cf. 3:16-17; 6:19-20; Eph. 2:20-22).

Matthew 5:17-26

This is the third in a series of five lessons from the Sermon on the Mount which was introduced in the comments on 5:1-12. The passage before us, 5:17-26, consists of two distinct units, verses 17-20 and 21-26. The discussion below will follow this natural division.

Matthew 5:17-20 contains four sayings of Jesus which probably existed earlier in different contexts but which have been drawn together here by Matthew. Of the four, only the second (verse 18) has a parallel elsewhere (Matt. 24:35; Mark 13:31; Luke 16:17; 21:23). The passage as a whole offers Jesus' relation to Judaism, the church's relation to the synagogue, the Gospel's relation to the law of Moses.

All the Gospels testify that the Christian movement was under attack for violating the sabbath, being lax about observance of fasts, not keeping the rituals of the faith, and in general eroding morals by associating with sinners and saints without proper discrimination. According to Matthew, Jesus refutes these charges against himself and his followers by a statement of complete fidelity to the law of Moses (verse 17). "The law and the prophets," the first two of the three divisions of the Hebrew Scriptures ("the writings" being the third), here are taken in the sense of commandments and not as prophecy of the messianic era, as in Luke 24:27, 44. In other words, Jesus and his disciples are no less serious than Judaism about matters of moral and ethical behavior. But the very statement, "Think not that I have come to abolish," indicates an ongoing debate on the relationship between law and grace. Paul's letters to the Galatians and the Romans and Acts 15 carry two perspectives on the issue. The point here is that following Christ does not mean being careless about conduct nor does grace mean permissiveness. On the contrary, the very opposite is the case, as verse 20 makes clear.

The last of the four sayings calls for a righteousness that exceeds that of the scribes and Pharisees (verse 20). Scribes and Pharisees are not synonymous terms; one is a profession, the other is a party. Pharisees were a lay group concerned primarily with interpreting and obeying the law of Moses. Because scribes were experts in the sacred texts, they naturally were associated with the Pharisees. The two groups were the persons most conscientiously committed to observance of the law. For Jesus to mention them was to say that his disciples were to exceed the best, not the worst.

Verse 20 also serves to introduce specific examples of what it means to practice this higher righteousness. In verses 21-48 there are six antitheses framed on the formula, "You have heard that it was said . . . but I say to you." In each case, following the basic antithesis there are one or more elaborations on Jesus' teachings representing Matthew's or the early church's attempts to apply Jesus' teachings to new and very real situations. This means that the teaching on each of the six subjects will consist of: the word of the law, the word of Jesus, and the interpretation and application of the teaching to a particular circumstance.

In the remainder of our lesson, verses 21-26, we have, then, the basic antithesis (verses 21-22*a*), an elaboration (verse 22*b*), a second elaboration (verses 23-24), and a third (verses 25-26). The basic antithesis states that the higher righteousness extends beyond the act of murder to the condition of anger that prompts it. To this has been added a pattern of instruction based on the idea of increasing seriousness of offense calling for increasing severity of punishment. To be angry with a brother places one before the judge; to insult (literally, to say, "Raca," an Aramaic term of derision) a brother places one before the council (the Sanhedrin, the supreme court); and to say, "You fool!" (moron, stupid, worthless) places one before the final judgment, the hell of fire. The second and third elaborations picture strained human relations in two very important settings, the sanctuary and the courtroom, and stress the urgency of reconciliation. The negative mood of punishment earlier (verses 21-22) is now balanced with instructions on taking the initiative to restore good relations. In the one case, reconciliation takes precedence over ritual (verses 23-24); in the other, over legal settlement (verses 25-26). Note: in both cases it is assumed that the disciple of Jesus is neither the offender ("your brother has something against you") nor the plaintiff ("make friends quickly with your accuser"). The teaching addresses victims but calls on them to take responsibility to restore the relationship. Evil is overcome with good.

Seventh Sunday After Epiphany (Proper 2)

Isaiah 49:8-13; Psalm 62:5-12; I Corinthians 3:10-11, 16-23; Matthew 5:27-37

The focus for last Sunday was the word of God for human behavior and relationships. Today the readings all relate the believer to God, each text offering a different perspective on God as the ground and center of the life of faith. Isaiah announces the continual restoration of God's people, always in comfort and compassion. The psalmist sings of God as our rock and salvation, apart from whom all is delusion. Paul also uses the image of a foundation in Jesus Christ whose temple we are and who relates us all to God. Matthew continues the Sermon on the Mount, with primary and concrete instruction on the nature of relationships that receive God's favor.

Isaiah 49:8-13

The lesson resumes where the Old Testament text for the Second Sunday After Epiphany left off. The original unit of speech probably was 49:7-12, preceded by the second Servant Song (49:1-6) and followed by a brief hymn of praise (49:13). As the first of the Servant Songs Isaiah 42:1-4 had been followed by a passage that interprets the servant as the people of Israel; this unit is an interpretation of the second Servant Song in a similar fashion.

Isaiah 49:7-12 is a prophetic announcement or proclamation of salvation, like a great many others in Second Isaiah, addressed to the people of Israel. The messenger formulas ("Thus says the Lord," verses 7-8) introduce the direct quotation of the words of God concerning what he is doing or about to do. These words are, without exception or qualification, good news for the people in exile in Babylon, and for the entire world. The glorious future is so certain that it can even be reported in the past tense.

"I have answered you" (verse 8) assumes that the people have been in prayer for deliverance. Their prayers would have been complaints or laments of the community such as those in Lamentations and Psalms 44; 74; 79. The prayers would have been part of ceremonies of petition such as reflected in Joel 1–2, in which the community reminded Yahweh of their troubles and asked why he did not answer. Now, says Second Isaiah, he has answered.

Even before describing the salvation in store for the people, the prophet reminds Israel of the larger divine purpose, namely, that they are to be "a covenant to the people" (verse 8; see also 42:6). The redemption of Israel from Babylon and their restoration in the land are not ends in themselves, but initiate the awareness of the lordship of Yahweh over the entire world, and implicitly ("covenant") the solidarity of all peoples.

The announcement of what is in store for Israel draws deeply upon the old salvation history. Yahweh will apportion the heritages, that is, divide up the land among the people, as in the time of Joshua. Prisoners will be released (verse 9), as the people of Israel were brought out of Egypt. They will be led through the desert, like Moses led them through the wilderness. The new miraculous preservation will be even more dramatic than the old, for the wilderness will be transformed into pastures (verse 9) with ample food and water (verse 10) along smooth highways (verse 11). The summary description of the return (verse 12) appears to include far more than the exiles in Babylon, since people will come from north and west, and as far as the southern part of Egypt ("Syene").

Verse 12 is a hymnic response to the proclamation of salvation. It begins with a call to praise, addressed to heavens, earth, and mountains, and then states the reason for praise, that the Lord has comforted his people (cf. 40:1).

It is tempting for the preacher to look for a "lesson" in every text, to find instruction or guidance for the congregation. Often, to be sure, that is the appropriate and responsible proclamation of the text in Christian worship. This reading, however, contains no instructions for the life of faith. Even the allusion to the people of God as "a covenant to the people" makes it clear that divine, not human, action is in view. It is God who will give such a covenant. The text is good news, and requires only to be proclaimed. God intends to set the captive people free, to transform the hostile environment of the desert into a highway. The only response is to sing a song of praise, accepting the gifts of God.

Psalm 62:5-12

These verses, also the reading for the Third Sunday After Epiphany, Year B, belong to a psalm whose fundamental theme is confidence and trust. The predominant form of address throughout is human-to-human speech with verse 12 being the single exception. Verses 1-2 and 5-7 are confessional, affirming the worshiper's faith. (Verses 1-2 and 5-6 are used almost like refrains but they are not totally identical.) Verses 3-4 describe the troublesome distress. Verse 8 is a direct admonition addressed to a human audience asking the hearers to offer confession and trust. Verses 9-11 are more homiletical in tone; they are more like proclamation and preaching than confession or admonition. The address to God (verse 12) closes out the psalm.

This psalm could have been utilized when a person sought refuge and safety in the sanctuary perhaps from some enemy. At any rate, the tone is that of having found safety and security in God. The hardships and tragedies of life and the enemies and obstacles to life's enjoyment are clearly in the background of this psalm but are there as something overcome.

Strong metaphorical imagery, which draws from military conditions, is found in verses 5-7 which describe God as the source of security—rock, salvation, fortress, deliverance, honor, refuge. These are matched by expressions of negativity in verses 3-4—set upon, shatter, leaning wall, tottering fence, thrust down, falsehood, curse. The psalm assumes that life is both tough and treacherous and that human beings are highly deceptive, blessing outwardly but cursing inwardly.

The psalmist claims God as the only source of real confidence and security in life and calls upon the audience to trust in him (verse 8). Trust in God (see Ps. 42:4) is balanced by the admonition to pour out one's heart, that is to make supplication and appeals to God (see Pss. 102:1; 142:2). Confidence in God but also verbalization of needs are both stressed.

The homiletical section (verses 9-10) takes a realistic, perhaps even a pessimistic, view of human nature warning one not to trust or have confidence in either humans of low estate or those of high estate. In other words, all humans are really very inconsequential, altogether nothing (see Isa. 41:24). Here the comparison of humankind—a breath, a delusion, lighter than a breath—is with the Deity (note the terms used in verses 5-7). Extortion and robbery (even *good* business) should not be the objectives of one's activity or the means for achieving goals. Even when goals are reached and "riches increase" one should not trust in them or be deceived about the meaning of life.

After all is said and done "power belongs to God" (verse 11). That is, people should not plan their lives, set their goals, and achieve their objectives on their own; even when they do, they may mean little, since it is God who counts. (The "once" and "twice" references probably mean no more than, "you can be/I am certain about what I say" (verse 11c).)

In prayer, the worshiper confesses that in God there is fidelity, assurance, and steadfast love, and thus God requites according to one's desserts.

I Corinthians 3:10-11, 16-23

The first part of today's lection picks up one of the three metaphors from the previous verse—God's building—and amplifies it. At least three facets are worth noting.

Paul as a skilled architect (verse 10). The "commission of God given to me" (RSV) is more literally rendered "according to the grace of God that was given me" (so NEB, JB, NIV). To be sure, when Paul experienced his apostolic call, it was for him a moment of divine grace (Rom. 1:5; 12:3, 6; 15:15; I Cor. 15:10; Gal. 2:9; also Eph. 3:2, 7-8; Col. 1:25).

What is striking here is Paul's description of himself as a "skilled architect" (RSV; cf. JB), "expert builder" (NIV), or "skilled master-builder" (NEB). The adjective used is "wise" *(sophos)*, which probably suggests the idea of being accomplished or highly skilled. The same phrase *(sophos architekton)* is used in Isaiah 3:3 of one of the various functionaries whom the Lord would remove from Jerusalem. It is rendered in the RSV as "skillful magician." Here, however, the image is clearly that of a builder who lays the courses of a foundation. It is not clear why he designates himself as a *wise* builder (cf. II Pet. 3:15), especially in light of his critique of wisdom in the earlier sections. Perhaps he is stressing that as their founding missionary and first minister he proceeded deliberately and methodically as he laid the groundwork for the church.

In any case, he now recognizes that his successor is adding another course to the foundation. His word of caution is that each successor should give careful attention to the quality of work that is done (verse 10b).

Christ as the foundation (verse 11). Even if Paul and Apollos have worked with the church at different stages (3:6), they are not to be seen as the originators or as the foundation. This role can only be occupied by Jesus Christ himself (verse 11). The foundational role of Christ is presupposed in Paul's advice to the Colossians to be "built up in him [Christ] and established in the faith" (Col. 2:7). The image of the foundation is slightly altered in Ephesians 2:19-22, where the church is said to be "a holy temple in the Lord" whose foundation consists of "the apostles and prophets." But within the foundation Christ is the cornerstone holding the whole structure together. The confession that Jesus is the Christ also serves as foundational (Matt. 16:18).

Paul's insistence that Christ is the only foundation has the same effect as his earlier claim that God was ultimately responsible for the church's growth (3:6-7). In each case, human work is given an ancillary role, important but ultimately derivative and subordinate. The substructure is provided by Christ, or God; the superstructure by human beings. It is a crucial difference.

The church as God's temple (verses 16-17). Paul's remarks here render the image of "building" in verse 9 more specific. The church is God's sanctuary *(naos)*. The metaphor is introduced later in the epistle (6:19), but there it is applied to the individual. Here the use is corporate: the church, or congregation as a whole, should be seen as the sanctuary in which God dwells (cf. II Cor. 6:16).

Once this is recognized, members of the church should be more judicious in their behavior. The warning in verse 17 is quite stern: the one whose behavior is responsible for bringing down the church, or who is intent on obstructing the work of the church, must be willing to confront the judgment of God. In this "sentence of holy law" we are reminded that the one who destroys God's work will be destroyed by God. To tamper with the sacred is to invite disaster.

The concluding section of our text returns to themes introduced earlier. Those who claim superior wisdom are addressed with slight irony: "If there is anyone among you who fancies himself wise . . ." (verse 18, NEB). The only solution to pretended wisdom is acknowledged folly. Echoing his sentiments in 1:18-24, Paul again insists that God looks at this world's wisdom and smiles (Job 5:12-13; Ps. 94:11). Human pretension is transparent to God who sees us for what we are and for who we really are.

Consequently, trust in human beings is misplaced trust. "So let no one boast of [humans]" (verse 21). All such boasting is excluded (1:29, 31; Rom. 3:27; Eph. 2:9). And why? Because it confuses being with the Source of all being. The hierarchy of being sketched in verses 21-23 is critically important. Granted, "all things are ours" in the sense that God's workers work in our behalf and all of reality is at our disposal. But finally because we belong to Christ, we are Christ's (Gal. 3:29; Rom. 14:8; cf. Mark 9:41). And because Christ is who he is because of God (1:30-31), Christ is God's (I Cor. 15:28). To be Son of God is to recognize that Christ is God's (cf. Luke 3:38).

At the top of the cosmic hierarchy is God. Like Christ, we ultimately define ourselves with respect to God. Our existence is ultimately derivative from God. Whether we are

God's workers, God's farm, God's temple, we are above all God's. It is God who is source of all being, the ground of being.

Once again, we find our text redefining human wisdom and human values. True wisdom consists in recognizing God as the One who knows us and finally judges us. To boast of anything, or anyone else, is utter folly.

Matthew 5:27-37

Last Sunday we treated the first of the six antitheses in Matthew 5 which provide concrete instances of the higher righteousness that Jesus demands of his disciples (verse 20). That first one dealt with murder (verses 21-26). Today we take up the second, third, and fourth antitheses: on adultery (verses 27-30), on divorce (verses 31-32), and on swearing (verses 33-37). As we noted last week, these teachings consist of the statement of Jewish law, Jesus' demand, and then an elaboration by Matthew or the early church in an attempt to apply Jesus' word to the actual situation of the church at that time. The preacher's first inclination may be to deal with only one of these three antitheses in a sermon. However, all three can receive attention in a single sermon if one focuses on the common theme running through not only these three but all six: the primary importance of person-to-person relationships. In verses 21-26 reconciled relations were urged as taking precedence over worship and litigation. Now the focus moves to the relationships between men and women (adultery and divorce) and to one's relationship to oneself (swearing).

The antithesis on adultery states the seventh commandment and then sets over against it Jesus' expectation that his disciples not harbor adulterous thoughts (verses 27-28). To this Matthew attaches two sayings on the right eye and right hand (verses 29-30), variations of which are found in Mark 9:43, 45, 47 and later in Matthew 18:8-9. These additional sayings were not to be taken literally, for self-mutilation would hardly immunize a sinful heart. Rather, they represent a forceful statement on the urgency of a life spiritually disciplined. In fact, one could argue that rather than blinding the eyes one would do better opening the eyes to see and learn more about the person who might be an object of inordinate desire. Lust is usually toward strangers or pictures in a book, but once those persons have names, families, dreams, plans, fears, and concerns—in other words, once one knows personally the other—the nature of the attraction is radically altered and takes on a wholeness of which sex is only a part. In the antithesis itself, it is assumed that the woman at whom a man "looks lustfully" is married since the issue is adultery. The law forbids coveting the neighbor's wife (Exod. 20:17) and the words "covet" and "lust" translate the same Greek word. The point is, a woman is not a thing, a property to be coveted so as to possess but a person to whom one relates with care and respect.

The antithesis on divorce (verses 31-32) is really an extension of the one on adultery. The issue of divorce was a thorny one for the early church as evidenced by Matthew's return to the subject in 19:2-9, paralleled with variations in Mark 10:2-12 and Luke 16:18. Mark's version speaks also of a woman divorcing her husband, indicating a non-Jewish context since that was not a possibility in Judaism. Paul struggles with the question of divorce in yet another setting (I Cor. 7:10-16). The law involved in this teaching was Deuteronomy 24:1-4, which assumed a man could divorce a wife in whom he found something unseemly, indecent, disturbing. Conservative Jewish teachers (school of Shammai) defined "unseemly" as unchastity while the liberals (school of Hillel) said it could mean anything, from a wart to inability to cook to constant talking. Matthew's phrase "except on the ground of unchastity" (verse 32) puts him in the conservative camp. However, most believe that phrase is Matthew's and is not from Jesus who would not have opened doors to divorce. Matthew 19:3-9 offers a fuller treatment in which Jesus appeals to creation as the ground for indissoluble marriage. Here the contrast is with Deuteronomy 24:1-4, which forbids the divorced woman, once remarried, from returning to her first husband. Jesus says she is not to be passed around at all, putting her in the position of becoming an adulteress and making whoever marries her an adulterer. Again, at the heart of the matter is the disregard for a person who was by ancient law, treated as property to be moved about.

The antitheses on swearing (verses 33-34*a*) has a rather detailed elaboration (verses 34*b*-37), an echo of which appears in James 5:12. The laws back of this teaching regulated perjury (Lev. 19:12) and failure to perform vows (Num. 30:2-15; Deut. 23:21-23). Under Judaic law swearing was not only permitted but commanded (Deut. 10:20). Jesus' teaching in contrast is predicated on strength and integrity of character which needs no scaffolding of an oath to persuade others of one's truthfulness. (Care must be taken to insure that the listeners do not confuse swearing with cursing or profanity. Popular usage is not careful to distinguish.) Jesus' teaching here says there is no need for a structure of oaths to support one's word, as though one were assumed to be a liar and hence had to have one's word guaranteed. If I am and know myself to be truthful, then self-respect demands that I offer my yes as yes and my no as no. Truth does not need to call in outside help.

Eighth Sunday After Epiphany (Proper 3)

Leviticus 19:1-2, 9-18; Psalm 119:33-40; I Corinthians 4:1-5; Matthew 5:38-48

Given the varieties of human relationships, pleasant and painful, friendly and hostile, the community of faith needs a polar star, a governing principle for any and all relationships. Matthew 5 concludes with Jesus reminding his hearers that neither friend nor foe determines behavior; rather we are to love as God loves. In a similar vein Leviticus holds before all relationships the constant of Israel's faith: I am the Lord your God. The psalmist understands this and prays for understanding and strength to please God through obedience and trust. Paul also reminds the Corinthians that it is God with whom we have to deal; hence we do not judge ourselves or one another. We belong to God.

Leviticus 19:1-2, 9-18

This reading is the only one from the book of Leviticus in the *Common Lectionary,* and its contents may come as a surprise to hearers familiar with the book mainly by its reputation. It is commonly assumed that Leviticus is concerned only with obscure matters of priestly ritual practice. Most of the book does indeed deal with the practice of worship, including sacrifices, the priesthood, the ritual calendar, the distinction between clean and unclean, and the definition of holiness. However, as this passage reveals, the book is concerned with the proper ordering of all of life before God, including life in society as well as in the cult. Leviticus, like ancient Israel in general, did not distinguish between "religious" and "secular" requirements.

Within the Pentateuch, the book of Leviticus is part of the account of what transpired at Mount Sinai. That report includes all of the material from Exodus 19 through Numbers 10:10, reporting the covenant, the law, and the initiation of Israel's life of worship, all through the mediation of Moses. The narrative framework of Leviticus comes from the latest of the pentateuchal sources, the Priestly Writer in the time of the Babylonian Exile or later, but most of the legislation itself is somewhat older in its literary formulation, and in many cases goes back to ancient oral tradition. Our reading comes from a distinct body of legislation, the so-called Holiness Code in Leviticus 17–26. This code includes instructions for both laity and priests. There are detailed regulations concerning diet, sexual relations, gifts and offerings, rituals, and ceremonies of worship.

Chapter 19 is addressed to the laity in general, and mainly concerns activities of everyday life outside the cult as such. Verses 1-2 give the narrative introduction to the chapter as a whole, stating the general command to the congregation and its reason: "You shall be [or "are"] holy; for I the Lord your God am holy."

The purpose of the regulations, then, is to define what it means for Israel to "be holy." Holiness is fundamentally a divine attribute and refers basically to what is distinct, radically different from the ordinary. Then it refers to holy places and things, such as cult objects, priestly attire, and offerings, sacred because of their proximity to God. Sacredness is contagious, so one must take care to maintain the proper distinctions between sacred and profane. The holy can also be dangerous, as the accounts of the calls of Moses (Exod. 3–4) and Isaiah (Isa. 6) reveal. Here, the people of Israel are holy because they are God's people, and they are to live out that holiness in all of life.

After the introduction, the instructions themselves appear as an almost random collection. Some are in the second person singular and some in the plural, and most are formulated like the apodictic laws of the Decalogue (Exod. 20). A refrain echoes no less than twelve times through the chapter, "I am the Lord," or "I am the Lord your God" (verses 3, 10, 11, 14, 16, 18, 25, 30, 31, 32, 34, 37). This means that the instructions define what it is to behave as the people of God. Verses 9-10 give some specific regulations for the harvest. Fields are not to be reaped all the way up to the border, what falls at random is not to be picked up, nor are vineyards to be stripped bare. Rather, something is to be left for those who have no fields or vineyards. Verses 11-12 contain a series of prohibitions, some of which are related to those in the Decalogue: theft, lying, and false oaths profane the name of Yahweh. Verses 13-14 prohibit oppression of the neighbor, including the day laborer who should be paid quickly and the blind. Verse 15 concerns justice in the law court. Since all Israelite citizens participated in the legal process it requires that no one should show partiality, either to the powerful out of fear or the weak out of pity. Verse 16 forbids slandering or cursing ("stand forth against the life") of the neighbor.

Verses 17-18 turn to the emotions and feelings that determine actions in society toward the neighbor. Instead of hating the brother one should reason with him; instead of taking vengeance or bearing a grudge one should love one's neighbor.

These final lines, "you shall love your neighbor as yourself," are neither unrealistic nor vague. Read in their context, they have a very specific and concrete force. All of the instructions in today's reading in effect define what it means to love one's neighbor. They concern the fair and equitable behavior that expresses concrete concern for the needy and the sort of justice that establishes and maintains a community of neighbors. The criterion for this love of neighbor is one's love of self. The refrain that runs through this chapter, "I am the Lord your God," already had laid the foundation for the combination of this command with the injunction to "love the Lord your God" (Deut. 6:5) as the summary of the law, a summary that was already known in the rabbinic tradition when it was cited by Jesus (Mark 12:31; Matt. 22:34-40; Luke 10:25-28). Each part defines the other. Love of neighbor rests upon and expresses love of God, which in turn is possible because God has chosen, and thereby expressed his love, for a people.

Psalm 119:33-40

These verses, like the reading for the Sixth Sunday After Epiphany, Year A (see page 163 and Propers 18 and 26, Year B and 24, Year C), come from the longest and most complex of the Psalms. Psalm 119, generally in prayer form, offers thanks and praise to God for his gracious gift of the "law."

In these verses, the eight lines of the text repeat eight of the synonymous terms used for law throughout the psalms: statutes, law, commandments, testimonies, ways, promise, ordinances, and precepts. (Elsewhere in the composition, "words" and "judgments" are also used.) This multiplicity of terminology leads to two basic conclusions: (1) The psalm is speaking about more than we normally include when we refer to "law" or Old Testament law. Law (or torah) is thus not just the Mosaic legislation or even the Pentateuch. It denotes the whole of what was considered the revelation of God and thus clearly included Torah or the law of Moses in the narrower sense. One should think of the psalmist as writing about the written laws, about what might be called customs, rules, and practices of everyday living and about divine judgments and decisions seen as reflected in the ongoing course of life; what we might call fate or what life hands us. In all of these areas, the law, however, is seen as good, as a beneficent possession of people and thus as a gift, not a burden, from God. (2) The diverse terminology indicates that the author was looking at the "law," the total revelation of God, from a wide angle of vision so as to stimulate thought and interest.

Each of the lines of this section provides interesting metaphors and highlights particular concerns that can be developed in preaching.

1. Verse 33 recognizes that "law" is not a natural possession of a person; it is not instinct, but must be taught. God as teacher occurs in other texts (Job 36:22; see Pss. 25:4, 9; 27:11; 86:11). Others could teach as representatives of God (see Deut. 24:8). The law is thus not identified with conscience or natural inclination but something requiring study—study being the dominant characteristic of the informed good person in later Judaism.

2. Understanding (verse 34) has always been seen as going

beyond the intellectual grasp. A person needs knowledge/ wisdom but he or she also needs understanding, the ability to use profitably what one knows. The ancient rabbis described this as follows: "He that has wisdom but no understanding is like a man with bread in his hand but nothing to eat it with. And he that has understanding, but has no wisdom, is like a man with a savory dish in his hand but no bread to eat with it. But he that has both wisdom and understanding is like a man with bread and a savory dish in his hand, who eats both and is full-fed."

3. Verse 35 concerns the need for continued guidance (see Prov. 4:11-19) and sees the commandments making life into a (mark-out and delineated) path not a road with uncertain shoulders and no signposts.

4. The heart (verse 36), the intellect, the will, the goal-setting organ needs to be inclined toward the law. The heart must be shaped or tilted, disposed toward a particular life-style. The psalmist realizes that God's torah and gain (or "covetousness," "unjust gain") are contrary goals.

5. Life and the eyes are brought together (verse 37; see Matt. 6:22-23). Visual imagery feeds the soul and thus tilts the heart's inclination. Here the psalmist asks that his/her eyes not look at vanity (either the materially unsubstantial or the morally corrupt).

6. The promise (or word) asked for in verse 38 may refer to either what is given to those who fear God or that which leads to fear of God. At any rate, it asks for assurance that God's way is the right way.

7. Verse 39 provides some problems: Does reproach refer to the psalmist's troubles, to the fear of failure, to judgment for failure, or to the scorn that may come from adherence to the law? Probably the latter. "Ordinances" here may mean judgments and refer to the judgment upon the scorners.

8. The final line of this stanza closes, like most prayers, with a request but also with an affirmation.

I Corinthians 4:1-5

How should ministers be regarded? As reference points for defining our religious loyalties (1:12-13)? As those whose preaching attracts us because of well-chosen words and well-turned phrases (1:17; 2:1-4)? As those in whom we boast (3:21)?

For Paul the answer is none of the above. For him, ministers *(diakonoi)* such as himself and Apollos were best regarded as "servants of Christ and stewards of the mysteries of God" (verse 1). Earlier he has stressed the servant-role of ministers (3:5). They are those through whom the Word of God does its work: "God's agents in bringing you to the faith" (3:5, NEB). Throughout he has stressed the subordinate role of ministers as God's servants, those discharged to an assigned work by their superior, doing the work the Lord has assigned them (3:5).

A steward *(oikonomos)* is someone entrusted with a particular responsibility, a trustee given charge of something that belongs to someone else. In this case, the minister is called a "steward of the mysteries of God" (verse 1). Earlier Paul has spoken of the higher wisdom that had been hidden from the world that is revealed to those who have received God's Spirit (2:6-13). As the recipient of God's revelation, the steward's primary responsibility is to be faithful in proclaiming God's will (cf. Luke 12:42; 16:1).

The important thing to note in both cases is that the minister's work is defined with respect to someone else: Christ and God. Ministers are not their own. They serve in behalf of Christ to whom they belong (II Cor. 10:7). They unfold mysteries of the faith that derive from God not from themselves.

Our text implies rather strongly that Paul is being judged negatively by some in the Corinthian church. He says as much later in the epistle (9:3). We are not quite sure of the precise nature of these negative judgments. In the Second Epistle the tone of the polemic rises as Paul mentions the unfavorable assessments of his preaching and personal demeanor (II Cor. 10:10-12; 11:6). This may already be foreshadowed in his remarks earlier (1:17; 2:1-5).

Whatever the nature of the criticisms he was receiving, Paul's response is instructive even now. First, the opinions of outsiders matter very little to him since he does not even judge himself (verse 3). Not that he knows anything against himself (verse 4). He could say with Job, "My conscience gives me no cause to blush for my life" (Job 27:6, JB). Having defined himself as living before God, acknowledging God as the source of all being (3:23), so does he defer all judgment to God: "It is the Lord who judges me" (verse 4). Since the sun neither rises nor sets with human beings, they cannot have the last word.

Second, he cautions against premature judgment (verse 5). His later remarks (4:8-13) suggest that some were claiming to have experienced Christian existence fully—they are already filled, rich, and reigning (4:8). Possibly this attitude stemmed from their realized eschatology, leading them to think that the future was now. If this were the case, then Paul's remarks here are apposite, for they serve to stem the tide against such presumption on the future. His advice is to let the future remain the future and not arrogate to ourselves the prerogative that belongs exclusively to the Lord at the final judgment (II Cor. 5:10).

Rather we are urged to understand truly what the Lord's judgment will ultimately mean: full disclosure of who we are and what we have done (Luke 8:17; Rom. 2:16). The darkened corners of our lives will be lit up with God's knowledge. The hidden will be revealed. God's light will eventually shine so that every deed is seen and assessed as if it were committed in the noonday sun.

Commendation may be in order, but in God's good time (verse 5).

Matthew 5:38-48

Matthew 5:21-48 contains six specific teachings of Jesus making concrete the general instruction of verse 20: "For I tell you, unless your righteousness exceeds that of the scribes and Pharisees, you will never enter the kingdom of heaven." The form of these six teachings is that of the antithesis: "You have heard that it was said . . . but I say to you." In each case, Matthew provides the command to Israel and the command of Jesus to his followers, to which is attached an elaboration showing how the early Christians applied Jesus' word to their situations. Today's lection consists of the last two of these antitheses: on retaliation (verses 38-42) and on relating to one's enemies (verses 43-48).

The *lex talionis,* the law of "retaliation in kind" is found in Exodus 21:22, with additional applications in Leviticus 24:19-20 and Deuteronomy 19:16-21. The law was for the due process of administering justice and not for private indulgences in getting even. Jesus states his demand as though the old law were individually carried out, and against such vengeful behavior he calls for actions free of revenge and attempts to even the score. The conduct of Jesus' disciples is in no way to be determined by that of the one who harms and hurts.

The principle "Do not resist one who is evil" (verse 39) is given four applications: when someone strikes you, when someone takes you to court, when someone forces you to go a mile, and when someone seeks a loan from you. In each of these it is assumed that the other person has taken the initiative to harm or victimize, but the disciple takes the initiative to act in kindness, without hostility. The teaching does not call simply for non-retaliation or passivity, but rather for positive acts of good. One may be victimized but one is not to think and act like a victim. Jesus was not a victim; he gave his life. So Jesus' followers take intentional steps of healing and helpful behavior toward those who are violent and abusive. The Mosaic law prohibited taking as a pledge the cloak of the poor (Deut. 24:10, 12-13), but Jesus says that to the one suing for your cloak, give your coat as well. Paul told the Corinthians it is better to be wronged, to be defrauded, than to be entangled in litigation (I Cor. 6:7). Going an extra mile involved not Jewish but Roman law by which soldiers could force non-citizens into service for one mile. The application of the principle to situations of begging or seeking loans is different from the other instances both because no "resisting an evil one" is involved and because Jesus' teaching really continues rather than alters the law of Moses. Moses wrote that loans to the poor were to be made, and without interest (Exod. 22:25; Lev. 25:36-37). Of these four applications, Luke's sermon on the plain contains three (6:29-30).

In the teaching on relating to one's enemies (verses 43-48;

see Luke 6:27-28, 32-36), the statement of the law of Moses is here offered differently. The law required love of neighbor (Leviticus 19:18) but not hatred of the enemy; that was an interpretation of the law's silence. If one is to love neighbors then surely one must hate enemies. Jesus rejected such distinctions: one is to love all regardless of friendliness or hostility. The behavior of Jesus' followers is not in response to, not a reaction to the conduct of another. Neither friends nor enemies dictate the life-style of disciples. The faithful take their pattern from the God who never reacts on the grounds of others' attitudes and behavior but who acts out of God's own nature, which is to love and to bless, both the good and evil, the just and unjust. God is even kind to the ungrateful and selfish (Luke 6:35). To be determined by the conduct of others is to be as tax collectors and Gentiles.

Behavior that loves without distinction or reaction is perfect because it is behavior like that of God who is perfect (verse 48). "Perfect" can also be translated "complete" or "mature." It is not here referring to moral flawlessness but to love that is not partial or immature. Partial and immature love embraces those who embrace us and rejects those who reject us. To be perfect is to love in the manner of our God who is without partiality.

Last Sunday After Epiphany (Transfiguration)

Exodus 24:12-18; Psalm 2:6-11; II Peter 1:16-21; Matthew 17:1-9

As Epiphany began with a proclamation of Christ to the nations, so the last Sunday after Epiphany is the occasion for an even more dramatic presentation of God's glory, this time from the mountaintop. Exodus 24 describes Moses' experience of God on the holy mountain. This text provides immediate background for Matthew's record of the Transfiguration of Jesus. By the time Second Peter was written the Transfiguration had been enshrined in the tradition and used as proof that Jesus was God's son. Psalm 2, a psalm of coronation, proclaims the king to be a son of God. The Christian movement was early drawn to the psalm for proclaiming Christ as King and Son of God, quoting it both at Jesus' baptism and transfiguration.

Exodus 24:12-18

The two paragraphs that comprise this reading on the one hand conclude the account of the ratification of the covenant on Mount Sinai (Exod. 19–24) and on the other hand introduce the Priestly Writer's instructions for the building of the tabernacle (Exod. 25–31). The context, especially chapters 19 and 24, breathes an air of mystery because of the awesome presence of Yahweh. This account of the dramatic theophany of the Lord and the ascension of Moses as the mediator of the law and the covenant informs the Gospel accounts of the Transfiguration of Jesus.

It is not easy to sort out the sequence of events in Exodus 24. Consequently, commentators have long recognized that the chapter combines a number of different sources and

188

traditions. In verse 1 the Lord calls Moses, Aaron, Nadab, Abihu, and the seventy elders to "worship afar off." Then, after a covenant ceremony involving the people (verses 3-8), those same parties "beheld God, and ate and drank" (verses 9-10). Later (verse 14), the elders are instructed to remain below while Moses—now another party, Joshua, appears (verse 13)—goes up on the mountain. Only some of the difficulties can be resolved by the traditional distribution of materials among the Pentateuchal sources. At least verses 15b-18 come from the Priestly Document. Moreover, chapter 24 seems to duplicate some of the events reported in chapter 19. This diversity attests to the importance of Sinai, the covenant, and Moses in Israelite tradition.

Verses 12-14, the first paragraph of our reading, report Yahweh's command to Moses to come up on the mountain to receive the tablets of the law. Tradition follows Exodus 34:28 in concluding that the tablets contained the Decalogue, but the contents are not defined here, and the Hebrew of verse 12 is problematic, leaving it uncertain what the narrator meant. This reference is a foreshadowing of the story of the broken tablets in Exodus 32. Exodus 31:18 is even more explicit about the form of the writing, stating that the tablets were "written with the finger of God." When Moses ascends the mountain, he has the elders wait, leaving Aaron and Hur responsible for resolving any disputes that arise.

The second paragraph, verses 15-18, gives an account of the theophany on the mountain. Significantly (compare Gen. 1), Moses waits for six days and on the seventh the voice of God calls to him. Attending the appearance of God are terrifying natural phenomena, the cloud (verses 15, 18) and the "devouring fire" (17). This contrasts with the description of the presence of God in verses 9-11, which seems to picture the floor of the divine throne room. More important, whereas verse 10 reports that Moses and Aaron, Nadab, and Abihu, and seventy of the elders "saw the God of Israel," here it is not God himself who appears, but "the glory of the Lord" (verses 16-17). Similarly, Ezekiel characterizes his vision of the presence of God as "the appearance of the likeness of the glory of the Lord" (Ezek. 1:28). God's "glory" is his visible manifestation. The purpose of this appearance of God is to communicate further instructions for the people.

Such texts as this one stress the holiness of God, the radical difference between the divine and the human. But the passage also reflects on how that gulf between divine and human is bridged. God is known as an awesome presence at particular places, such as Sinai, and, later, Jerusalem. God is known not directly but through his "glory." Finally, God is known through a mediator of the covenant, Moses.

Psalm 2:6-11

This portion of Psalm 2 fits nicely into the themes of Transfiguration Sunday. (The entire psalm is one of the readings for the Second Sunday of Easter, Year C.) In Matthew 17:5, Jesus is declared the Son of God; in like manner Psalm 2 speaks of the ancient Judean monarch as son of God.

In verses 6-11, there are three (maybe two) different speakers and three different speeches. All of these can be understood against the background of the ritual of the coronation of a king for which this psalm was written. (For the features of the coronation ritual, see I Kings 1:32-40 and II Kings 11:12.) Verse 6 is given as divine speech to a human audience (probably spoken by a priest or prophet in the ritual). Verses 7-9 are the new king's address to his subjects, reporting on the divine promises proclaimed to the king in the enthronement ritual (the testimony given to the king in II Kings 11:12?). In verses 10-12, the new Judean monarch addresses the rulers of the nations of the world, calling upon them to submit to God's act manifest in his enthronement.

The king reigning on Zion was the messiah (= the anointed in verse 2; see I Sam. 26:9). Verse 6 holds together two factors: the Judean (Davidic) king as God's appointed ruler (see II Sam. 7) and Zion as God's chosen place of abode (see Pss. 46, 48, 76).

The promises to the king, spelled out in verses 7-9, are two-pronged, the first being directly connectible with the divine address to Jesus at the Transfiguration. The first (verse 7) illustrates the close intimacy, the filial relationship between the Deity and the king. The ruling monarch was the son of God, having been so begotten on the day of the coronation (see Isa. 9:1-6). Sonship here is clearly seen as a special status granted the king in terms of the monarch's adoption on the day of his coronation and anointment. The position and status of messiah was not something one was born with; it was a status bestowed upon one and recognized by the people. As the messiah, the chosen ruler, the king, was also the son of God (see Ps. 89:26). The second promise (verses 8-9) declares that the new king will have a universal rule extending from one end of the earth to the other and that he will destroy kings and nations through his power. (Note how the view of the Messiah in the Gospel text has Jesus as the Messiah exercising that office through humiliation, not through conquest and battle.)

The final stanza, verses 10-12, calls upon the rulers of the world to accept what has occurred in the coronation and to offer their submission to the Davidic messiah.

II Peter 1:16-21

This text is chosen as the epistolary lection because of its explicit reference to the Transfiguration of Jesus in verses 17-18. It is a remarkable text because it appears to be the only New Testament text outside the Gospels that refers to the Transfiguration. It clearly presupposes knowledge of the Synoptic account (Matt. 17:1-13; Mark 9:2-13; Luke 9:28-36), though it is briefer and exhibits a different tone.

Mention of the Transfiguration is introduced in the context of a discussion of the "power and coming of our Lord Jesus Christ" (verse 16). There is some dispute as to whether the "coming" (*parousia*) referred to here is the Lord's first coming in the Incarnation or his Second Coming at the end of time. The word *parousia* is typically used for his Second Coming (Matt. 24:3; I Cor. 15:23; I Thess. 2:19; 3:13; 4:15; 5:23; II Thess. 2:1, 8-9; James 5:7-8; 1 John 2:28). It is similarly used later in the Epistle of Second Peter (3:4, 12). In fact, this epistle is written in response to those who were denying in some sense the Second Coming. Since the Lord had not yet appeared, they concluded that he would never appear (3:4). They argued that things were pretty much as they had always been and that they were unlikely to change.

Thus if we take seriously the overall context of the epistle, it looks as if our text has in mind the Lord's Second Coming. The exegetical difficulty here is why the author introduces the Transfiguration to make this more plausible. Presumably, if he had in mind the first coming, it would make sense to mention the Transfiguration as an instance in which he served as an eyewitness. But it may be that he introduces it to establish credibility in the Second Coming by showing that Christ had already exhibited honor and glory as the Son of God. If such a graphic demonstration of his sonship could occur during his ministry, why not at the end of time? His majesty had been seen once by eyewitnesses in the Transfiguration, and it would be seen again at his Second Coming.

This helps explain the author's opening statement that the apostolic tradition did no consist of "cleverly devised myths" (verse 16; cf. I Tim. 4:7; 6:20; II Tim. 2:16). The opponents, or "scoffers" (cf. 2:1-3; 3:4), had apparently classified certain parts of the apostolic testimony with other incredible tales. Our text insists that this could not be the case because such events as the Transfiguration were verified by "eyewitnesses of his majesty" (verse 16). The letter, of course, is attributed to the apostle Peter (1:1), although it is now widely recognized as being pseudonymous. In any case, the claim here is that Peter, the author, had witnessed this event, indeed had been with Christ on the holy mount (verse 18).

The second part of today's lection (verses 19-21) moves to another topic: the reliability of the prophetic witness. First there is the reminder that prophecy is not a matter of private interpretation (verse 20). This seems directed at the heretics who would often appeal to novel interpretations to support their position. It suggests that interpretation of Scripture must somehow be answerable to a wider public. The apostolic tradition serves as one norm against which Scripture interpretation is to be judged (1:12-15).

Second, there is a reminder that Scripture itself is not the product of individual initiative. It is not as if the prophets were self-motivated. They were rather impelled by the Holy

Spirit to speak for God (cf. II Tim. 3:16; also Acts 2:1-6; 28:25). Even though this passage presents several exegetical difficulties, it provides useful images for preaching on the Transfiguration. We should note the vivid images in verse 19: the lamp shining in darkness, the dawning of the day (Luke 1:78), and the rising of the morning star (cf. Rev. 2:28): Each of these extend the image of Majestic Glory (verse 17). The full significance of the Transfiguration could only be stated symbolically: dazzling light signified the presence of God and the divine confirmation of Jesus as God's Son. In the same way that God's radiance broke through in the ministry of Jesus, a similarly dazzling display may be expected at the Lord's Second Coming.

Matthew 17:1-9

Just as the Gospel for the first Sunday after Epiphany always recalls the baptism of Jesus, so the reading for the last Sunday always recalls the Transfiguration. The two records have many parallels: in both Jesus is passive, being acted upon; in both God reveals who Jesus really is. Both experiences immediately follow occasions that point up the humble obedience of Jesus. The Transfiguration follows after Jesus announces his coming death (16:21). Both the baptism and the Transfiguration are epiphanies, or more precisely, Christophanies.

The story in 17:1-9 is that of a Christophany by means of a metamorphosis ("transfiguration" is derived from the Latin translation). The word occurs in II Corinthians 3:18 and Romans 12:2. Jesus' whole being is transformed, including his clothing. There is no reason to argue that this is a misplaced resurrection story or Parousia story. That which someday "every eye will see" (Rev. 1:7) is here revealed to Peter, James, and John, the inner circle (Mark 5:37; 14:33), and through them to the reader; that is, the glory of the eternal status of the divine Son. That which flesh, blood, and human observation could not perceive but which God revealed to Simon Peter at Caesarea Philippi (16:17), here shines through the face and frame of Jesus of Nazareth. Jesus is the Son of God.

In telling the story, Matthew follows closely Mark 9:2-8, as does Luke (9:28-36) although with more variations. Many of the details are drawn from Old Testament accounts of theophanies: after six days (Exod. 24:16), the shining of the face (Exod. 34:29-35), and being overshadowed (Exod. 40:35). Bright light is, of course, everywhere mentioned as a symbol of the divine presence (Rev. 3:4; 7:9; Col. 1:12; Heb. 1:1-3). The presence of Moses and Elijah confirm the witness of the law and the prophets to Jesus Christ, and Peter's suggestion of building booths recalls the Feast of Booths during which Israel commemorated very special times being led of God in the wilderness by means of the cloud and the fire (Lev. 23:39-43). While Mark introduces Simon Peter's fear at the appearance of the three figures, which fear prompts him to speak (9:5-6), Matthew says fear came upon all three at the voice from the cloud, "This is my beloved Son, with whom I am well pleased; listen to him" (verses 5-6). These disciples did not hear this voice and the similar message at Jesus' baptism (3:17), but the reader recalls that account. At baptism, when Jesus submitted to the call of John to prepare for the kingdom, the voice from heaven announces who Jesus really is. At his prediction of death, when Jesus will submit to the experience common to us all (16:21), the divine voice again says who Jesus really is, and adds that he, not Moses or Elijah, is to be obeyed (verse 5). Given these two occasions brightened by heaven's attestation, one might anticipate that the confirming voice would come appropriately one more time, at the cross. But it did not, and the crowds were persuaded that Jesus, without heaven's voice or divine rescue, was not from God (27:39-43).

It is only at verse 7 that Jesus speaks or acts (this verse has no parallel in Mark). Jesus comes to them, a rare expression given the fact that throughout the Gospel others come to Jesus. Here he approaches them, as he does in the post-resurrection scene in 28:16-20. The phrase could carry the force of a descent, of a kind of Parousia. Jesus' touch and his words bless and assure. It was enough to embolden them to open their eyes and the vision was over. There is no reason to think they understood what had occurred, but in subsequent Christian history the event was enshrined as occurring on "the holy mountain" and was offered as proof of the truth of the apostolic witness to Jesus (II Pet. 1:17-18).

Our lection closes with a post-transfiguration note: "Tell no one the vision, until the Son of man is raised from the dead" (verse 9). If the disciples understood who Jesus was only after the resurrection, there certainly was no reason to assume the crowds could. After all, if the baptism and the prediction of passion seemed a contradiction of the terms "Messiah" and "Son of God," how much more would the cross? The people are not ready for the Transfiguration story because the disciples are not ready to tell it.

Holy Name of Jesus;
Solemnity of Mary,
Mother of God, January 1

Numbers 6:22-27; Psalm 67; Galatians 4:4-7 or *Philippians 2:9-13; Luke 2:15-21*

Celebrating the beginning of the new year on January 1 goes back to the mid-first century B.C., when Julius Caesar restructured the civil calendar. Prior to that time, March 1 marked the beginning of the new year. From the outset, it was a festive celebration that easily gave way to excesses of various kinds. In response, the Roman church called on Christians to open the new year with prayer, fasting, and penitential devotions. Another way to provide an alternative to raucous festivals was to designate January 1 as a time for honoring Mary the Mother of God. In the Roman calendar the day was designated *Natale Sanctae Mariae*, the Feast of Saint Mary.

Even though the particular emphasis given to January 1 has shifted through the centuries, in modern times, and especially in the Roman church, this day has received a dual emphasis. First, it is a time to recall the naming of Jesus, hence the designation the "Holy Name of Jesus." This aspect of its celebration is closely related to the custom, going back at least to the sixth century, of celebrating the Feast of the Circumcision of the Lord on this day. Second, it is an occasion for commemorating Mary, hence the designation the "Solemnity of Mary, Mother of God."

The selection of readings for this day echoes these themes. The Old Testament reading is chosen because of its emphasis on the bestowal of the divine name on the people Isarel.

Psalm 67 closely parallels Numbers 6:22-27 in the form of the blessing it contains. The epistolary readings in different ways pick up on both themes: the Galatians passage embodies a pre-Pauline tradition in which Christ is confessed as one "born of woman, born under the law," while the Philippians reading lays stress on the exalted name that God bestowed on the risen Lord. The Gospel text, of course, combines both themes: the central role of Mary as the one who pondered the divine mystery in her heart and the circumcision of Jesus as the occasion when he received the holy name.

Numbers 6:22-27

Doubtless this passage found its place on this day in the lectionary because of its concluding verse, "So shall they put my name upon the people of Israel, and I will bless them." It thus serves to emphasize, and to interpret, the account of the naming of Jesus in Luke 2:15-21.

Numbers 6:22-27 is the report of the institution of what must have been a regular religious practice in ancient Israel, the Aaronic blessing. Introducing the blessing itself is a concise but complicated narrative in verse 22. Yahweh instructs Moses to instruct Aaron and his sons to bless the people of Israel in a particular way. Thus the blessing comes from God himself, transmitted through intermediaries. Recall that Moses, when he was called to deliver Israel, protested that he was not eloquent, so his brother Aaron was designated to speak on his behalf (Exod. 4:10-16). The real addressees of these instructions, however, are "the sons of Aaron," that is, the priests throughout later generations who are descendants of Moses' brother. Thus the text gives to the Aaronic priests a special gift and a particular responsibility.

The introduction also makes clear what is known throughout the Old Testament, namely, that blessing—like curse—can be transmitted, and by words. Moreover, those words are known to be powerful. Sometimes they refer to very specific gifts, as in the case of Isaac's blessing given to Jacob instead of to Esau (Gen. 27), or Jacob's blessings on his sons (Gen. 49).

A blessing is in effect a prayer for the well-being of the person so addressed, either in general terms, or for a particular gift. Thus one can read each line of this blessing, with the TEV, "May the Lord . . . ". Given the context, then, Yahweh gives the priests the words of the prayer they are to address to him.

Polished by centuries of oral delivery, the blessing itself is in poetry. It contains three sentences, each with two parts, and all in typical Hebrew parallelism. The first half of each sentence concerns the Lord's attitude toward the one blessed: "bless you," "make his face to shine upon you," "lift up his countenance upon you." Each one of these asks that Yahweh look favorably upon the people. The second half of each sentence concerns the Lord's activity on behalf of the ones blessed: "keep you" (or "watch over you," NEB), "be gracious to you," "give you peace." The care and divine generosity of the first two is taken up in the third, for "peace" (*shalom*) is a comprehensive term for well-being.

By uttering the blessing over the people, the priests put the "name" of Yahweh upon them, and God will bless them (verse 27). Placing the name of the Lord on the people may refer to the utterance of that name in prayer in their presence and on their behalf. But it probably means more than that. To put the name of the Deity on them is to identify them with their Lord, to make it clear whose they are, and consequently, who they are. They are, and are to remain, Yahweh's own people. In that naming they are blessed.

In reflecting upon the text, we may identify with both the people and the priests. As the people of God, we are known by that name and are recipients of the blessing. But the people of God are a "nation of priests," so it is the responsibility of all to transmit such blessing, to utter this prayer over others, to identify them as blessed by God's name.

Psalm 67

Psalm 67 contains both request to receive blessing and thanksgiving for blessing received. Verses 1 and 6-7 speak about God, while verses 2-5 directly address God and thus are in prayer form. Verses 3 and 5 are a refrain. Probably different groups of the people or different choirs sang the prayerful requests of verses 2 and 4 and the refrains of verses

3 and 5. The psalm thus has some of the characteristics of a lament (petitions for blessing) and of a thanksgiving.

The tension in the psalm can also be seen in its stress on both the particular (the people of Israel; the "us" of the psalm) and the universal (the nations; the peoples of the world). The request for blessing upon the more restricted community, that is, the "us" of verses 1, 6, and 7, has as its ultimate goal, the recognition of God by foreigners and the praise of the nations.

The analogies between this psalm and Christians, holy family, and Mary the mother of Jesus might be seen as the following. The birth of a child has very specific, very limited connotations. The child is very particular: the particular offspring of a particular locale. The birth is always to a particular "us." Yet the birth of Jesus is proclaimed as possessing universal ramifications that reach out to the nations and the peoples of the world. The Incarnation is at once a most particular and a universal event. At the same time, a birth is a blessing and an occasion for thanks (verses 6-7) and yet it looks forward to the future, to the expectation and intercession of blessings to come.

Three elements or emphases in the psalm are of interest and could be developed in preaching. There is, first of all, the benedictory character of the opening verse. In this text, the congregation requests divine favor and blessing. For the "face to shine upon" someone was a way of saying "show favor toward." It is equivalent to our saying, may God "smile" on us. Both in terminology and concern, this opening verse is very similar to the great priestly blessing found in Numbers 6:24-26, truly one of the great texts of the Hebrew Scriptures.

Second, the psalm has a strong universal emphasis. This is expressed in three ways. (1) The request for divine blessing on the Israelite community has, as its rationale, a universal goal. Bless us, it requests, "that thy way may be known upon earth, thy saving power among all nations." Divine blessing on the worshiping community is thus seen as the means for God to bear witness to himself among other people. (2) The psalm petitions God to let the nations of the world (the Gentiles) join in the praise of him. This envisions others joining the chosen people in the worship of their God but not necessarily their conversation. (3) God is declared ready to be the judge and guide for the nation, a role that he exercises with equity. Such a declaration clearly affirms a universal rule for the Deity.

Finally, the psalm offers thanksgiving for the earth's increase. Verses 6-7 suggest that this psalm may have been used in conjunction with either the spring or the fall harvest seasons. The divine blessing is related, however, not to the worshiping community's own self-enjoyment but as an instrument for the universal acknowledgment and fear of God.

Galatians 4:4-7

This text serves as the epistolary reading for the First Sunday After Christmas in Year B. The reader may wish to consult our remarks in *Advent, Christmas, Epiphany, Year B*. It also serves as one of the options for the epistolary lesson in all three years for this special day of celebration of the name of Jesus or Mary as the mother of God. Our comments on this passage under the "Special Days" section in the *Advent, Christmas, Epiphany* volume for Year C might prove useful as well.

The phrase from this epistolary passage that makes it a suitable text for this special day is "born of woman" (verse 4). Although Mary is not mentioned by name, she is clearly in mind in what appears to be a pre-Pauline kerygmatic summary. What makes it remarkable is that it is one of the few times that Paul refers to the tradition of Jesus' birth (cf. Rom. 1:3). In fact, in none of Paul's writings does he ever refer to Mary, the mother of Jesus, by name (cf. Rom. 16:6). For that matter, she is referred to only once by name outside the Synoptic Gospels (Acts 1:14).

Even so, this single reference achieves a prominence, if for no other reason than because it is exceptional. The preacher's task on this occasion is to highlight its significance within this Pauline passage rather than treating it as Paul's slighting Mary.

Given the prominence of this phrase, and its companion

phrase "born under the law," within this passage, we should observe first that Paul anchors the Incarnation in time and history. In this respect, he shares Luke's view of the Christ-event as an event that is part of world history (cf. Luke 2:1-3; 3:1-2). In this respect, the epistolary reading nicely complements the Gospel lesson from Luke with its distinctive interest in the role of Mary in the birth and infancy story (cf. Luke 1:26-56; 2:5-7, 16, 19, 22-35, esp. verses 34-35, 48, 51).

By focusing on Mary, the preacher might explore her role in the following respects:

1. As the one through whom "the fullness of time" occurred (verse 4). One of the characteristic ways of interpreting the Christ-event was to see it as the end of one era and the beginning of a new era. The "time" of the old era came to an end with the coming of Christ, hence the story of Jesus begins with the announcement, "The time has come" (Mark 1:15, NEB; cf. I Cor. 10:11, Eph. 1:10; Heb. 1:2; 9:26; I Pet. 1:20).

2. As the one through whom the sending of God's Son occurred (verse 4). We might compare this metaphor with others used of the Incarnation. "Sending" suggests a commissioning for a particular task (Rom. 8:3; cf. John 5:36; I John 4:9), whereas "giving" suggests a sacrificial image (Rom. 8:32; cf. John 3:16).

3. As the one through whom liberation from the law occurred (verse 5). This must be understood within the context of Paul's special agenda in the Epistle of Galatians, where he emphasizes Christ's role as rescuing us from the curse of the law (3:13). The image is rendered especially well in the NEB: "to purchase freedom for the subjects of the law" (verse 5; cf. I Cor. 6:20; 7:23; I Pet. 1:18-19).

4. As the one through whom our adoption as children occurred (verse 5). Earlier Paul has insisted that our becoming "sons of God" was made possible in Christ (3:26). But the contrast here is between being slaves and being children (verse 7; 3:29; Rom. 8:16-17). The crucial difference, of course, is that being a child means being a heir (3:29). This was not an entirely new status—being children of God (cf. Deut. 14:1). But being a child has been redefined by Christ.

5. As the one through whom our status as children is validated by the Spirit of Christ (verse 6). Our text speaks of two sendings: God's sending of the Son and God's sending of the Son's Spirit. The one sending has occurred in the world, the other within our hearts. The role of the Spirit receives particular definition as the one who utters the words of Jesus in Gethsemane, "Abba, Father" (Mark 14:36). It is Christ's Spirit who utters within us the words of filial obedience that continually confirm our status as children.

Obviously, each of the above claims is true primarily with reference to Christ. The one danger of this way of appropriating the text is that the role of Christ may easily become subsumed under the role of Mary. And yet none of this would have been possible had Christ not been "born of woman."

Philippians 2:9-13

The fuller version of this well-known Pauline text (2:1-13) serves as the epistolary reading for Proper 21 in Year A. The reader may wish to consult our remarks in *After Pentecost, Year A*. This text also overlaps with the standard epistolary lesson (2:5-11) that is used for Passion/Palm Sunday in all three years. Additional remarks may be found in the *Lent, Holy Week, Easter* volumes for Years A, B, and C.

Today's text consists of two parts. Verses 9-11 comprise the second major part of the christological hymn that begins in verse 6. Verses 12-13 provide an exhortation based on the hymn.

The exaltation of Christ (verses 9-11). What makes this part of the passage appropriate for the day set aside for honoring the Holy Name of Jesus is the double reference to "the name" in verses 9-10. In the first instance, the "name which is above every name" is doubtless a reference to "Lord," which is made clear in the confession "Jesus Christ is Lord" (verse 11; I Thess. 1:1; Eph. 1:21). This name is bestowed as a result of Christ's resurrection, here referred to as his exaltation, which in other texts is rendered even more vividly as an enthronement at God's right hand (cf. Acts 2:33; 5:31). Elsewhere the exalted name is "Son of God" (Rom. 1:3), which according to the Epistle to the Hebrews is incomparably superior to the name of angels (Heb. 1:4-14).

Yet the Lord is clearly identified with the historical figure Jesus, for it is "at the name of Jesus" before which the universe will bow in submission (verse 10). The language is doubtless supplied by Isaiah 45:23, where Yahweh calls on the nations of the earth to recognize him as the only God before whom there is none other, promising that eventually "to me every knee shall bow, every tongue shall swear." This universal recognition of Yahweh's preeminent status equalizes our status (Rom. 14:11). In our text, however, the name of Jesus has replaced the name of Yahweh as the name of universal recognition and submission.

Bowing before the name of Jesus finally expresses itself as confession. The confession that embodies the sum and substance of the Christian faith in its simplest terms, which at one time defined earthly loyalties (Rom. 10:9; I Cor. 12:3; II Cor. 4:5; Col. 2:6), now reconfigures heavenly loyalties.

The exhortation to believers (verses 12-13). Confession properly understood should translate into an appropriate form of life. Here we are urged to make our salvation actual by allowing God to be at work within us. The form of the exhortation seems strange coming from Paul, the chief critic of salvation by works. Yet we are urged to "work out [our] own salvation with fear and trembling" (verse 12). The language is difficult to square with Pauline theology as expressed in Romans and Galatians, but it probably suggests that we should actualize or realize God's saving work in our lives by adopting a stance of healthy fear before God (cf. II Cor. 7:15; Eph. 6:5; I Pet. 1:17).

We should perhaps note his reference to their obedience (verse 12), which might suggest that the obedient life is the form in which our salvation becomes concrete. Paul's injunction to us is qualified somewhat by his insistence that it is actually God who is working in us, or energizing us, to carry out the divine will (cf. 1:6; II Cor. 3:5).

As we can see, the text presents several exegetical problems with which the preacher must grapple before deciding how to use this text on a day honoring the name of Jesus. What should not be ignored, however, is the honorific

203

tone of the passage and the central claim of the ultimate preeminence of Christ's name.

Luke 2:15-21

The tradition that calls for this special service on January 1 carries with it a double focus, either one of which may be central to the liturgy and sermon for any given year of the lectionary. Primary attention may be given to Mary or it may be given to the child upon the occasion of circumcision and naming. In either case it means for the preacher a return to the Lukan text treated earlier as the Gospel (along with John 1:1-14) for the season of Christmas. Only verse 21 is added to the earlier reading. This return will be no strain either on the familiar text or on the preacher's imagination if the special focus of this service is kept in mind. We will here discuss Luke 2:15-21 with attention first upon Mary and then upon the eight-day-old child, leaving to the preacher the choice of accent. For the recovery of the whole narrative (Luke 2:1-20) the reader may wish to review the comments on the Christmas lection.

In Luke 2:15-20, Mary is in the unusual position of hearing from strange visitors, the shepherds, the testimony about her son's significance in God's gracious purpose for "all the people" (verse 10). The shepherds receive from heaven's messenger the good news of a Savior; the shepherds hear the angelic choir; the shepherds are given a sign for confirmation. Mary, the child's mother, hears all this, not directly, but through their testimony. Not that there is anything wrong with hearing it the way the whole world receives it (24:47-48; Acts 1:8). But his young mother, in pain, away from home, uncomfortably housed in a stable, would surely have been cheered and encouraged by a brief return of the angel who visited her nine months earlier. Nine months is a long time; in fact, plenty of time to doubt one's own experience, plenty of time to wonder about the adequacy of one's answers to inquiring relatives and friends.

But our quiet wish for Mary is not her own wish. She keeps these things in her heart, pondering, remembering (verse 19). The witness of the shepherds confirms what Gabriel had said (1:26-38) and what her kinswoman Elizabeth had told her (1:39-45). Soon Simeon would add to this testimony, as would Anna, and the child himself at age twelve, causing Mary to ponder further the meaning of all this (2:22-51). Mary was not, however only a ponderer: she believed God's word and was obedient to it (1:38, 45); she had strong confidence and hope in God (1:46-55); and she became a disciple of her firstborn, joining his other followers in Jerusalem as they prayerfully waited for the Holy Spirit he had promised (Acts 1:5, 14). No fear of an excessive adoration of Mary should blind us to Luke's portrayal of her as a true disciple.

Verse 21 provides the second perspective in today's lesson, the naming of Jesus. Luke, who alone among the Evangelists records this moment in Jesus' life, conveys three messages in the one sentence devoted to it. First, there is the name itself. Jesus is a form of the name Joshua which means "salvation from Jehovah." Luke has already called Jesus "Savior" (2:11), but it is Matthew who states more directly the choice of the name: "and you shall call his name Jesus, for he will save his people from their sins" (1:21).

Luke's second point is that the naming of Jesus both fulfills and confirms the word of God delivered by the angel (1:31). To say the word was fulfilled is to acknowledge a pattern of promise/fulfillment very important to Luke both in the Gospel (4:16-21; 24:44) and in Acts (2:17-36). More consistently in Luke than in any other New Testament writer the theme of continuity between the Old Testament and the New is developed. To say the word of God was confirmed is to say that the event of naming the child Jesus confirmed the divine revelation. The same was true in the case of John. The name was given to Zechariah in a revelation (1:13) and so the child was called John, much to the surprise of relatives and neighbors (1:57-63). Both John and Jesus are of families which hear, believe, and obey the word of God.

And finally, Luke wants it understood that there was nothing about Jesus and his followers which violated the law of Moses. In chapter 2 alone Luke cites repeated observances of the law: circumcision, dedication at the temple, purification of the mother, journey to Jerusalem at age twelve for the Passover. Luke's Jesus worships regularly in the synagogue (4:16), and following his death, the disciples continue to worship God in the temple (24:53). Jesus and his disciples do not represent a breach of ancient law and covenant but rather continuation and fulfillment of God's gracious purpose as revealed in the law, the prophets, and the writings (24:27, 44-47).

Presentation, February 2

Malachi 3:1-4; Psalm 84 or 24:7-10; Hebrews 2:14-18; Luke 2:22-40

This special service commemorates the presentation of the child Jesus in the temple in the rite of dedicating him to God. The temple is important in Luke's story of Jesus and the early church, and there is no shortage of Old Testament texts to join him in that affirmation of the temple as central in the life of God's people. Malachi pictures the awful day of the Lord's coming to the temple to cleanse and purify. The psalmist sings not only of the Lord's coming to the temple but also of the beauty and attractiveness of the temple for all those who trust in God. The Hebrew text shifts the image, portraying Christ as the meeting place of the eternal and holy God and the people who are but flesh and blood. In order to be for us a place to meet God, Christ came from God to be one of us, made in every way like his brothers and sisters.

Malachi 3:1-4

The Book of Malachi originated in the postexilic period, between 520 B.C., when the temple was rebuilt, and 400 B.C., when the law was instituted by Ezra. Sacrifices and offerings in the temple seem to have become a regular part of the life of worship. Judah would have been a province of the Persian Empire, with its own "governor" (Mal. 1:8).

Nothing is known about the life of the prophet himself, not even his name. "Malachi" is not a proper name but the title, "my messenger," apparently taken from the passage before us (3:1). The person responsible for the book continues the ancient prophetic tradition of speaking in the name of the Lord concerning the immediate future, and he is willing to

207

challenge current beliefs and practices. He was deeply interested in priestly matters, and likely was identified with the Levites (Mal. 2:4-9).

The reading for today is part of a unit that begins in 2:17 and concludes with 3:5. It is a disputation between the prophet, speaking on behalf of the Lord, and persons whose words he quotes. They have "wearied" the Lord by saying, "Every one who does evil is good in the sight of the Lord, and he delights in them," and by asking, "Where is the God of justice?" (2:17) In short, because evildoers prosper, they question the presence of a God of justice.

Malachi 3:1-4 is the prophetic response to such objections. The prophet hears the Lord announcing the arrival of a messenger, the messenger of the covenant, who will prepare for the appearance of the Lord himself in the temple. The day of arrival, elsewhere called the Day of the Lord, will be a terrible time, for no one can stand before him. It will be a day of refining and purification, particularly of the Levites, who will then present offerings that "will be pleasing to the Lord" (verse 4).

Next, the Lord himself will appear in judgment, punishing "every one who does evil" (2:17), including sorcerers, adulterers, and those who deal unjustly with the weak, such as hirelings, widows, orphans, and resident aliens (3:5).

Where is the God of justice? God is sending a messenger to prepare the way, cleansing the priesthood and worship in the temple, and then God himself will approach as judge. Sinners may prosper, but not for long.

The passage has echoed in various ways through Christian tradition. Mark took the messenger to be John the Baptist and quoted the initial line of verse 1 to introduce the account of John's appearance and his baptism of Jesus. On the commemoration of Presentation, read with Luke 2:22-40, the ambiguities of verse 1 take on added significance. Is Jesus the messenger, or the Lord himself, who "will suddenly come to his temple"? The somber, apocalyptic tone of the passage from Malachi underscores the threatening aspects of the presentation of Jesus in the temple (Luke 2:34-35). Behind this serious note, however, the good news of Malachi is unmistakable. God will establish justice, and the arrival of his

messenger will restore the means of communion with God
(3:4).

Psalm 84

The two psalms selected for reading in celebration of Jesus'
presentation at the temple are both concerned with devotion
to the temple. Psalm 84 may have been once used in
conjunction with a pilgrimage made to Jerusalem at festival
time, although verse 9 seems to suggest it was used by the
king. Psalm 24 contains words spoken at the time when
pilgrims entered the sanctuary precincts.

Psalm 84:5-7 probably talks about the route to Zion taken
by pilgrims as they made their way along the roads to the
city. At the time of the fall festival, some of the early autumn
rains may already have fallen, reviving the parched land.
"Strength to strength" could be translated "stronghold to
stronghold," that is, the people move from one village
outpost to another.

The piety of the worshiper and the psalm composer can be
seen in various ways in the text. One way of analyzing the
materials is to note the three groups whom the writer
declares "blessed" (or "happy" which is a better translation
of the Hebrew word used in all three cases).

1. First, a happy company is the birds that dwell
continuously in the temple (verses 3-4). The sparrows and
swallows that nest in the sacred precincts have the advantage
of constantly dwelling in the house of God where they can
sing God's praise forever.

2. Happy are those who go on pilgrimage to Jerusalem
(verses 5-7). To visit the temple and Zion is to experience
happiness and to see "the God of gods."

3. Happy are those who trust in God (verse 12), who find
their confidence in him. Here we have a sort of generalizing
pronouncement that moves beyond the specificity of temple
piety.

Verse 10 may be taken as embodying the overall sentiment
of the psalm: to visit the temple and worship in its courts
were some of the supreme experiences for the ancient
Hebrews.

Psalm 24:7-10

Of all the Psalms, Psalm 24 probably illustrates most clearly the fact that the Psalms were used as the spoken part of cultic rituals. Throughout verses 3-10, the material is comprised of a series of questions and answers probably recited by pilgrims and priests.

The psalm opens (verses 1-2) with a hymnic praise of Yahweh which identifies the God of Israel as the possessor of the world and all that is in it. The ownership of the terrestrial kingdom is his by right of creation. He is the one who anchored the earth in the midst of the seas and established it firmly upon the rivers (or streams) of the deep that ancients believed lay underneath the dry land. (Such a belief is partially based on the presence of springs and wells which suggest that water lies beneath the earth.)

The questions in verse 3 were addressed by the pilgrims to the priests inside the temple as the pilgrims arrived at the gates of the temple. The questions concern the qualifications demanded of those allowed to enter the sacred precincts: "Who shall ascend the hill of the Lord [who can enter the temple precincts]? Who shall stand in his holy place [in the temple in the presence of God]?" The priestly answer in this catechism of admission (verses 4-5) brings together two pairs of ethical qualifications: purity of outward deeds (clean hands) and purity of thought or inward truthfulness (pure heart) followed by purity of religious practice or unadulterated faith (not lifting up the soul to what is vain) and purity in speaking (does not swear deceitfully). These four principles in themselves provide a rather comprehensive perspective of ethical demands and requirements. If such demands as these were made as part of the worship, then one surely cannot condemn ancient worship services of being free from ethical interests and demands.

Verse 6 provides the worshipers' response to the requirements for entrance: "Those are the kind of people we are." Thus they claim the promises of verse 5—blessing and vindication from God.

With verse 7, the focus shifts from humankind and the moral values of living to God himself. The pilgrims or choir outside the sanctuary address the temple gates demanding that they be lifted up so that the King of glory can come in. But how could God enter the sanctuary? No doubt, the ark, the symbol of God's presence, had been carried out of the temple to reenter with the pilgrims on a high holy festival day. The choir or priests within offer a response in the form of a question, "Who is this King of glory?" God is then described as the one strong and mighty, mighty in battle. Perhaps part of the festival involved the proclamation of God's triumph over the forces of evil.

Hebrews 2:14-18

For comments on this epistolary lection, see the discussion of the readings for the First Sunday After Christmas, Year A, in this volume. Since this text serves as the epistolary text for Presentation in all three years, the reader may wish to consult our remarks on this passage in connection with Presentation in the *Advent, Christmas, Epiphany* volume for Year C.

Luke 2:22-40

The text which provides a Gospel basis for the service of the Presentation of Jesus is found only in Luke (2:22-40). In fact, Luke places between the nativity (2:1-20) and Jesus beginning his public life at age thirty (3:23) three stories: the circumcision and naming when the child was eight days old (2:21; see the special service for January 1); the presentation in the temple when he was about forty days old (2:22-40; Lev. 12:1-4); and the visit to the temple at age twelve (2:41-52). All this is to say that the Jesus who began his ministry at age thirty was thoroughly grounded and rooted in his tradition, that observance of the law and attendance to temple duties were very important, and that although he was a Galilean, neither he nor his disciples scorned Jerusalem. In fact, says Luke alone, Jesus' disciples were to remain in Jerusalem after his ascension and from Jerusalem were to launch their mission (24:47-48). "And they returned to Jerusalem with great joy, and were continually in the temple blessing God" (24:52-53). It is no wonder that Jesus, the true Israelite, went to the synagogue on the sabbath, "as his custom was" (4:16). Jesus and some of the religious leaders disputed over the tradition, to be sure, but it was a tradition he knew and kept from childhood.

When one looks at the presentation account itself, it is evident that there is the story line (2:22-24, 39-40) into which two sub-stories have been inserted: that of Simeon (verses 25-35) and that of Anna (verses 36-38). The principal story line seems to have as its basic purpose the demonstration that in the life of the Christ Child the law of Moses had been meticulously observed (verses 22, 23, 24, 27, 39). In the course of making that point Luke has conflated two regulations: a mother was to be ceremonially purified after childbirth (Lev. 12:1-4; in cases of poverty, Lev. 12:6-8 was applied), and a firstborn male was to be dedicated to God (Exod. 13:2, 12-16). Of course, provision was made for parents to redeem their son from the Lord (Num. 18:15-16) so they could keep him as their own. Luke says nothing about the redemption of Jesus; perhaps his silence serves to prepare the reader for the next story in which Jesus in the temple at age twelve said to his parents, "Did you not know that I must be in my Father's house?" (verse 49). That story, along with verses 40 and 52 make it evident that Luke is echoing the story of the boy Samuel who was dedicated to God and who lived in the temple (I Sam. 1-2).

In the persons of Simeon (verses 25-35) and Anna (verses 36-38) Luke tells how the Israel that is true, believing, hoping, devout, and temple-attending responded to Jesus. Simeon's acknowledgment of Jesus as "the Lord's Christ" was inspired by the Holy Spirit (verse 26) and Anna's was that of a true prophetess who fasted and prayed continually (verses 36-37). Simeon longed for "the consolation of Israel" (verse 25), a phrase referring to the messianic age. The Nunc Dimittis (verses 29-32) may have been a portion of a Christian hymn familiar to Luke and his readers. Simeon's words make it clear that Israel's consolation would not be a time of uninterrupted joy; hostility and death would be aroused by the appearance of the deliverer. Good news always has its enemies. Mary herself would pay a heavy price: "and a sword will pierce through your own soul also" (verse 35).

Devout and obedient Israel, as portrayed in the old prophetess Anna, also saw in Jesus "the redemption of Jerusalem" (verse 38). Her thanks to God and her witness concerning Jesus provide a model of the Israel which accepted Jesus and saw in him the fulfillment of ancient hopes. Luke will write later of that portion of Israel which rejected Jesus and turned a deaf ear to the preaching of the early church. But in Luke's theology, they are thereby rejecting their own tradition and their own prophets as it was interpreted to them by one who was a true Israelite, Jesus of Nazareth. He not only kept the law, held Jerusalem in great affection (13:34), and was faithful to the synagogue, but also his teaching was in keeping with all that was written in Moses, the prophets, and the writings (24:44). No prophet is so powerful and so disturbing as the one who arises out of one's own tradition and presents to the people the claims of that tradition.

Scripture Reading Index

Table of Readings and Psalms

(Versification follows that of the *Revised Standard Version*)

		First Sunday of Advent	Second Sunday of Advent	Third Sunday of Advent	Fourth Sunday of Advent
A.	Lesson 1	Isaiah 2:1-5 Psalm 122	Isaiah 11:1-10 Psalm 72:1-8	Isaiah 35:1-10 Psalm 146:5-10	Isaiah 7:10-16 Psalm 24
	Lesson 2	Romans 13:11-14	Romans 15:4-13	James 5:7-10	Romans 1:1-7
	Gospel	Matthew 24:36-44	Matthew 3:1-12	Matthew 11:2-11	Matthew 1:18-25
B.	Lesson 1	Isaiah 63:16-64:8 Psalm 80:1-7	Isaiah 40:1-11 Psalm 85:8-13	Isaiah 61:1-4, 8-11 Luke 1:46b-55	II Samuel 7:8-16 Psalm 89:1-4, 19-24
	Lesson 2	I Corinthians 1:3-9	II Peter 3:8-15a	I Thessalonians 5:16-24	Romans 16:25-27
	Gospel	Mark 13:32-37	Mark 1:1-8	John 1:6-8, 19-28	Luke 1:26-38
C.	Lesson 1	Jeremiah 33:14-16 Psalm 25:1-10	Baruch 5:1-9 *or* Malachi 3:1-4 Psalm 126	Zephaniah 3:14-20 Isaiah 12:2-6	Micah 5:2-5a (5:1-4a) Psalm 80:1-7
	Lesson 2	I Thessalonians 3:9-13	Philippians 1:3-11	Philippians 4:4-9	Hebrews 10:5-10
	Gospel	Luke 21:25-36	Luke 3:1-6	Luke 3:7-18	Luke 1:39-55

	Christmas, First Proper (Christmas Eve/Day*)	Christmas, Second Proper (Additional Lessons for Christmas Day)	Christmas, Third Proper (Additional Lessons for Christmas Day)
A. Lesson 1	Isaiah 9:2-7 Psalm 96	Isaiah 62:6-7, 10-12 Psalm 97	Isaiah 52:7-10 Psalm 98
Lesson 2	Titus 2:11-14	Titus 3:4-7	Hebrews 1:1-12
Gospel	Luke 2:1-20	Luke 2:8-20	John 1:1-14

*The readings from the second and third propers for Christmas may be used as alternatives for Christmas Day. If the third proper is not used on Christmas Day, it should be used at some service during the Christmas cycle because of the significance of John's prologue.

		First Sunday After Christmas*	January 1—Holy Name of Jesus Solemnity of Mary, Mother of God	January 1 (when observed as New Year)	Second Sunday After Christmas**
A.	Lesson 1	Isaiah 63:7-9 Psalm 111	Numbers 6:22-27 Psalm 67	Deuteronomy 8:1-10 Psalm 117	Jeremiah 31:7-14 or Ecclesiasticus 24:1-4, 12-16 Psalm 147:12-20
	Lesson 2	Hebrews 2:10-18	Galatians 4:4-7 or Philippians 2:9-13	Revelation 21:1-6a	Ephesians 1:3-6, 15-18
	Gospel	Matthew 2:13-15, 19-23	Luke 2:15-21	Matthew 25:31-46	John 1:1-18
B.	Lesson 1	Isaiah 61:10—62:3 Psalm 111		Ecclesiastes 3:1-13 Psalm 8	
	Lesson 2	Galatians 4:4-7		Colossians 2:1-7	
	Gospel	Luke 2:22-40		Matthew 9:14-17	
C.	Lesson 1	I Samuel 2:18-20, 26 or Ecclesiasticus 3:3-7, 14-17 Psalm 111		Isaiah 49:1-10 Psalm 90:1-12	
	Lesson 2	Colossians 3:12-17		Ephesians 3:1-10	
	Gospel	Luke 2:41-52		Luke 14:16-24	

*Or the readings for Epiphany.

**Or the readings for Epiphany if not otherwise used.

	Epiphany	Baptism of the Lord (First Sunday After Epiphany)*	Second Sunday After Epiphany	Third Sunday After Epiphany	Fourth Sunday After Epiphany
A. Lesson 1	Isaiah 60:1-6 Psalm 72:1-14	Isaiah 42:1-9 Psalm 29	Isaiah 49:1-7 Psalm 40:1-11	Isaiah 9:1-4 Psalm 27:1-6	Micah 6:1-8 Psalm 37:1-11
Lesson 2	Ephesians 3:1-12	Acts 10:34-43	I Corinthians 1:1-9	I Corinthians 1:10-17	I Corinthians 1:18-31
Gospel	Matthew 2:1-12	Matthew 3:13-17	John 1:29-34	Matthew 4:12-23	Matthew 5:1-12
B. Lesson 1		Genesis 1:1-5	I Samuel 3:1-10 (11-20)	Jonah 3:1-5, 10	Deuteronomy 18:15-20 Psalm 111
Lesson 2		Psalm 29 Acts 19:1-7	Psalm 63:1-8 I Corinthians 6:12-20	Psalm 62:5-12 I Corinthians 7:29-31 (32-35)	I Corinthians 8:1-13
Gospel		Mark 1:4-11	John 1:35-42	Mark 1:14-20	Mark 1:21-28
C. Lesson 1		Isaiah 61:1-4	Isaiah 62:1-5	Nehemiah 8:1-4a, 5-6, 8-10	Jeremiah 1:4-10
Lesson 2		Psalm 29 Acts 8:14-17	Psalm 36:5-10 I Corinthians 12:1-11	Psalm 19:7-14 I Corinthians 12:12-30	Psalm 71:1-6 I Corinthians 13:1-13
Gospel		Luke 3:15-17, 21-22	John 2:1-11	Luke 4:14-21	Luke 4:21-30

*In leap years, the number of Sundays after Epiphany will be the same as if Easter Day were one day later.

	Fifth Sunday After Epiphany	Sixth Sunday After Epiphany (Proper 1)	Seventh Sunday After Epiphany (Proper 2)	Eighth Sunday After Epiphany (Proper 3)	Last Sunday After Epiphany Transfiguration
A. Lesson 1	Isaiah 58:3-9a Psalm 112:4-9	Deuteronomy 30:15-20 *or* Ecclesiasticus 15:15-20 Psalm 119:1-8	Isaiah 49:8-13 Psalm 62:5-12	Leviticus 19:1-2, 9-18 Psalm 119:33-40	Exodus 24:12-18 Psalm 2:6-11
Lesson 2	I Corinthians 2:1-11	I Corinthians 3:1-9	I Corinthians 3:10-11, 16-23	I Corinthians 4:1-5	II Peter 1:16-21
Gospel	Matthew 5:13-16	Matthew 5:17-26	Matthew 5:27-37	Matthew 5:38-48	Matthew 17:1-9
B. Lesson 1	Job 7:1-7 Psalm 147:1-11	II Kings 5:1-14 Psalm 32	Isaiah 43:18-25 Psalm 41	Hosea 2:14-20 Psalm 103:1-13	II Kings 2:1-12a Psalm 50:1-6
Lesson 2	I Corinthians 9:16-23	I Corinthians 9:24-27	II Corinthians 1:18-22	II Corinthians 3:1-6	II Corinthians 4:3-6
Gospel	Mark 1:29-39	Mark 1:40-45	Mark 2:1-12	Mark 2:18-22	Mark 9:2-9
C. Lesson 1	Isaiah 6:1-8 (9-13) Psalm 138	Jeremiah 17:5-10 Psalm 1	Genesis 45:3-11, 15 Psalm 37:1-11	Ecclesiasticus 27:4-7 *or* Isaiah 55:10-13 Psalm 92:1-4, 12-15	Exodus 34:29-35 Psalm 99
Lesson 2	I Corinthians 15:1-11	I Corinthians 15:12-20	I Corinthians 15:35-38, 42-50	I Corinthians 15:51-58	II Corinthians 3:12-4:2
Gospel	Luke 5:1-11	Luke 6:17-26	Luke 6:27-38	Luke 6:39-49	Luke 9:28-36

	Ash Wednesday	First Sunday of Lent	Second Sunday of Lent	Third Sunday of Lent	Fourth Sunday of Lent
A. Lesson 1	Joel 2:1-2, 12-17a	Genesis 2:4b-9, 15-17, 25-3:7	Genesis 12:1-4a (4b-8)	Exodus 17:3-7	I Samuel 16:1-13
	Psalm 51:1-12	Psalm 130	Psalm 33:18-22	Psalm 95	Psalm 23
Lesson 2	II Corinthians 5:20b-6:2 (3-10)	Romans 5:12-19	Romans 4:1-5 (6-12), 13-17	Romans 5:1-11	Ephesians 5:8-14
Gospel	Matthew 6:1-6, 16-21	Matthew 4:1-11	John 3:1-17 *or* Matthew 17:1-9	John 4:5-26 (27-42)	John 9:1-41
B. Lesson 1		Genesis 9:8-17	Genesis 17:1-10, 15-19	Exodus 20:1-17	II Chronicles 36:14-23
		Psalm 25:1-10	Psalm 105:1-11	Psalm 19:7-14	Psalm 137:1-6
Lesson 2		I Peter 3:18-22	Romans 4:16-25	I Corinthians 1:22-25	Ephesians 2:4-10
Gospel		Mark 1:9-15	Mark 8:31-38 *or* Mark 9:1-9	John 2:13-22	John 3:14-21
C. Lesson 1		Deuteronomy 26:1-11	Genesis 15:1-12, 17-18	Exodus 3:1-15	Joshua 5:9-12
		Psalm 91:9-16	Psalm 127	Psalm 103:1-13	Psalm 34:1-8
Lesson 2		Romans 10:8b-13	Philippians 3:17-4:1	I Corinthians 10:1-13	II Corinthians 5:16-21
Gospel		Luke 4:1-13	Luke 13:31-35 *or* Luke 9:28-36	Luke 13:1-9	Luke 15:1-3, 11-32

	Fifth Sunday of Lent	Lent 6 when observed as Passion Sunday	Lent 6 when observed as Palm Sunday*
A. Lesson 1	Ezekiel 37:1-14 Psalm 116:1-9	Isaiah 50:4-9a Psalm 31:9-16	Isaiah 50:4-9a Psalm 118:19-29
Lesson 2	Romans 8:6-11	Philippians 2:5-11	Philippians 2:5-11
Gospel	John 11:(1-16), 17-45	Matthew 26:14-27:66 *or* Matthew 27:11-54	Matthew 21:1-11
B. Lesson 1	Jeremiah 31:31-34 Psalm 51:10-17	Same as A Psalm 31:9-16	Same as A Psalm 118:19-29
Lesson 2	Hebrews 5:7-10	Same as A	Same as A
Gospel	John 12:20-33	Mark 14:1-15:47 *or* Mark 15:1-39	Mark 11:1-11 *or* John 12:12-16
C. Lesson 1	Isaiah 43:16-21 Psalm 126	Same as A Psalm 31:9-16	Same as A Psalm 118:19-29
Lesson 2	Philippians 3:8-14	Same as A	Same as A
Gospel	John 12:1-8	Luke 22:14-23:56 *or* Luke 23:1-49	Luke 19:28-40

*These readings are provided for the liturgy or procession of palms for churches which have not had the tradition of readings-and-procession and also for an early "said" service in the Episcopal tradition.

HOLY WEEK

	Monday	Tuesday	Wednesday	Holy Thursday* **	Good Friday
A. Lesson 1	Isaiah 42:1-9 Psalm 36:5-10	Isaiah 49:1-7 Psalm 71:1-12	Isaiah 50:4-9a Psalm 70	Exodus 12:1-14 Psalm 116:12-19	Isaiah 52:13–53:12 Psalm 22:1-18
Lesson 2	Hebrews 9:11-15	I Corinthians 1:18-31	Hebrews 12:1-3	I Corinthians 11:23-26	Hebrews 4:14-16; 5:7-9
Gospel	John 12:1-11	John 12:20-36	John 13:21-30	John 13:1-15	John 18:1–19:42 *or* John 19:17-30
B. Lesson 1				Exodus 24:3-8 Psalm 116:12-19	
Lesson 2				I Corinthians 10:16-17	
Gospel				Mark 14:12-26	
C. Lesson 1				Jeremiah 31:31-34 Psalm 116:12-19	
Lesson 2				Hebrews 10:16-25	
Gospel				Luke 22:7-20	

*For those who want the feet washing emphasis every year, "A" readings are used each year.
**Psalm 116 is used at the Lord's Supper on Holy Thursday. Psalm 89:20-21, 24, 26 is used at the "chrism" service.

EASTER VIGIL*

Old Testament Readings and Psalms (A, B, C)

Genesis 1:1–2:2
Psalm 33
Genesis 7:1-5, 11-18; 8:6-18; 9:8-13
Psalm 46
Genesis 22:1-18
Psalm 16
Exodus 14:10–15:1
Exodus 15:1-6, 11-13, 17-18
Isaiah 54:5-14
Psalm 30

Isaiah 55:1-11
Isaiah 12:2-6
Baruch 3:9-15, 32–4:4
Psalm 19
Ezekiel 36:24-28
Psalm 42
Ezekiel 37:1-14
Psalm 143
Zephaniah 3:14-20
Psalm 98

Second Reading (A, B, C)

Romans 6:3-11
Psalm 114

Gospel

A. Matthew 28:1-10
B. Mark 16:1-8
C. Luke 24:1-12

---

*This selection of readings and psalms is provided for the Easter Vigil. A minimum of three readings from the Old Testament should be used, and this should always include Exodus 14.

	Easter* **	Second Sunday of Easter	Third Sunday of Easter	Fourth Sunday of Easter	Fifth Sunday of Easter
A. Lesson 1	Acts 10:34-43 *or* Jeremiah 31:1-6 Psalm 118:14-24	Acts 2:14a, 22-32 Psalm 16:5-11	Acts 2:14a, 36-41 Psalm 116:12-19	Acts 2:42-47 Psalm 23	Acts 7:55-60 Psalm 31:1-8
Lesson 2	Colossians 3:1-4 *or* Acts 10:34-43	I Peter 1:3-9	I Peter 1:17-23	I Peter 2:19-25	I Peter 2:2-10
Gospel	John 20:1-18 *or* Matthew 28:1-10	John 20:19-31	Luke 24:13-35	John 10:1-10	John 14:1-14
B. Lesson 1	Acts 10:34-43 *or* Isaiah 25:6-9 Psalm 118:14-24	Acts 4:32-35 Psalm 133	Acts 3:12-19 Psalm 4	Acts 4:8-12 Psalm 23	Acts 8:26-40 Psalm 22:25-31
Lesson 2	I Corinthians 15:1-11 *or* Acts 10:34-43	I John 1:1-2:2	I John 3:1-7	I John 3:18-24	I John 4:7-12
Gospel	John 20:1-18 *or* Mark 16:1-8	John 20:19-31	Luke 24:35-48	John 10:11-18	John 15:1-8

*See next page for Easter Evening.
**If the Old Testament passage is chosen for the first reading, the Acts passage is used as the second reading in order to initiate the sequential reading of Acts during the fifty days of Easter.

	Easter*	Second Sunday of Easter	Third Sunday of Easter	Fourth Sunday of Easter	Fifth Sunday of Easter
C. Lesson 1	Acts 10:34-43 *or* Isaiah 65:17-25 Psalm 118:14-24	Acts 5:27-32 Psalm 2	Acts 9:1-20 Psalm 30:4-12	Acts 13:15-16, 26-33 Psalm 23	Acts 14:8-18 Psalm 145:13b-21
Lesson 2	I Corinthians 15:19-26 *or* Acts 10:34-43	Revelation 1:4-8	Revelation 5:11-14	Revelation 7:9-17	Revelation 21:1-6
Gospel	John 20:1-18 *or* Luke 24:1-12	John 20:19-31	John 21:1-19 *or* John 21:15-19	John 10:22-30	John 13:31-35

Easter Evening*

A. Lesson 1	Acts 5:29-32 *or* Daniel 12:1-3 Psalm 150
Lesson 2	I Corinthians 5:6-8 *or* Acts 5:29-32
Gospel	Luke 24:13-49

*If the first reading is from the Old Testament, the reading from Acts should be second.

	Sixth Sunday of Easter	Ascension*	Seventh Sunday of Easter	Pentecost**	Trinity Sunday
A. Lesson 1	Acts 17:22-31 Psalm 66:8-20	Acts 1:1-11 Psalm 47	Acts 1:6-14 Psalm 68:1-10	Acts 2:1-21 or Isaiah 44:1-8 Psalm 104:24-34	Deuteronomy 4:32-40 Psalm 33:1-12
Lesson 2	I Peter 3:13-22	Ephesians 1:15-23	I Peter 4:12-14; 5:6-11	I Corinthians 12:3b-13 or Acts 2:1-21	II Corinthians 13:5-14
Gospel	John 14:15-21	Luke 24:46-53 or Mark 16:9-16, 19-20	John 17:1-11	John 20:19-23 or John 7:37-39	Matthew 28:16-20
B. Lesson 1	Acts 10:44-48 Psalm 98	Psalm 47	Acts 1:15-17, 21-26 Psalm 1	Acts 2:1-21 or Ezekiel 37:1-14 Psalm 104:24-34	Isaiah 6:1-8 Psalm 29
Lesson 2	I John 5:1-6		I John 5:9-13	Romans 8:22-27 or Acts 2:1-21	Romans 8:12-17
Gospel	John 15:9-17		John 17:11b-19	John 15:26-27; 16:4b-15	John 3:1-17

*Or on Seventh Sunday of Easter.

**If the Old Testament passage is chosen for the first reading, the Acts passage is used as the second reading.

	Sixth Sunday of Easter	Ascension*	Seventh Sunday of Easter	Pentecost**	Trinity Sunday
C. Lesson 1	Acts 15:1-2, 22-29 Psalm 67	Psalm 47	Acts 16:16-34 Psalm 97	Acts 2:1-21 or Genesis 11:1-9 Psalm 104:24-34	Proverbs 8:22-31 Psalm 8
Lesson 2	Revelation 21:10, 22-27		Revelation 22:12-14, 16-17, 20	Romans 8:14-17 or Acts 2:1-21	Romans 5:1-5
Gospel	John 14:23-29		John 17:20-26	John 14:8-17, 25-27	John 16:12-15

*Or on Seventh Sunday of Easter.

**If the Old Testament passage is chosen for the first reading, the Acts passage is used as the second reading.

		Proper 4* Sunday between May 29 and June 4 inclusive (if after Trinity Sunday)	Proper 5 Sunday between June 5 and 11 inclusive (if after Trinity Sunday)	Proper 6 Sunday between June 12 and 18 inclusive (if after Trinity Sunday)	Proper 7 Sunday between June 19 and 25 inclusive (if after Trinity Sunday)	Proper 8 Sunday between June 26 and July 2 inclusive
A.	Lesson 1	Genesis 12:1-9 Psalm 33:12-22	Genesis 22:1-18 Psalm 13	Genesis 25:19-34 Psalm 46	Genesis 28:10-17 Psalm 91:1-10	Genesis 32:22-32 Psalm 17:1-7, 15
	Lesson 2	Romans 3:21-28	Romans 4:13-18	Romans 5:6-11	Romans 5:12-19	Romans 6:3-11
	Gospel	Matthew 7:21-29	Matthew 9:9-13	Matthew 9:35-10:8	Matthew 10:24-33	Matthew 10:34-42
B.	Lesson 1	I Samuel 16:1-13 Psalm 20	I Samuel 16:14-23 Psalm 57	II Samuel 1:1, 17-27 Psalm 46	II Samuel 5:1-12 Psalm 48	II Samuel 6:1-15 Psalm 24
	Lesson 2	II Corinthians 4:5-12	II Corinthians 4:13-5:1	II Corinthians 5:6-10, 14-17	II Corinthians 5:18-6:2	II Corinthians 8:7-15
	Gospel	Mark 2:23-3:6	Mark 3:20-35	Mark 4:26-34	Mark 4:35-41	Mark 5:21-43
C.	Lesson 1	I Kings 8:22-23, 41-43 Psalm 100	I Kings 17:17-24 Psalm 113	I Kings 19:1-8 Psalm 42	I Kings 19:9-14 Psalm 43	I Kings 19:15-21 Psalm 44:1-8
	Lesson 2	Galatians 1:1-10	Galatians 1:11-24	Galatians 2:15-21	Galatians 3:23-29	Galatians 5:1, 13-25
	Gospel	Luke 7:1-10	Luke 7:11-17	Luke 7:36-8:3	Luke 9:18-24	Luke 9:51-62

*If the Sunday between May 24 and 28 inclusive follows Trinity Sunday, use Eighth Sunday After Epiphany on that day.

	Proper 9 Sunday between July 3 and 9 inclusive	Proper 10 Sunday between July 10 and 16 inclusive	Proper 11 Sunday between July 17 and 23 inclusive	Proper 12 Sunday between July 24 and 30 inclusive	Proper 13 Sunday between July 31 and Aug. 6 inclusive
A. Lesson 1	Exodus 1:6-14, 22–2:10 Psalm 124	Exodus 2:11-22 Psalm 69:6-15	Exodus 3:1-12 Psalm 103:1-13	Exodus 3:13-20 Psalm 105:1-11	Exodus 12:1-14 Psalm 143:1-10
Lesson 2	Romans 7:14-25a	Romans 8:9-17	Romans 8:18-25	Romans 8:26-30	Romans 8:31-39
Gospel	Matthew 11:25-30	Matthew 13:1-9, 18-23	Matthew 13:24-30, 36-43	Matthew 13:44-52	Matthew 14:13-21
B. Lesson 1	II Samuel 7:1-17 Psalm 89:20-37	II Samuel 7:18-29 Psalm 132:11-18	II Samuel 11:1-15 Psalm 53	II Samuel 12:1-14 Psalm 32	II Samuel 12:15b-24 Psalm 34:11-22
Lesson 2	II Corinthians 12:1-10	Ephesians 1:1-10	Ephesians 2:11-22	Ephesians 3:14-21	Ephesians 4:1-6
Gospel	Mark 6:1-6	Mark 6:7-13	Mark 6:30-34	John 6:1-15	John 6:24-35
C. Lesson 1	I Kings 21:1-3, 17-21 Psalm 5:1-8	II Kings 2:1, 6-14 Psalm 139:1-12	II Kings 4:8-17 Psalm 139:13-18	II Kings 5:1-15ab ("... in Israel") Psalm 21:1-7	II Kings 13:14-20a Psalm 28
Lesson 2	Galatians 6:7-18	Colossians 1:1-14	Colossians 1:21-29	Colossians 2:6-15	Colossians 3:1-11
Gospel	Luke 10:1-12, 17-20	Luke 10:25-37	Luke 10:38-42	Luke 11:1-13	Luke 12:13-21

	Proper 14 Sunday between August 7 and 13 inclusive	Proper 15 Sunday between August 14 and 20 inclusive	Proper 16 Sunday between August 21 and 27 inclusive	Proper 17 Sunday between August 28 and Sept. 3 inclusive	Proper 18 Sunday between September 4 and 10 inclusive
A. Lesson 1	Exodus 14:19-31 Psalm 106:4-12	Exodus 16:2-15 Psalm 78:1-3, 10-20	Exodus 17:1-7 Psalm 95	Exodus 19:1-9 Psalm 114	Exodus 19:16-24 Psalm 115:1-11
Lesson 2	Romans 9:1-5	Romans 11:13-16, 29-32	Romans 11:33-36	Romans 12:1-13	Romans 13:1-10
Gospel	Matthew 14:22-33	Matthew 15:21-28	Matthew 16:13-20	Matthew 16:21-28	Matthew 18:15-20
B. Lesson 1	II Samuel 18:1, 5, 9-15 Psalm 143:1-8	II Samuel 18:24-33 Psalm 102:1-12	II Samuel 23:1-7 Psalm 67	I Kings 2:1-4, 10-12 Psalm 121	Ecclesiasticus 5:8-15 or Proverbs 2:1-8 Psalm 119:129-136
Lesson 2	Ephesians 4:25–5:2	Ephesians 5:15-20	Ephesians 5:21-33	Ephesians 6:10-20	James 1:17-27
Gospel	John 6:35, 41-51	John 6:51-58	John 6:55-69	Mark 7:1-8, 14-15, 21-23	Mark 7:31-37
C. Lesson 1	Jeremiah 18:1-11 Psalm 14	Jeremiah 20:7-13 Psalm 10:12-18	Jeremiah 28:1-9 Psalm 84	Ezekiel 18:1-9, 25-29 Psalm 15	Ezekiel 33:1-11 Psalm 94:12-22
Lesson 2	Hebrews 11:1-3, 8-19	Hebrews 12:1-2, 12-17	Hebrews 12:18-29	Hebrews 13:1-8	Philemon 1-20
Gospel	Luke 12:32-40	Luke 12:49-56	Luke 13:22-30	Luke 14:1, 7-14	Luke 14:25-33

		Proper 19 Sunday between September 11 and 17 inclusive	Proper 20 Sunday between September 18 and 24 inclusive	Proper 21 Sunday between Sept. 25 and Oct. 1 inclusive	Proper 22 Sunday between October 2 and 8 inclusive	Proper 23 Sunday between October 9 and 15 inclusive
A.	Lesson 1	Exodus 20:1-20 Psalm 19:7-14	Exodus 32:1-14 Psalm 106:7-8, 19-23	Exodus 33:12-23 Psalm 99	Numbers 27:12-23 Psalm 81:1-10	Deuteronomy 34:1-12 Psalm 135:1-14
	Lesson 2	Romans 14:5-12	Philippians 1:21-27	Philippians 2:1-13	Philippians 3:12-21	Philippians 4:1-9
	Gospel	Matthew 18:21-35	Matthew 20:1-16	Matthew 21:28-32	Matthew 21:33-43	Matthew 22:1-14
B.	Lesson 1	Proverbs 22:1-2, 8-9 Psalm 125	Job 28:20-28 Psalm 27:1-6	Job 42:1-6 Psalm 27:7-14	Genesis 2:18-24 Psalm 128	Genesis 3:8-19 Psalm 90:1-12
	Lesson 2	James 2:1-5, 8-10, 14-17	James 3:13-18	James 4:13-17; 5:7-11	Hebrews 1:1-4; 2:9-11	Hebrews 4:1-3, 9-13
	Gospel	Mark 8:27-38	Mark 9:30-37	Mark 9:38-50	Mark 10:2-16	Mark 10:17-30
C.	Lesson 1	Hosea 4:1-3, 5:15-6:6 Psalm 77:11-20	Hosea 11:1-11 Psalm 107:1-9	Joel 2:23-30 Psalm 107:1, 33-43	Amos 5:6-7, 10-15 Psalm 101	Micah 1:2; 2:1-10 Psalm 26
	Lesson 2	I Timothy 1:12-17	I Timothy 2:1-7	I Timothy 6:6-19	II Timothy 1:1-14	II Timothy 2:8-15
	Gospel	Luke 15:1-10	Luke 16:1-13	Luke 16:19-31	Luke 17:5-10	Luke 17:11-19

	Proper 24 Sunday between October 16 and 22 inclusive	Proper 25 Sunday between October 23 and 29 inclusive	Proper 26 Sunday between October 30 and Nov. 5 inclusive	Proper 27 Sunday between November 6 and 12 inclusive	Proper 28 Sunday between November 13 and 19 inclusive
A. Lesson 1	Ruth 1:1-19a Psalm 146	Ruth 2:1-13 Psalm 128	Ruth 4:7-17 Psalm 127	Amos 5:18-24 Psalm 50:7-15	Zephaniah 1:7, 12-18 Psalm 76
Lesson 2	I Thessalonians 1:1-10	I Thessalonians 2:1-8	I Thessalonians 2:9-13, 17-20	I Thessalonians 4:13-18	I Thessalonians 5:1-11
Gospel	Matthew 22:15-22	Matthew 22:34-46	Matthew 23:1-12	Matthew 25:1-13	Matthew 25:14-30
B. Lesson 1	Isaiah 53:7-12 Psalm 35:17-28	Jeremiah 31:7-9 Psalm 126	Deuteronomy 6:1-9 Psalm 119:33-48	I Kings 17:8-16 Psalm 146	Daniel 7:9-14 Psalm 145:8-13
Lesson 2	Hebrews 4:14-16	Hebrews 5:1-6	Hebrews 7:23-28	Hebrews 9:24-28	Hebrews 10:11-18
Gospel	Mark 10:35-45	Mark 10:46-52	Mark 12:28-34	Mark 12:38-44	Mark 13:24-32
C. Lesson 1	Habakkuk 1:1-3; 2:1-4	Zephaniah 3:1-9	Haggai 2:1-9	Zechariah 7:1-10	Malachi 4:1-6 (3:19-24 in Hebrews)
Lesson 2	Psalm 119:137-144 II Timothy 3:14-4:5	Psalm 3 II Timothy 4:6-8, 16-18	Psalm 65:1-8 II Thessalonians 1:5-12	Psalm 9:11-20 II Thessalonians 2:13-3:5	Psalm 82 II Thessalonians 3:6-13
Gospel	Luke 18:1-8	Luke 18:9-14	Luke 19:1-10	Luke 20:27-38	Luke 21:5-19

Proper 29 (Christ the King) Sunday between November 20 and 26 inclusive

	Lesson 1	Lesson 2	Gospel
A.	Ezekiel 34:11-16, 20-24 / Psalm 23	I Corinthians 15:20-28	Matthew 25:31-46
B.	Jeremiah 23:1-6 / Psalm 93	Revelation 1:4b-8	John 18:33-37
C.	II Samuel 5:1-5 / Psalm 95	Colossians 1:11-20	John 12:9-19

All Saints, November 1*

	Lesson 1	Lesson 2	Gospel
A.	Revelation 7:9-17 / Psalm 34:1-10	I John 3:1-3	Matthew 5:1-12
B.	Revelation 21:1-6a / Psalm 24:1-6	Colossians 1:9-14	John 11:32-44
C.	Daniel 7:1-3, 15-18 / Psalm 149	Ephesians 1:11-23	Luke 6:20-36

Thanksgiving Day**

	Lesson 1	Lesson 2	Gospel
A.	Deuteronomy 8:7-18 / Psalm 65	II Corinthians 9:6-15	Luke 17:11-19
B.	Joel 2:21-27 / Psalm 126	I Timothy 2:1-7	Matthew 6:25-33
C.	Deuteronomy 26:1-11 / Psalm 100	Philippians 4:4-9	John 6:25-35

*Or on first Sunday in November.
**Readings *ad libitum*, not tied to A, B, or C.

Annunciation March 25

	Lesson 1	Lesson 2	Gospel
A.	Isaiah 7:10-14 / Psalm 45 or 40:6-10	Hebrews 10:4-10	Luke 1:26-38

Visitation May 31

Lesson 1	Lesson 2	Gospel
I Samuel 2:1-10 / Psalm 113	Romans 12:9-16b	Luke 1:39-57

Presentation February 2

Lesson 1	Lesson 2	Gospel
Malachi 3:1-4 / Psalm 84 or 24:7-10	Hebrews 2:14-18	Luke 2:22-40

Holy Cross September 14

Lesson 1	Lesson 2	Gospel
Numbers 21:4b-9 / Psalm 98:1-5 or 78:1-2, 34-38	I Corinthians 1:18-24	John 3:13-17

Titles of Seasons, Sundays, and Special Days

Advent Season

First Sunday of Advent..............The Sunday occurring November 27 to December 3
Second Sunday of Advent..............The Sunday occurring December 4 to December 10
Third Sunday of Advent..............The Sunday occurring December 11 to December 17
Fourth Sunday of Advent..............The Sunday occurring December 18 to December 24

Christmas Season

Christmas Eve/Day..............December 24/25
First Sunday After Christmas..............The Sunday occurring December 26 to January 1
New Year's Eve/Day..............December 31 to January 1
Second Sunday After Christmas..............The Sunday occurring January 2 to January 5

Epiphany Season

Epiphany..............January 6 or first Sunday in January
First Sunday After Epiphany (Baptism of the Lord)..............The Sunday occurring January 7 to January 13
Second Sunday After Epiphany..............The Sunday occurring January 14 to January 20
Third Sunday After Epiphany..............The Sunday occurring January 21 to January 27
Fourth Sunday After Epiphany*..............The Sunday occurring January 28 to February 3
Fifth Sunday After Epiphany*..............The Sunday occurring February 4 to February 10
Sixth Sunday After Epiphany (Proper 1)*..............The Sunday occurring February 11 to February 17
Seventh Sunday After Epiphany (Proper 2)*..............The Sunday occurring February 18 to February 24
Eighth Sunday After Epiphany (Proper 3)*..............The Sunday occurring February 25 to February 29
Last Sunday After Epiphany (Transfiguration Sunday)

*Except when this Sunday is the Last Sunday After Epiphany.

Lenten Season

Ash Wednesday: Seventh
   Wednesday Before Easter
First Sunday of Lent
Second Sunday of Lent
Third Sunday of Lent
Fourth Sunday of Lent
Fifth Sunday of Lent

Holy Week

Passion/Palm Sunday
Monday in Holy Week
Tuesday in Holy Week
Wednesday in Holy Week
Holy Thursday
Good Friday
(Holy Saturday)

Easter Season

Easter Vigil
Easter
Easter Evening
Second Sunday of Easter
Third Sunday of Easter
Fourth Sunday of Easter
Fifth Sunday of Easter
Sixth Sunday of Easter
Ascension (fortieth day, sixth Thursday of Easter)
Seventh Sunday of Easter
Pentecost

Season After Pentecost

Trinity Sunday (First Sunday After Pentecost)
Propers 4-28 (See note below.)
Proper 29, Christ the King: the Sunday occurring
   November 20 to 26

Special Days

Some special days observed by many churches are included in the table, with appropriate readings and psalms.

NOTE: Easter is a movable feast, and can occur as early as March 22 and as late as April 25. When Easter is early, it encroaches on the Sundays after Epiphany, reducing their number, as necessary, from as many as nine to as few as four. In similar fashion the date of Easter determines the number of Sunday Propers after Pentecost. When Easter is as early as March 22, the numbered Proper for the Sunday following Trinity Sunday is Proper 3.